How Ar

The Importance of father's men n

By

Mark Williams BCAH

ISBN: 9781916981669

If you're struggling to let go of a painful experience, you may benefit from talking to a professional. Sometimes it's difficult to implement information on your own, and you need an experienced professional to help guide you through the process.

The Author

Mark Williams BCAh FRSA is a Keynote Speaker, Author and International campaigner.

In 2010, he became very unwell and entered community mental health services. He founded International Fathers Mental Health Day and #Howareyoudad campaign to make sure all parents have support for the whole family. Mark has worked in many areas of youth and mental health since 2005 and has spoken to thousands of parents in many countries since 2011.

Mark has spoken on television and radio stations around the world while working with Dr Jane Hanley who have both published articles on Fathers Mental Health together. Mark was awarded Inspirational Father of the year and Local Hero at the Pride of Britain Awards in 2012 even invited to meet The Royal Family on World Mental Health Day also awarded the Point Of Light Award by the Prime Minister in 2019.

Mark published the report called "Fathers Reaching Out - Why Dads Matter" to explain the importance of paternal mental health which has far better outcomes for the whole family and the development of the child when we include fathers.

Mark has contributed to over twenty books about fathers' mental health. He has trained, Midwives and Health Visitors on paternal mental health and other professionals. Also, as a consultant for many organisations including the National Health Service, Movember, and Tommy Tippe while delivering talks to companies including Google.

Helped produce the film Daddy Blues based on Mark's journey is now available on Amazon Prime. Ambassador for

Mother's for Mother's and Mother's Matter charities. Started the Campaign to reopen the mother and baby unit in Wales, which was reopened seven years later.

Mark has delivered talks all around the world, face-to-face and online since becoming a keynote speaker in 2012. He has spoken at over 300 conferences to date and delivered a TEDx Talk on the importance of father's mental health.

In 2023, Mark was awarded the British Citizens Award for Healthcare at Westminster for work in changing policies and becoming a pioneer in mental health. He is now a member of the Fatherhood All-Party Parliamentary Group and a Human Rights activist.

Foreword

Mark Williams's enthusiasm and passion are more than enough to fuel a PowerStation to supply energy to the whole world. Since I have known Mark, his desire to make a difference has been unwavering.

I was introduced to him as we both had a special interest in fathers' mental health. At that time, little was known about this as a 'condition', as most of the research and support focused on mothers' mental health. The recognition of the mental health of mothers during the perinatal period was in its infancy, with reputable researchers and clinicians highlighting the importance of good mental health in both pregnancy and the postnatal period.

Some of the consequences of mental illnesses and disorders for mothers and infants were accepted, and healthcare professionals and practitioners were able to adapt their practice to accommodate the needs of the mothers and their infants. The role of fathers was not, on the whole, acknowledged.

There was little regard for their mental health and how that may be affected by the process of the pregnancy, delivery, and postnatal period. When perinatal mental health support services were in place, there were few for fathers. Fathers were often not included in the conversations and yet they were left holding the baby. That is until Mark started his campaigns. 'Yes', he was told 'of course fathers are included as part of our services' but in reality, fathers admitted to Mark that they felt they were' marginalised' 'left out of the plans' 'not considered when discussing mental health issues', 'their feelings were neglected. Fathers talked to Mark because of his rapidly increasing popularity.

Mark had been there, done that, got the tee shirt, and caught the illness! He knew firsthand what it was like to watch helplessly as his wife suffered trauma. He understood how it felt to be powerless to support his wife and tiny infant when they too experienced despair. He was aware that, with one or two exceptions, current National Health Services were not equipped to help him, or even acknowledge how he may be feeling. He knew he could not be alone and knew that something should be done about it.

Mark generated by these events, and the love of his family, started his campaigns. It is difficult to recollect how many times Mark and I met to discuss the next moves. Historically It was meetings in the Harvester Inns, with notepad and pen we would outline who needed to be contacted and why. Start and the top and work down to the bottom or vice versa? We knew education and training would be a good place to start. Mark's lived experience, speaking with parents and my background knowledge was an ideal recipe.

We did, and met with members of the Welsh Assembly, putting our case forward about the lack of services for parents in Wales. Some listened, some not, but those that did, including Mark Drakeford, the current First Welsh Minister, ensured that money was ringfenced for perinatal mental health services. That service, although few may recognise it, is due to the efforts of many of us, pushing, shoving and never giving up.

Mark, naturally, did not stop there. Next, it was the Houses of Parliament, meeting with the members. Once again, we talked about perinatal mental health, but this time the concentration was on the mental health of fathers. Some feigned interest, others were more committed. It was, after all a new, different, and controversial area. Mark's effervescent personality ensured that this was taken seriously. Important people started to take note and there was significantly more talk about it.

Slowly more men, who were familiar with the symptoms Mark described, came forward and joined in the campaign. Some, impressed by Mark's talks and knowledge, have branched off to form companies, coalitions, and campaigns. The UK can be proud of the many services currently offered by these fathers, which are the envy of the world.

The world is another area. Mark was conscious that, amongst others, Dr Angela Barton in Canada, started the first World Maternal Mental Health Day. There was no first World Fathers' Mental Health Day until Mark founded one. He gathered experts, clinicians, practitioners, lived experience and researchers to design and develop the Day, which is held annually, to emphasise the importance of understanding and supporting fathers during this crucial period in their life.

Mark has written many articles and has co-authored two books on perinatal mental health with me. One book is due out next Summer. Some of Mark's work was recently recognised at Westminster, where he was awarded the prestigious British Citizen Award for Health care.

Writing, like talking, does not earn fortunes. I have often rebuked Mark for subsidising the work he does, which is mostly for free. He is often on the early Mega Bus from Cardiff as it is less expensive than traveling by train, driving the length and breadth of the country to deliver his messages to a captivated audience, shaking hands with those who earn more in a day than Mark does in a year.

Yet, his enthusiasm and passion remain undaunted. Mark knows he can and does make a huge difference to fathers, and the world of perinatal mental health, and it is my honor and pleasure to have worked and to work with him in the future. Who needs fossil fuels when you have Mark?

Dr Jane Hanley Honorary Senior Lecturer, former President, and current executive member, of the International Marcé Society for Perinatal Mental Health.

I first met Mark in 2014 at a Marce International Society meeting in Swansea. His passion for making a difference for fathers inspired me. I had already been working with mothers' mental health for almost 10 years at that point, but it was then that I realised how much we needed to add fathers to that work. Mark's own experience was the trigger for him to start the campaigning. For many years, it must have been like shouting into the wind; no one wanted to hear. But, Mark never gave up.

For most of us who work in this field, Mark has been the inspiration that motivated us to help make that difference. The monumental changes that we have seen in support of fathers are also more than just my professional and academic work; it's personal. As a grandfather multiple times over, I have seen the impact of perinatal challenges on my daughters and their partners. I am so grateful that we know so much more and can provide more help than ever before. I truly believe that we can all thank Mark for leading these campaigns in the first place.

All too often, husbands and partners are overlooked when it comes to providing support and information on mental health. Evidence suggests that the risk factors, and impact, of perinatal mental health are reduced when mums have a supportive partner. Furthermore, fathers can develop 'perinatal mental health' problems (either as a result of their spouse's/partner's illness or independently).

There is often little guidance available for men to understand the causes, risk factors, treatments and prognosis of perinatal mental illness, quite apart from what support they can give to their partner. Fathers also need information on how to improve their mental health. On this page, you will find some information about the latest campaigns that I am involved with, some media stories that have been run about that, and an overview of resources and support for fathers.

It is worth starting by restating why I feel fathers' mental health matters. For me, there are three key areas that we need to focus on: what information and support do fathers need to help their wives/partners should experience poor mental health in the perinatal period; what support do we need to give to fathers to deal with their mental health in the perinatal period; and what information and support do we need to give to a father should his wife/partner experience what might be a traumatic birth.

We also need to give fathers resources to help them support their wives/partners should they develop mental health problems in the perinatal period. We often hear that men have limited knowledge about what they can do and where they can access information. While we are beginning to see some appropriate mental health support directed at mothers during the perinatal period, including signposting and information, their partners are all too frequently disregarded. In some further research at Bournemouth University, we sought to explore fathers' perceptions about what information and support they received (and needed) to enable them to help their partner. The outcomes from that research have now been published.

One theme that was consistent across all of the work we have undertaken so far is that fathers are saying that some health professionals do not regard them as part of the birthing experience or give them due consideration when it comes to perinatal mental health. To that end, we have just finished collecting data from UK health visitors, where we asked what support, they can give fathers. I hope to report those findings soon.

We also know that enduring poor mental health can mean that the relationship between the father and his baby can be deeply affected. A strong bond is needed between an infant and both parents to ensure a healthy development for that child. We need to provide more support for fathers' mental health and enhance their relationship with their infants. I will be working on some projects around that soon too.

In 2018, I reported the exciting news that NHS England had announced how they would now screen some fathers for their mental health. This decision was largely based on data that I (and others, such as Mark Williams, The Fatherhood Institute, and many more) had provided on what was needed. “The recent trends in support for Fathers’ Mental Health is testimony to the hard work undertaken by so many inspirational people over these last few years,

Perhaps that turning point of the announcement in 2018 for NHS England that fathers would now be screened for their mental health in the perinatal period. Since then, despite a few potentially serious setbacks in the wake of the Covid pandemic, we are beginning to see so much more support emerging for fathers. The evidence base in quality research is also expanding rapidly.

Research with mothers who have had a traumatic birth is still in its infancy. However, until now, nothing has been done with fathers (who have witnessed that trauma). At Bournemouth University, we undertook research to explore this vitally important area of work. We wanted to examine fathers' experiences, especially around the information and support given to them at this time.

Campaigning is not likely to be successful without evidence, especially when trying to convince NHS commissioners or the Government. Until recently, that evidence has been limited. I am honored to work with some great professionals, academics, and dads on those campaigns. Most of that has been undertaken with my great friend Mark Williams.

I am honored to have been part of the campaigning, and for contributing to published research. There are countless names I could cite who have been inspirational in helping us to be where we are now. However, I feel that none of this would have been possible without the pioneering work and dogged determination of Mark Wiliams.

"Mark Williams is (by my book) the leading voice in the UK on Fathers' Mental Health".

Lecturer Bournemouth University and Campaigner. Dr Andrew Mayers

The need for support for fathers has greatly come to light over the last few years with campaigners such as Mark Williams who has pro-actively researched and campaigned for this cause, using his own lived experience as motivation to help other fathers.

We know that between 25-50% of men who have a partner who has perinatal mental illness will then go on to experience poor mental health themselves.

We also know from the dads we speak to, that their mental health does not feel heard, or considered and does not exist in many NHS or parental-related appointments from conception through to birth and beyond. Yet the expectations of the responsibilities of parenting are equal, and the consideration of mental health appears to be one-sided which has a detrimental effect on the entire family unit.

Postnatal depression is now, finally clinically recognised in men, and it is the courage and support from Dads who share their perinatal mental health journeys that then inspires and encourages many more men to share how they are feeling and ultimately get the support that they need.

The stigma of mental health is considerably reduced thanks to much work by many different individuals and organisations and even becoming en -vouge as a theme, which is pleasing and a positive movement. Men's maternal mental health is still very much stigmatised, and the acknowledgment of perinatal mental health is considered 'real' within men is so desperately needing movement in the general attitude towards it, without overlooking or undermining a dad as a parent's mental health being equally considered int he parental journey as a vital part of the family unit.

Loss of identity, feeling like a spare part, and lack of bonding with a new baby particularly to do with feeding early on, are all things that Dads tell us that make them feel anxious, stressed and with the inclusion of sleep deprivation early on after a new baby is born this can quickly develop into postnatal depression for men.

GPs, Health visitors, midwives, and networks of people involved in the parental journey need to be proactively asking Dads, with meaning how they are to ensure that no Dad feels alone in his journey as a parent and that support can be there when needed.

Annie Belasco Head of UK Charity PANDAS Foundation (Pre and Postnatal Depression Advice and Support)

Testimonials

Mark Williams is a force of nature and has done a huge amount to raise awareness of perinatal mental health. By talking about his experiences, he has focused our attention on the effects that perinatal mental illness can have on the family including partners, and reminded us of the importance of Dads. The world of Maternal Mental Health owes Mark a huge vote of thanks."

National Centre for Mental Health Professor Ian Jones, Director.

"Dear Mark, I would like to say that the work you have been doing about fathers is really valuable. There is now much attention given to perinatal mental illness in mothers, but the suffering of fathers, and how this can affect the rest of the family remains largely neglected. You speak eloquently on this and have really helped to bring awareness of this important topic to the wider public."

Imperial College London Vivette Glover, Professor of Perinatal Psychobiology

"Mark is a tower of inspiration, strength and dedication when speaking out for dads and families. It's a pleasure and privilege working with him."

Maternal Mental Health Alliance Dr Alain Gregoire, Consultant and Honorary Senior Lecturer in Perinatal Psychiatry and Chair

Thank you, Mark. It's heartening to know that there has been that kind of positive effect. I greatly admire your work."

Prof Paul Ramchandani Faculty of Medicine, Department of Medicine. Reader in Child and Adolescent Psychiatry

Mark is a truly authentic passionate speaker who delivers a story detailing lived experience of mental health, particularly surrounding childbirth and parenting. Mark's messages for health professionals are compassionate and courageous - he is a unique individual who stimulates learning in an engaging and compelling way. Mark is super friendly, kind and caring and I am honoured to have him in my life.

Sheena Byrom OBE was one of the UK's first consultant midwives and Author.

Thank you so much for your really fantastic talk today and yesterday. I know the audiences really enjoyed hearing from you. You are such a good speaker and communicate such a lot in terms of experience and work, with great thoughtfulness, honesty, humour and energy.

Dr Liz McDonald, The Royal Collage of Psychiatrists

Mark is an advocate for all parents. He brings insights informed by his own family's experience and the voices of the very many families that he has worked with over the years, together with understanding vital aspects when working in parental mental health, including safeguarding and the need for supervision.

Dr Zoe Darwin University of Huddersfield inspiring global professionals

"Mark Williams is a true legend and inspiration for all of us. His commitment to improve the mental health in general and of the fathers in particular is phenomenal. He is a great speaker, author campaigner, and trainer in mental health. He spoke in one of my events at the House of Commons which was very well received by the attendees. I attended some of his talks and his knowledge and passion were exceptional."

Dr Raja Gangopadhyay Dr Raja Gangopadhyay is a consultant obstetrician and gynaecologist with a special interest in perinatal mental health.

"Mark is a true inspiration! His vision for equality and his fortitude in pursuing it, are exemplary! I have known Mark in different capacities since 2015 and in that time, I have seen him elevate the cause of perinatal, paternal mental health from the fringes to widely accepted of needing attention and care." –

Chris Stein, Future Men

INTRODUCTION

MY STORY

Becoming a father is indeed a life-changing event. It brings about a new sense of responsibility, love, and care that can profoundly change one's perspective on life. It's a journey filled with joy, challenges, learning, and unforgettable moments. What is often never talked about in society, is that parents' experiences can vary and often many parents struggle during the perinatal period and beyond. It is an area that is often dismissed, and even mental health charities have been unaware of perinatal mental health.

In 2004, I suffered my first ever panic attack at thirty years of age and I didn't have a clue what was happening to me. It was the day my son was born. My wife Michelle was taken to the theatre for an emergency C-section, and I honestly thought she was going to die. I was terrified.

During this period, I experienced nightmares about Michelle and Ethan dying in the theatre. I would wake up thinking it was real. Sadly, Michelle went on to develop severe postnatal depression and my world changed forever.

I had never known anyone with the illness. I was so uneducated about mental health that I used to wonder: 'How can people be depressed?'. Within weeks of Michelle's diagnosis, I had to give up my job to care for Michelle and Ethan. I loved the social side of my job, and I was isolated. Sometimes I wouldn't get out the front door for days. Within months, my personality changed, and I was drinking in an attempt to cope.

I became angry. It got to the point where, if I did manage to get out with friends, I wanted to fight the doorman. I had this strange need to get hurt to try and stop what I was feeling and the thoughts that were going through my head. It was another way of self-harming.

I began to have uncontrollable suicidal thoughts but never acted on them.

At the time, I felt like I couldn't talk to anyone. I was raised in a working-class community where my father and grandfather were coal miners. Growing up, we looked up to 'hard men' who didn't show their emotions and now I was feeling emotional – and I was feeling weak. I kept telling myself I just had to 'man up' and everything would be okay.

After five years of suffering in silence since my son was born, and after losing my grandfather and my mother getting diagnosed with cancer within weeks apart, my mental health got worse.

One day, whilst sitting in my car before walking into work, I had a complete breakdown, or breakthrough I tend to call it. I just literally couldn't get out of the car, I was shaking, crying and suicidal thoughts were racing through my mind.

After going through community mental health teams, I was eventually diagnosed with anxiety and depression and later attention deficit hyperactivity disorder (ADHD). I was never asked once about my mental health in 2004 and was never diagnosed with postnatal depression or post-traumatic stress disorder when after speaking with professionals at conferences, would often say that I would have been if an assessment was in place.

Therapy, medication, and learning coping skills through Cognitive Behavioural Therapy all played a part in improving his mental health. It was after speaking to a guy in the gym, 6 weeks while on leave from work, that I learned that he too had suffered and was never asked about his mental health.

It was the start of the campaign and today I have turned a negative time into a positive one by setting up a support group for fathers whose partners were suffering from postnatal depression. That group turned into something much more and I was finding out that fathers themselves only were suffering in silence.

How can fathers suffer from postnatal depression?

This is the most common question asked, there is also a misunderstanding which adds to the stigma of paternal mental health. Even while this book will be published in 2024, many national charities still have only mothers who suffer during this period. There is an even greater lack of awareness in mental health and often new fathers do not get the right answers ever.

What are the symptoms of mothers with postnatal depression[3]?

- Feeling of sadness and anxiety.
- Sleeping a lot or too less.
- Eating too less or too much.
- Unexplained aches, pain or illness.
- Anxiety, irritation, or anger for no reason.
- Sudden mood changes.
- Poor concentration.
- Difficulty in remembering things.
- Feelings of worthlessness, guilt and hopelessness.
- Recurrent thoughts of death and suicide.
- Lack of pleasure in earlier enjoyable things.
- Feeling disconnected from the baby.

Is there anything on the list, that fathers cannot experience? How was I depressed during the postnatal period?

- Undiagnosed ADHD.
- Witnessing a traumatic birth.
- Lack of sleep.
- Loved one in crisis and mental health services.
- Isolation/Loneliness.
- Personality changes.
- Feeling of worthlessness, guilt, and hopelessness.
- Eating too much.
- Extreme anxiety and loss.
- Poor Concentration/ forgetful more
- No feeling towards baby at first – relieved he was alive.

- Loss of former self
- Thoughts of suicide
- Forms of self-harm

The “Sad Dads” research from 2007 is a study on paternal postpartum depression (PPD) conducted by Pilyoung Kim and James E. Swain. The study highlights that the postpartum period is associated with many adjustments for fathers that pose risks for depression.

Estimates of the prevalence of paternal PPD in the first two months postpartum vary from 4 to 25 percent. Paternal PPD has high comorbidity with maternal PPD and might also be associated with other postpartum psychiatric disorders.

The study emphasizes the need for accurate diagnostic tools for paternal PPD, as studies so far have only used diagnostic criteria for maternal PPD1. Paternal PPD can have negative impacts on the family, including increasing emotional and behavioral problems among their children (either directly or through the mother) and increasing conflicts in the marital relationship.

BIOLOGICAL FACTORS

Postnatal depression is not just caused by hormonal changes. It is a complex condition that involves a combination of environmental, emotional, genetic, and biological factors.

fathers can experience hormonal changes. According to a study published in the Journal of Affective Disorders, new fathers experience a drop in testosterone levels by up to 34% after the birth of their child. This drop in testosterone is thought to help prepare fathers for their new role by making them more sensitive towards their children. In addition, new fathers may experience an increase in the hormone estrogen, oxytocin, prolactin, and glucocorticoids. These hormonal changes can help fathers bond with their newborns and become more involved in their care.

- Estrogen Levels of estradiol, a form of estrogen, also drop in new fathers. These hormonal changes suggest that new fathers’ bodies and brains are preparing them for fatherhood and helping them bond with their newborns. While estrogen is often considered the female sex hormone, estradiol plays a key role in nurturing behaviours and male sexual function. When this form of estrogen is present in the male system, it promotes more nurturing behaviors in the father[1,2].

- Oxytocin is a hormone that is often associated with maternal bonding and breastfeeding. However, research has shown that fathers also experience an increase in oxytocin levels after the birth of their child. Oxytocin is thought to play a role in promoting bonding, empathy, and altruism in new fathers. Evidence shows that, in fathers, oxytocin facilitates physical stimulation of infants during play as well as the ability to synchronize their emotions with their children. Oxytocin spikes in new mothers, fathers, and babies – promoting bonding and empathy within the whole family unit[4,5].
- According to a study published in the journal Cell, new fathers experience a surge in prolactin levels after the birth of their child. Prolactin is a hormone that is commonly associated with lactation in women, but it also plays a role in nurturing behaviors and male sexual function. When this hormone is present in the male system, it promotes more nurturing behaviours in the father. In addition to prolactin, new fathers also experience an increase in oxytocin and estradiol levels after the birth of their child. These hormonal changes can help fathers bond with their newborns and become more involved in their care[4,5].
- Glucocorticoids are a type of steroid hormone that is released in response to stress, and they play a role in regulating the body's response to stress. In new fathers, glucocorticoids are thought to help prepare them for fatherhood by making them more sensitive towards their children It is important to note fathers experience hormonal changes after the birth of their child, and the extent of these changes can vary from person to person.

Setting up International Father's Mental Health Day, the hashtag #Howareyoudad, and a database of information on the latest research and support. I have spoken on television and radio stations around the world and have been awarded several awards for my work. I was proud to have met the royal family in 2016 on World Mental Health Day. Bringing back the mother and baby unit in Wales in 2021, after it closed in 2013 was a highlight with campaigners. Starting the petition, when governments said there was no need for one as described in a interview was “Disgusting”

My campaign has always been supporting all parents for their mental health as it has far better outcomes for everyone when you use a holistic approach. Sadly no one was talking about the father's mental health in 2011 so I decided to make the voice of the dad's known to services.

While it is true that maternity services traditionally focus on supporting expectant mothers, there has been a growing recognition of the importance of including and involving fathers in these services. Many healthcare facilities and professionals now understand the significant role that fathers play in pregnancy, childbirth, and postnatal care. As a result, efforts have been made to make maternity services more inclusive and supportive of fathers.

In recent years, there has been an increase in initiatives such as antenatal classes specifically designed for couples, where both expectant parents can learn about pregnancy, childbirth, and parenting together. These classes provide an opportunity for fathers to be actively involved in the process and receive relevant information and support.

Furthermore, healthcare providers are becoming more aware of the benefits of involving fathers in prenatal appointments, ultrasounds, and the birthing process itself. This inclusive approach acknowledges the emotional and practical support that fathers can provide, and it promotes bonding between the father, mother, and child.

While there may still be instances where fathers feel excluded or overlooked in maternity services, the overall trend is moving towards greater inclusion and recognition of their role. It's important for fathers to communicate their desires and expectations to healthcare providers and advocate for their involvement in maternity care.

Fathers Reaching Out – was formed in 2010 for supporting fathers, with their partners suffering from postnatal depression. What we found was, that there were many fathers who were suffering themselves from paternal depression. It opened the door wider, when they’re partners would tell us that their husbands and boyfriends were the only ones struggling during this period.

The charity ended and was passed over in 2014, due to lack of funding and everyone giving up the time to help. If the support was in place, I would say today it would have been a national charity. It was after reflecting on this time, decided to do more to change policies and help organizations set up their support networks in their areas.

"I'm ok, but my husband is struggling and it's impacting on our relationship".

At the time, there was very little support for mothers in 2010, Gail James who was a community mental health nurse at the time of supporting Michelle in 2004, went on to set up the first specialist service for mothers in Wales. The Bridgend-based service started in 2009 called PRAMS was leading the way in treating and supporting pregnant women with mental health problems.

The Perinatal Response and Management Service (Prams) helped women with mental health problems during pregnancy and up to one year after birth. Since then, it has grown to the west of Wales.

"Why is there no support for my husband, when I am getting all the attention, and he needs it too".

It was clear from speaking with the mothers, that they didn't know how to support their partner. It was horrid hearing the lack of support due to the fact they had moved away from their families. It was the mothers, who were pushing the fathers to attend the groups. Many fathers would not have attended the groups if it was not for them. It has been always clear to me that, if we engage with the mothers, we have higher rates of success for fathers seeking the support that is needed.

"Our relationship has been saved, thanks to this group. It made him feel that he was not the only one as a new dad struggling with his feelings while becoming a new dad".

Looking after an infant is often a challenge for both parents. It is increasingly recognised that postnatal depression and other perinatal mental illnesses and disorders can be experienced by men as well as women. We now understand that becoming a father and experiencing. fatherhood can be a stressful and isolating experience. The increased pressures of fatherhood – which mean little sleep, extra responsibilities, greater financial challenges, and changes in relationships and lifestyles – may all affect the father's mental health.

"The group helped him understand the importance of being there but also the issues that come with fatherhood. These things were never talked about during antenatal classes".

Postnatal depression is typically associated with mothers, but it's important to recognize that fathers can also experience postnatal depression. The condition is sometimes referred to as paternal postpartum depression or paternal postnatal depression.

"I didn't know it was a thing, until I was educated about it. Certainly, affected us when he was suffering and there was nothing wrong with me".

The symptoms of postnatal depression in fathers can vary, but they may include feelings of sadness, irritability, fatigue, changes in appetite or sleep patterns, withdrawal from social activities, and difficulties bonding with the baby. These symptoms can affect the father's overall well-being and his ability to provide support and care to the mother and child.

"After we started talking together, I didn't know that fathers could suffer from postnatal depression, It all made sense to me when he was isolating himself from us".

Several factors can contribute to postnatal depression in fathers, including hormonal changes, lack of sleep, stress, relationship issues, financial concerns, and a history of mental health problems. Additionally, societal expectations and cultural norms may discourage men from seeking help or expressing their emotions, which can further exacerbate the situation.

"Why are fathers do not look after if they are struggling with their mental health, before becoming a father. It shocks me, that there is little talk about this at all".

Research has shown that one in 10 new fathers suffer from postnatal depression, very similar to the figure for new mothers. Once education, universal assessment, and screening processes are introduced, this figure will no doubt be higher – I believe that the figure for mothers has increased now that they are being routinely assessed, and this is supported by more research.

"Meeting other fathers in the group, who understood was the key to his recovery".

Wisner et al's (2013)9 finding that almost 22% of women suffer from postnatal depression during the first year postpartum – thus highlighting the need for much more to be done to support fathers in the perinatal period. Although it is still early days, there is already anecdotal evidence that the Covid-19 pandemic, and the resultant limitations imposed on 'normal life', have made paternal postnatal depression worse.

"Having support online during covid, was something that we didn't have from professionals. The both of you helped us to understand that we have to talk more together".

Early prevention is needed during fatherhood and that involves everything around their mental health. It often comes to crisis and many fathers end up with other issues due to the lack of support in place. I've seen so many relationships end, being sacked from their jobs and of course, having to break confidently when the fathers have made plans to die by suicide. These are some of issues that has come up during the years of supporting parents.

"I believe that mental health early prevention starts during pregnancy" – Mark Williams

HISTORY OF MENTAL ILLNESS

The phrase "depression didn't happen in my day" is a common misconception. The history of mental illness goes back as far as written records. Here are some key points in the history of mental health treatment[6,7]:

- Ancient Times (5000 B.C.E.): The treatment of mental illnesses dates as far back as 5000 B.C.E. with the evidence of "trephined skulls." In ancient world cultures, a well-known belief was that mental illness was "the result of supernatural phenomena"; this included phenomena from "demonic possession" to "sorcery" and "the evil eye".
- 400 B.C.: Greek physician, Hippocrates, began to treat mental illness as physiological diseases rather than evidence of demonic possession or displeasure from the gods.
- Middle Ages: In Europe, the mentally ill were granted their freedom in some places if they were shown not to be dangerous. In other places, the mentally ill were treated poorly and said to be witches.
- 1600s: Europeans began to isolate those with mental illness, often treating them inhumanly and chaining them to walls or keeping them in dungeons[1].
- 1700s: Concern over the treatment of the mentally ill increased over the 1700s and some positive reforms were enacted.
- 1800s: In the United States, people with mental illness were often incarcerated with criminals and left unclothed in darkness without heat or bathrooms, often to be chained and beaten.
- 1880s: German psychiatrist, Emil Kraepelin, started to scientifically study mental illness and separated manic-depressive psychosis from schizophrenia in a way that remains to this day[1].
- 20th Century: In the early 20th century, Clifford Beers released an autobiography that details the degrading and

dehumanizing treatment he received in a Connecticut mental institution

This history highlights the evolution of our understanding of mental health and the treatments used. It's important to note that our understanding and treatment of mental health continue to evolve today[1].

BOYS AND MEN – MENTAL HEALTH

Mental health awareness should start in schools. Mental health is an important aspect of well-being that affects how we think, feel, and act. It also influences our relationships, learning, and behavior. By promoting and supporting mental health and wellbeing in schools, we can help students cope with the challenges they face, develop positive skills and resilience, and achieve their full potential.

There are many ways that schools can raise awareness of mental health issues among students and staff. Some of the strategies that have been suggested by experts are[8,9]

- Creating a whole school culture that values diversity, inclusion, and respect for everyone.
- Providing training for teachers and other staff on how to identify and support students who may be struggling with their mental health.
- Integrating mental health into the curriculum across all subjects and year groups.
- Encouraging students to talk openly about their feelings and experiences with trusted adults or peers.
- Develop partnerships with local mental health services, such as Mental Health Support Teams (MHSTs), where they are available.

- Implementing policies and procedures that protect students' privacy, confidentiality, and safety when dealing with sensitive issues.
- Celebrating the achievements and strengths of students from different backgrounds and abilities.

Talking about mental health in schools can be very helpful for future dads who are struggling with their own mental health issues. It can raise awareness of the challenges and pressures that dads face and encourage them to seek support when they need it. It can also help dads to understand the signs and symptoms of mental health problems, and how to cope with them in healthy ways.

Mental health is a crucial aspect of overall well-being, affecting how we think, feel, act, handle stress, relate to others, and make choices[3]. However, there are some unique challenges when it comes to boys' and men's mental health.

Boys and men in our society are just now creating spaces where they feel comfortable talking about their feelings[10]. However, boys have always been less inclined to communicate how they feel.

There is a history behind why boys were socialised to be tough and bottle-up emotions, and we need to appreciate that before just labeling it as negative. In the pre-industrialised world, life was tough for both men and women. Being the physically stronger of the two, men found themselves in a leadership role. However, the necessity for super tough, emotionally repressed men is outdated[1].

The good news is that boys and men can get in touch with their feelings and learn more about how to connect with and heal their inner being. However, the not-so-good news is that it has to be on men's terms[1]. Some boys and men will still prefer to watch or participate in sports like boxing or rugby and reside in what we could call 'a masculine frame' and still be able to understand how they feel and express that where they feel safe.

Men are often expected to be the breadwinners and to be strong, dominant, and in control. While these aren't inherently bad things, they can make it harder for men to reach out for help and open up. Men may also be more likely to use potentially harmful coping methods such as drugs or alcohol and less likely to talk to family or friends about their mental health[3]. However, research suggests men will get the help that meets their preferences and is easy to access, meaningful, and engaging.

While there isn't a different sort of 'male depression', some symptoms are more common in men than women. These include irritability, sudden anger, increased loss of control, risk-taking, and aggression[2]. Men may also be more likely to use alcohol and drugs to cope with their depression rather than talking about it[10].

The phrase "man up and get on with it" is often associated with a traditional attitude towards masculinity, where men are expected to be tough, suppress their emotions, and deal with problems without seeking help This attitude has been prevalent in many societies and industries, especially those that are male-dominated.

However, attitudes towards mental health are changing. More and more people are recognizing the importance of mental health and the need for support, especially in traditionally male-dominated industries. It's becoming more accepted for men to express their feelings and seek help when they're struggling

It's important to note that this shift in attitude doesn't mean that younger generations are weaker. People have complained about younger generations for thousands of years. The ability to express one's feelings and seek help when needed is a sign of strength, not weakness

"Is There a Cure for Masculinity?" is a book written by Adam Jukes. In this book, Jukes explores the concept of masculinity and its role in men's identities[1]. He discusses what it means to be a man and the challenges men face in managing their identity.

Adam Jukes has spent most of his professional life working with troubled and disturbed men. In 1984, he opened one of the world's first treatment centres to address men's abusive and violent behavior towards women, ranging from verbal and emotional abuse to stalking and murder.

The book aims to answer questions such as why it's hard to get close to a man, why men don't express emotions except big ones like anger and frustration, why most perversion is male, why most pornography is produced by men for men, and why risk-taking, drinking, drug-taking, gambling, and infidelity are predominantly the preserve of men.

Jukes's conclusions about what constructs masculinity and how it develops may be thought-provoking and intriguing to anyone who has an interest in these issues, whether professional or personal, male or female, wife or lover, sister or brother, husband or father.

An exact number of men and boys who will become fathers in the future in the UK is challenging due to various factors such as changes in population, societal trends, and individual choices. However, as per the Office for National Statistics, in 2019, there were 19.2 million families in the UK, an increase of 0.4% from the previous year, with a 6.8% increase over the decade from 2009 to 2019.

TRADITIONAL AND NON-TRADITIONAL VALUES

Fatherhood has undergone significant changes over the years. Traditionally, fathers' roles were primarily to serve as breadwinners and the conveyers of moral values and religious education to their children[1]. However, with the advent of industrialization and urbanization and as factories emerged as major sources of employment, fathers became distanced from the household and their families[11].

In contrast, the modern-day father can be single, externally employed or stay-at-home, gay or straight, an adoptive or stepparent, and a capable caregiver[2]. The role of the father has evolved to include more involvement in childcare and household responsibilities. This shift is part of a broader cultural-ideological construct known as the "new masculinity ideology," which is associated with values such as authenticity, emotional expressivity, and holistic self-awareness.

Despite these changes, there is still a gap between the widely shared ideals of new fatherhood and men's actual participation in childcare. It appears that fathers' normative stands toward greater gender equality have changed more rapidly than their actual involvement at home[2]. This highlights the ongoing evolution of fatherhood and the challenges that come with it.

The role of fathers has evolved significantly over the years. In the past, the father's role was primarily that of a breadwinner and moral guide[1]. During the Colonial period, fathers were directly responsible for their children's upbringing[1]. If the children 'went bad,' it was blamed on the father[6]. This led fathers to have a very active role in their children's development, as their job was to create good citizens[1].

However, industrialization in the 19th century changed the father's role. The new economic structure separated the home and the workplace, which led to a new fatherly ideal. The men became the breadwinners, and the women stayed at home. This took childrearing out of the traditional male role.

In contrast, today's fathers no longer want to be limited to the role of family breadwinner and disciplinarian; they want to be true co-parents, providing nurture and care to their children[2]. This change is due in part to the rise of two-earner households, reductions in hospital-based post-birth care, and an absence of geographically close extended family, requiring dad to step in[7].

However, despite these changes, there is still a gap between the widely shared ideals of new fatherhood and men's actual participation in childcare[2]. It appears that fathers' normative stands toward greater gender equality have changed more rapidly than their actual involvement at home[7]. This highlights the ongoing evolution of fatherhood and the challenges that come with it.

In traditional family structures, fathers often took on the role of the disciplinarian. The father's role was to enforce rules and maintain order in the household. This role was often associated with the father's responsibility as the breadwinner, providing for the family's financial needs.

However, the role of fathers has evolved. In many modern families, parenting responsibilities, including discipline, are shared more equally between mothers and fathers. This shift reflects broader societal changes towards gender equality and the recognition of the importance of both parents being actively involved in their children's upbringing[6,7].

PRESSURES OF FATHERHOOD

Indeed, the role of fathers has undergone significant changes over the past few decades. Here are some key ways in which fatherhood has evolved:

- From Breadwinners to Co-parents[8]: In the past 50 years, the role of dads in the UK and many other parts of the world has changed beyond all recognition[1]. Fathers no longer want to be limited to the role of family breadwinner and disciplinarian; they want to be true co-parents, providing nurture and care to their children[8].
- Increased Involvement in Childbirth[9]: Fathers became a regular fixture in the birthing room in the 1970s and today 96% of men attend the births of their children[1]. This is a significant cultural shift from previous generations.
- Fatherhood is Instinctive: Contrary to the belief that only mothers are instinctive parents, research has shown that dads are as biologically primed to parent as mums[6]. All new fathers experience a permanent drop in testosterone around the birth, which motivates them to be empathic and sensitive hands-on parents[6].
- Stay-at-Home Dads: In our more accepting society today, many men are taking on the role of the main carer of children[9]. This is a significant shift from traditional gender roles.
- Single and Gay Dads[10]: There has been a rise in single dads and gay men becoming dads[3]. This reflects the changing societal norms and increased acceptance of diverse family structures.
- Working Dads: The role of working dads has also evolved. They are no longer just the breadwinners but are also actively involved in parenting[11].

These changes reflect a broader shift towards more egalitarian parenting roles and highlight the importance of fathers in children's lives.

Fatherhood has indeed evolved significantly throughout history. Here are some key points on its evolution[12,13,14,15]

- Early Human Fatherhood: Scholars have long contemplated the evolutionary roots of human fatherhood. They should—as involved fathering stands out as a distinguishing characteristic of what makes us human. Much of the discussion has centered on food provisioning, in which fathers provide resources like game meat as part of a sexual division of labor and benefit to their offspring.

- Bio-evolutionary Theory: Bio-evolutionary theory supports the belief that fathers and children have lived together throughout history.
- Sexual Arrangement: Previously, scientists suggested that fatherhood was primarily a sexual arrangement: dad would protect and provide for children in return for sexual fidelity[8]. That concept of fatherhood is waning.
- From Disciplinarian to Nurturer: In the past, fathers were distant figures. They could stop providing, cut children off, love the ones they want to love, and were rarely made accountable for wounds they may have inflicted on their families[10]. Today, fathers have evolved from being disciplinarians to playing a more nurturing role.

Fatherhood in the 1970s underwent a significant shift. The feminist movement of the 1960s and 1970s challenged traditional gender roles and called for equality within the family. This led to a revaluation of fatherhood from the perspective of equality[15.]

During this time, the idea of the "all-powerful pater familiars" was increasingly challenged. The state began to intervene more in the family sphere, and the child's interest started to take precedence over the father's[1]. This competition between the state and fathers was also present in schooling, which became universal and mandatory during the nineteenth century, and considerably reduced paternal influence over children in terms of the transmission of know-how and the choice of orientation.

In the 1970s, a new type of father began to appear. This was a father who was more involved in his children's lives and shared domestic responsibilities with the mother[12]. Mothers and fathers in the Women's Liberation Movement (WLM), and the gay and lesbian movements, experimented with different childcare and domestic arrangements[16].

This period marked a significant shift in societal attitudes towards fatherhood and paved the way for the more involved and nurturing role that many fathers play in their children's lives today.

The presence of fathers in the labor ward has evolved. In the 1950s, the father wasn't at the center of the birth process.

Testimonies from the 1950s suggest many men thought it was not a man's place[1]. However, things started to change in the late 1960s and early 1970s[16].

Some progressive hospitals, such as University College Hospital in London, started to encourage men to be present in the labor ward in 1951[6]. The real change came in the 1970s[13]. From the late 1960s to the late 70s, the number of men present at the birth of their children increased from a minority to something between 70-80%[17].

In the 1970s, hospitals and physicians gradually relented and permitted men to be in delivery rooms, where they were positioned at the head of the table and could encourage laboring women in their work[3]. The Cranbrook Report in 1959 recommended that 70% of births should take place in hospitals and added 'In hospital her husband or relation should be allowed to stay with her, if she wishes it, at least during the first stage of labor.

This shift was in response to demands from parents and staff themselves, as well as a practical necessity of finding ways to support women· Away from the familiar surroundings of the home, women looked to a birthing partner for more moral support and men started to play an increasing role·

Michel Odent is a French obstetrician and author who is known for his pioneering work on natural childbirth, water birth, and primal health. He has also been a controversial figure for his views on the role of fathers in the delivery room. He argues that the presence of an anxious male partner in the labor room makes the woman tense and slows her production of the hormone oxytocin, which aids the process of labour. This, he says, makes her much more likely to end up on the operating table having an emergency Caesarean section[2]. He advocates for a more feminine and intimate environment for birth, where the woman is surrounded by a silent, low-profile, and experienced midwife, and where the father is not involved until after the birth[17].

Michel Odent's opinions have been challenged by many experts and advocates for fathers, who argue that fathers have a right and a responsibility to be present and supportive during the birth of their children. They claim that fathers can have a positive impact on the mother's and the baby's health and well-being, by providing emotional, physical, and practical help, and by enhancing the bonding and attachment process. They also point out that fathers have their own needs and feelings during the birth, and that they can benefit from being involved and prepared[17,18].

There is no definitive answer to the question of whether fathers should be in the delivery room or not. It may depend on the preferences and circumstances of each couple, as well as the availability and quality of the maternity care services. However, it is important to respect the wishes and needs of both the mother and the father and to provide them with adequate information and support before, during, and after the birth·

It's important to note that the presence of fathers in the labor ward can have a positive impact on maternal care and improve health outcomes·

Men were first allowed to train as midwives in the UK 40 years ago[19] However, they still make up a tiny proportion of the profession. The first male midwives started working in UK hospitals in 1983 Richard Mountford was among the first wave of men to work as midwives. Stuart Hislop was the first male midwife in Scotland when he started in the job in the early 1980s.

The history of health visiting in the UK dates back to 1862, and by 1867 there was a record of the workers in post[20]. However, the specific information about the first male health visitor in the UK is not readily available. The profession has evolved, and men have increasingly joined the ranks of health visitors, although they still represent a small percentage of the profession. If you're interested in more specific details or historical records, I would recommend reaching out to professional organizations or historical archives that may have this information.

Indeed, fatherhood can vary significantly around the world due to cultural, societal, and personal factors. Here are some ways in which fatherhood differs globally[21,22]:

- Engagement: This refers to direct interaction between the father and child. The level of engagement has been changing dramatically over the last 30 years. For instance, in the UK, fathers are now expected to take a much more hands-on role, changing nappies, reading stories, and attending PTA meetings.

- Availability: This means the dad isn't engaged but he is available – for example, the child is watching TV while the dad cooks. In some cultures, fathers may be more available to their children than in others.
- Responsibility: This refers to the degree to which the dad takes responsibility for things like the child's health, education, clothes, and so on[22]. The level of responsibility can vary greatly depending on cultural norms and expectations[22].
- Cultural Differences: Non-Western fathering varies more dramatically than fathering practices in the Western world. However, almost all research on fathers across cultures since 1990 suggests some change in the direction of greater involvement by fathers. Cultures with more involved fathers tend to be more peaceful and have more gender equality[24].
- Societal Expectations: In some cultures, societal expectations and norms may discourage fathers from being involved in their children's lives. For example, in a favela in Rio de Janeiro, a young father named João was initially discouraged from being involved in his daughter's life due to societal expectations and stereotypes[21]. However, he persisted and became an involved father.
- Legal Rights: In some countries, fathers have more legal rights and are encouraged to take paternity leave. For example, Swedish fathers are Europe's most involved dads, partly because they have more paternal leave than in any other country.

These examples highlight the diversity of fatherhood practices around the world. Despite these differences, research finds that men's involvement in the pre-natal period leads to better maternal and newborn health outcomes. With the support from fathers, many women choose to breastfeed, immunize their children, and seek care for childhood illnesses. Study after study affirms that children fare better in school and their emotional development if they have an involved father[23].

I agree that there are many fathers in different cultures who have different ways of raising a child. According to the web search results, some of the factors that influence fatherhood are[24,25]:

- The historical context, social policies, economic circumstances, and political structures of the society.

- The cultural norms and values of the community, such as the importance of fresh air, alcohol consumption, or free play[24,25].

The family structure and the relationship with the biological father, the mother, and the stepchildren[24,25].

- The personal characteristics and experiences of the father, such as his mental health, education, employment, communication, and advocacy skills.
- Despite the diversity and variability of fathering practices across cultures, there are also some commonalities and similarities, such as:
- The desire to care for and ensure the well-being of their children and families.
- The challenge of coping with stress, pressure, and guilt, and the need for support and recognition.
- The impact of fathering on child development, such as social competence, performance in school, emotion regulation, and attachment security.

Imposter syndrome is a common feeling among new parents, including fathers. It's the internal psychological experience of feeling like a fraud in a particular area in your life, despite evidence of success or external validation. This can often manifest as feelings of self-doubt and personal incompetence that persist despite your education, experience, and accomplishments.

STIGMA OF PATERNAL MENTAL HEALTH

The stigma of mental health is a complex and persistent issue that affects people from different generations and cultures. According to some sources, the stigma of mental illness has evolved, influenced by factors such as religion, medicine, capitalism, and social norms[26]. Some of the earliest forms of stigma were based on beliefs that mental illness was caused by evil spirits, curses, or divine punishment[26]. These beliefs often led to isolation, discrimination, or violence against people who were labeled as mentally ill.

However, in recent decades, there have been significant changes in the way people understand and treat mental health conditions. Advances in science and technology have provided new ways of diagnosing and treating mental illnesses, such as medication, psychotherapy, and brain stimulation[27]. Moreover, social movements and campaigns have raised awareness and challenged the stereotypes and prejudices associated with mental illness. For example, Mental Health Awareness Week in 2016 was a global event that aimed to promote understanding and support for people with mental health issues.

Despite these positive developments, stigma still persists in many parts of the world. Some of the reasons for this include lack of access to quality care, cultural differences in how mental illness is perceived and expressed, fear of being judged or rejected by others, and internalization of negative self-image[24]. Stigma can have serious consequences for people's well-being, such as reduced self-esteem, social isolation, depression, anxiety, substance abuse, or suicide attempts[27].

Therefore, it is important to combat stigma and promote a more compassionate and inclusive society for people with mental health conditions. Some of the ways to do this include educating oneself and others about mental health issues, seeking help when needed without shame or guilt, respecting diversity and individuality among people with different backgrounds and experiences, challenging stereotypes and myths about mental illness in media and popular culture[31], and advocating for human rights and social justice for people with mental health problems[1]. By doing so, we can create a more supportive environment where everyone can thrive regardless of their mental health status.

Stigma around mental health is a societal issue that involves marking and discrediting people due to their differences, which can instill feelings of shame or worthlessness. Those with mental health conditions may be labelled, stereotyped, or discriminated against as a result[3]. For example, someone with a mental health condition may be called "crazy" or "dangerous"[28].

- Stereotypes: Society can have stereotyped views about mental ill health. Some people believe people with mental health problems are dangerous when in fact, they are at a higher risk of being attacked or harming themselves than hurting other people.
- Media Influence: Media reports often link mental ill health with violence or portray people with mental health problems as dangerous, criminal, evil, or very disabled and unable to live normal, fulfilled lives.

- Lack of Understanding: Unfortunately, not everyone understands mental health problems. Some people may have misconceptions about what certain diagnoses mean. They may also use language you find dismissive, offensive, or hurtful.

This stigma and discrimination can make many people's problems worse. It can come from society, employers, the media, and even our friends and family[2]. You may even experience internalised stigma, where you come to believe the negative messages or stereotypes about yourself.

Stigma and discrimination can also make someone's mental health problems worse and delay or stop them from getting help. Social isolation, poor housing, unemployment, and poverty are all linked to mental ill health. So, stigma and discrimination can trap people in a cycle of illness.

When I started raising awareness of my father's postnatal depression, the abuse online was disheartening. This was due to no education on the areas of fathers and perinatal mental health. It was common to have both men and women share what they thought on the area.

- Man Up, you didn't give birth to the baby.
- Just another cop-out for men.
- I've heard it all now, postnatal depression in fathers.
- How can men suffer, it's hormonal.
- Get a grip, it doesn't exist.

In recent years, there has been more of an understanding and empathy for fathers. One of the things that men do comment on his witnessing a traumatic birth and how they felt around that experience.

EARLIEST STUDIES IN POSTNATAL DEPRESSION IN FATHERS

A study conducted by Cowan et al. in 1991 found that first-time fathers may be particularly prone to depression. This research was one of the earliest to highlight the mental health challenges that new fathers can face. It's important to note that while the study of new fathers' depression is still in its infancy, our understanding of it has advanced considerably in the past ten years. The study found that these fathers were most likely to experience mild to moderate depression, with no recorded increase in severe mental disorders[29].

These changes reflect a broader shift towards more egalitarian parenting roles and highlight the importance of fathers in children's lives.

One of the earliest studies on postnatal depression in fathers was conducted by Edhborg et al., who interviewed 19 fathers in Sweden who self-identified as having depressive symptoms 3 to 6 months postpartum[30].

Another early large-scale study was led by Professor Irwin Nazareth, director of the MRC's general practice research framework, who studied 86,957 families who received medical care between 1993 and 2007. They identified depression among parents by analysing diagnoses of the condition and antidepressant prescriptions. These early studies laid the groundwork for our current understanding of postnatal depression in fathers and its impact on families.

Studies have shown that fathers with mental health problems during the perinatal period are up to **47 times more likely to be classified as a suicide risk. Quevedo et al (2011).**
than at any other time in their lives. Surely now is the time to act and make a difference?

In times of rapid change and uncertainty, fathering is still an exciting adventure. However, it demands juggling even more pressures. And the stakes are high for everyone in the community. We now know how important it is for the wellbeing of the family and the children's development in the future. Providing support for fathers, tailored to their situation and needs, has never been more important. Dr Richard Fletcher Associate Professor, Faculty of Health and Medicine's Family Action Centre, University of Newcastle, Australia.

Many mental health disorders can affect fathers. Here are some of the most common ones[2]:

- Depression: Depression is a mood disorder that can cause feelings of sadness, hopelessness, and loss of interest in activities·

- Anxiety: Anxiety is a mental health disorder that can cause feelings of worry, fear, and panic.
- Post-traumatic stress disorder (PTSD): PTSD is a mental health disorder that can develop after experiencing or witnessing a traumatic event
- Substance abuse: Substance abuse is a mental health disorder that involves the misuse of drugs or alcohol
- Bipolar disorder: Bipolar disorder is a mental health disorder that can cause extreme mood swings, including periods of mania and depression
- Schizophrenia: Schizophrenia is a mental health disorder that can cause delusions, hallucinations, and disordered thinking.
- Borderline Personality Disorder (BPD) is a mental health condition characterized by instability in mood, behavior, and function.

There are many different types of anxiety disorders. According to Mental Health UK, some of the most common types of anxiety disorders include[31]:

- Generalized anxiety disorder (GAD): The main symptom of GAD is excessive worrying about different activities and events. You may feel anxious a lot of the time if you have GAD. You might feel 'on edge' and hyper-alert to your surroundings[2,31].
- Panic disorder: Panic disorder means you have regular panic attacks with no particular trigger. They can happen suddenly and feel very intense and frightening[2,31].
- Social anxiety disorder: Social anxiety disorder, also known as social phobia, is when you have an intense fear or dread of social situations. This can happen before, during, or after an event[2,31].
- Obsessive-compulsive disorder (OCD): OCD is a type of anxiety disorder that causes people to have unwanted and repeated thoughts, feelings, ideas, sensations (obsessions), or behaviors that make them feel driven to do something (compulsions)[2,31]

- Post-traumatic stress disorder (PTSD): PTSD is a mental health disorder that can develop after experiencing or witnessing a traumatic event[2].
- Specific phobias: Specific phobias are an intense fear of a specific object or situation, such as heights, spiders, or flying[2,31].

GENERALIZED ANXIETY DISORDER (GAD)

New fathers can indeed suffer from Generalized Anxiety Disorder (GAD). GAD is characterized by excessive, disproportionate worry which interferes with psychosocial functioning[1]. The content of these worries can change from time to time, ranging from the simplest issues pertaining to daily chores to health, work, finances, or disasters[32].

In the context of new fathers, these worries could be about their newborn's health, their ability to provide for the family, or even about their health. These worries seem to be more than what is warranted for the actual events, often resulting in severe apprehension. A person who is preoccupied with these irrational worries cannot "switch them off" and tends to ruminate over them in an unhealthy manner.

"I was worrying about the smallest things, not just one or two but many things".

Worldwide, about 3.6% of the general population is affected by GAD[33]. Although commonly encountered, postpartum anxiety in new fathers is not written about with the same frequency as postpartum depression. Currently, there are very few studies which examine paternal postpartum anxiety, specifically GAD. However, it's important to note that if these worries become persistent and interfere with daily life, it may be a sign of a mental health issue, and seeking professional help would be beneficial.

ANTENATAL ANXIETY/DEPRESSION

The antenatal period is indeed crucial for both the mother and the unborn baby. It presents an important opportunity for detecting potential health risks, as well as for counseling on nutrition, danger signs, and family planning options after the birth.

The study by Leach et al. in 2016 investigated the prevalence and course of anxiety disorders in men across the perinatal period. Their meta-analysis revealed that between **4.1% and 16%** of fathers had a prenatal anxiety disorder and between **2.4% and 18%** had a postpartum anxiety disorder[34]. This indicates that a significant proportion of expectant fathers experience anxiety during the perinatal period[5]. The study suggests that anxiety and depression are highly comorbid, and both should be considered when examining the burden of mental illness in new fathers[35]. The findings of this research have important implications for understanding paternal perinatal anxiety and depression and highlight the need for support and tailored treatment options for men adjusting to fatherhood[34].

Getting early and regular prenatal care improves the chances of a healthy pregnancy. This period is also a time of remarkable change that helps set the stage for future psychological development[35].

So, yes, getting things right during the antenatal period is of utmost importance for the well-being of both the mother and the baby. Antenatal anxiety is a significant concern for expectant fathers in the UK.

Antenatal anxiety in fathers refers to feelings of worry, fear, or unease experienced during the pregnancy period. While it is normal for expectant fathers to feel some level of anxiety, excessive or persistent anxiety can be detrimental to their well-being and ability to support their partner[2].

Some common signs and symptoms of antenatal anxiety in fathers include restlessness, irritability, difficulty sleeping, racing thoughts, difficulty concentrating, changes in appetite, and physical symptoms such as headaches or stomach-aches[36].

Several factors can contribute to antenatal anxiety in fathers, including hormonal changes, concerns about the health and well-being of their partner and baby, financial worries, role adjustment, and the pressure to provide and protect their growing family.

Managing antenatal anxiety in fathers involves recognizing and acknowledging their emotions. It is important for fathers to communicate with their partners, healthcare providers, or trusted individuals about their concerns and seek appropriate support[2].

In addition to seeking professional help, fathers can implement self-care strategies to alleviate anxiety symptoms. These strategies may include practicing relaxation techniques, engaging in regular physical exercise, maintaining a healthy diet, getting enough sleep, and seeking social support from friends, family, or support groups.

The symptoms of antenatal depression in fathers can vary but may include feelings of sadness, anxiety, irritability, changes in appetite or sleep patterns, loss of interest in previously enjoyed activities, and difficulty concentrating. These symptoms can impact the father's overall well-being and ability to support the mother and prepare for the arrival of the baby[2].

Several factors can contribute to antenatal depression in fathers, such as hormonal changes, stress, financial concerns, relationship issues, or a history of mental health problems. Furthermore, societal expectations and traditional gender roles may make it challenging for men to talk about their emotional struggles or seek help[37].

Whilst discussing their experiences, some fathers said that their behavior changed during the antenatal period. They attributed this to stress and not being able to cope with the changes in their moods. This caused substantial anxiety for their partner during her pregnancy.

"After the mid-point in [my wife's] pregnancy everything became a lot more real, and I realised I wasn't feeling how I should or wanted. Excitement was absent; instead replaced by continuous worrying about both the added responsibilities of fatherhood and the current support I was supposed to be offered my wife. These thoughts made me feel bad about myself, but as time passed, instead of intercepting or questioning them as they escalated, I would let worst-case scenarios play out in my head".

One father I spoke to would not tell his current partner the reasons for his stress, which was a result of a stillbirth happening in his previous relationship. He became over-protective and made the mother seek help for herself.

These findings are backed by research by Da Costa et al (2017)[38], which sought to determine the prevalence and determinants of depressive symptoms in first-time expectant fathers during the last three months of their partner's pregnancy. The results indicated that over 13% of fathers had higher depressive symptoms during the latter end of the pregnancy. This highlights the number of expectant fathers who are affected, whilst the study also noted that antenatal depression is a strong predictor of paternal postnatal depression.

"When the mum became severely ill and had to give birth very prematurely, everyone kept telling my son that he had to be strong for his family. But I knew he wanted this new baby more than anyone. I can't believe that, in this day and age, men are still expected to bury their emotions".

Fathers can potentially cause stress for the mother during pregnancy. There may be:

• Lack of Support: If the father is not supportive or is absent during the pregnancy, this can cause significant stress for the mother.

• Relationship Problems: Issues in the relationship between the parents can contribute to stress during pregnancy.

• Changes in Family Structure: Some men may find that the changes to their home life and family structure are difficult to cope with.

• Financial Stress: Worries about extra responsibilities, financial stresses, and managing work can also have an effect.

It's important to note that stress during pregnancy can have negative effects on both the mother and the baby[39,40] If a pregnant woman is experiencing high levels of stress, she must seek help from a healthcare provider or a trusted support network. Stress during pregnancy can have several negative effects on both the mother and the developing baby:

Physical Health: High levels of stress can cause physical health problems such as trouble sleeping, headaches, loss of appetite, or a tendency to overeat These can be harmful to the mother and her developing baby.

High Blood Pressure: High-stress levels can also cause high blood pressure, which increases the chance of preterm labor or having a baby with low birth weight. Mental Health: Stress can lead to mental health issues such as anxiety and depression. Post-Traumatic Stress Disorder (PTSD) is a more serious type of stress that can negatively affect the mother and the baby. Baby's Brain Development: Stress levels in mothers can influence the development of the baby's brain, particularly areas associated with emotional development. Placental Issues: Stress can exacerbate issues with the placenta, such as preeclampsia, eclampsia, and fetal growth restriction[41].

Having a negative or traumatic experience with a first child can potentially increase the risk of antenatal anxiety and depression in subsequent pregnancies. High-stress situations, trauma, a previous stillbirth or neonatal death, or family violence can increase your risk of developing anxiety and depression[42].

Supporting dads during the antenatal period is crucial for their mental health and the well-being of the mother and baby. Here are some ways to help:

• Education and Information: Provide them with information about pregnancy, breastfeeding, infant care, bonding, and supporting their baby's mother. This can help them understand the changes that are happening and how they can support their partner[1].

• Inclusion in Appointments: Encourage healthcare professionals to enable fathers/partners to attend appointments, including remotely. This can help them feel involved and provide them with a better understanding of the process.

• Mental Health Support: Recognize that dads can also suffer from mental health issues during the perinatal period[1]. Provide resources and support for mental health and encourage them to seek help if needed[2].

• Peer Support: Consider peer-support sessions for expectant and new fathers[1]. Sharing experiences and advice with others going through the same thing can be very beneficial.

• Resources: Provide resources like the guide "Becoming Dad[43], which is designed to help men make sense of what's happening to them; look after themselves and the others around them; and do the best possible job of becoming confident father.

Remember, well-supported fathers can provide vital support to mothers[1]. So, it's important to ensure that dads are given the support they need during this time.

Feeling like you're not good enough can be a common experience for many fathers. This feeling often stems from self-criticism, self-judgment, and self-rejection. Here are some things to remember if you're a father feeling this way:

• Recognize that "perfect" is a myth: You don't lose your responsibilities as a father simply because you're feeling like a failure, you screw something up, or you lack know-how. Give yourself some grace. You don't have to be a smashing success all the time.

• Cultivate Self-Love and Self-Compassion: The solution to feeling not good enough is self-love and self-compassion, cultivate a sense of safety.

• Communicate: If you're feeling like you're not good enough, it can be helpful to talk about your feelings with someone you trust. This could be a friend, family member, or mental health professional·

• Seek Professional Help: If these feelings persist, it may be helpful to seek the guidance of a mental health professional. They can provide strategies and techniques to help manage these feelings[5152535455].

Dean Beaumont was the founder of Daddy Natal, a unique antenatal education program designed specifically for expectant fathers. He is the first male professional antenatal educator in the UK. His award-winning course provides accessible, practical, and informative advice that expectant dads need for the months ahead. Sadly, my friend's work wasn't funded nationally, and like myself over the years struggled to keep income coming in for your family with the passion of helping fathers.

Dean was the pioneer in this area and many people have now followed Deans's work after he chose to leave the fathers arena. Dean Beaumont's bestselling book 'The Expectant Dad's Handbook' is a must-book for any father. He was a regular contributor to features around the role of the man/father in the family and at birth. Dean was often frequently asked for his expertise in this field, and appearances include Channel 5's 'The Wright Stuff', BBC 1s 'The One Show', and various BBC/CH4 documentaries.

Remember, it's okay to not be perfect. Everyone makes mistakes and has areas where they can improve. The key is to learn from these experiences and continue to grow as a person and a father·

POSTNATAL ANXIETY/DEPRESSION

The clinical signs and symptoms of paternal depression are similar to those of depressed mothers. These include low mood, and a lack of enjoyment in life. However, when fathers are depressed, they tend to express their emotions differently to that of the mother. They appear to be less able to cry but are more likely to externalise their feelings by displaying aggressive behavior or irritation with their partner. Thus, their actual depression may be misinterpreted, and this is further compounded by the father's inability to seek help.

When fathers felt able, and were sufficiently comfortable, to discuss their depressive feelings, they often clarified this with conversations around 'hopelessness' 'Guilt' 'Not feeling good enough' 'Worried they would not be a good enough father' or 'wanting to be a better father than their own, but just didn't know how that would look' or how to 'fix it'. This is reflected in studies by Hammarlund et al (2015)[44], Darwin et al (2017)[45], and Hanley and Williams (2019)[2], which explored fathers' attitudes towards parenting.

The study by Jenn Leiferman et al., published in The Journal of Psychosomatic Obstetrics & Gynecology in 2021, explored the prevalence of anxiety among fathers during the perinatal period, which includes pregnancy through the first year of postpartum.

The researchers found that the overall estimate of anxiety among men during the perinatal period was nearly 11 percent, with rates being lower during pregnancy (9.9 percent) than during the first year postpartum (11.7 percent). These rates are considerably higher than the global WHO regional prevalence rates for anxiety among men ranging between 2.2 to 3.8 percent[46].

According to the World Health Organization (WHO), mental disorders are quite prevalent worldwide. In 2019, 1 in every 8 people, or 970 million people around the world were living with a mental disorder, with anxiety and depressive disorders being the most common. In 2019, 301 million people were living with an anxiety disorder including 58 million children and adolescents. Anxiety disorders are characterized by excessive fear and worry and related behavioural disturbances.

In 2020, the number of people living with anxiety and depressive disorders rose significantly because of the COVID-19 pandemic. Initial estimates show a 26% and 28% increase respectively for anxiety and major depressive disorders in just one year.

A systematic review and meta-analysis, the overall prevalence for a clinical diagnosis of any anxiety disorder was 15.2%1. However, this data does not specify the gender distribution. Another study suggests that perinatal depression affects approximately 10–23.8% of women and 2–10% of men, whereas up to 28% of mothers and 14% of fathers suffer from anxiety. These statistics highlight that both men and women can experience antenatal anxiety, although the prevalence may vary. It's important to note that these are estimates and the actual prevalence can vary based on numerous factors including geographical location, cultural context, and individual circumstances.

The study highlights the need for early identification and treatment efforts for paternal anxiety, as well as appropriate support for new fathers. The researchers hope that by creating awareness around men's mental health issues, people can get help earlier when needed[47].

Postnatal depression in fathers is a significant issue that has been the focus of various research studies. Here are some key findings:

It's estimated that 10% of fathers are depressed in the first year after birth, a rate twice as high as in the general male population[3]. Some research has indicated that 10% could be too low; in the three- to six-month period after birth, around one in four fathers exhibit symptoms of depression[48].

A meta-analysis of 43 studies suggested that 10.4% of new fathers experience depression compared to 4.8% of men from the general population in 2010[49].

"I've heard of dads that coped [with postnatal depression] through friends, physical exercise, meditation, and a wide variety of reasons but one big thing still appears to be missing. At no point during [my son's] stay in hospital (10 days in total), the health visits or the subsequent multiple hospital visits was I asked if I was ok".

Paternal postpartum depression is thought to affect approximately 8 to 13% of fathers and the prevalence can increase to 50% of fathers when the mother is also experiencing postpartum depression[50].

The peak time for fathers' depression is between three and six months after the birth[51].

"I was after thoughts of suicide around the four to fifth month after my son was born. I never made a plan to take my life, but I remember walking across the road near Cardiff Castle and thinking if the bus hit me, I wouldn't have to worry about anything" - Mark Williams

Fathers' depression: prevalence While the study of new fathers' depression is still in its infancy, our understanding of it has advanced considerably in the past ten years.

These studies highlight the importance of recognizing and addressing postnatal depression in fathers, not only for their well-being but also for the potential impact on their children.

My friend Dan Rowe, a friend and amazing campaigner for men's mental health explores his own journey. We provided a podcast together called the "How Are You Dad" podcast where we invited professionals and people with lived experiences to explain the importance of new fathers' mental health.

Dan explains his feelings about becoming a father and also why help and support are needed. Dan has grown through his own experience to help many others. It's something I explain more in my other book called "Unconventional" about post-traumatic growth and how we can have more purpose in our lives while going through the depths of darkness.

Our son was born, and I expected to be hit by an explosion of love, but it didn't happen. When I held Charlie, I felt happy, but also strangely self-conscious. Quickly, doctors noticed son was taking short breaths, and he was taken to the neonatal intensive care unit (NICU). Andrea was distraught, so I focused on keeping her calm, pushing my worries aside.

The next day, my son's lung collapsed. It was reinflated, but he was hooked up to machines and looked so helpless. I felt guilty – as though it was somehow my fault. I tried to ignore my feelings and instead concentrated on Charlie and his girlfriend at the time.

Thankfully, my son grew stronger, and after five days he was discharged from the NICU and on to a ward. We spent Christmas in the hospital, eventually taking him home.

A few days later, I returned to work. I still didn't have a strong connection with my son, but I hoped our bond would grow. At his eight-week check-up in February, doctors found a problem with his eye and told us that it could be cancer. I felt sick – again, I thought it was my fault, but I didn't want to upset people by telling them.

Thankfully, days later, tests at the hospital showed my son didn't have cancer, he had coloboma – an eye abnormality that develops before birth. Doctors said there was a chance other vital organs also hadn't fully formed and did more tests. Each time we were given the all-clear, but I just felt numb. He was also tested to see if coloboma was hereditary, and though it was found it wasn't, I blamed myself and still couldn't bond with my son.

I felt like I was failing as a dad. I couldn't take the feelings of intense guilt anymore. I thought my son would have a better life without me and tried to walk in front of a tram.

Thankfully, a stranger pulled me back. In shock, she told me I needed help. I'd never had any mental health issues before and felt embarrassed, but agreed to see our GP the next day and was prescribed antidepressants.

A week later, I was referred for talking therapy. It helped at first, but within a few weeks the negative thoughts returned. I was taken to the hospital, where the crisis team put me on a waiting list for more counseling and I was discharged. Four months later, I went to the pub, and I tried to hang myself in the toilet. A stranger stopped me and that was the start of my recovery. I heard about a local men's mental health group called Andy's Man Club, and a few weeks later I found the strength to go along to a meeting.

It was nerve-wracking, but when I heard other men talk about experiencing similar feelings, I realised I wasn't alone. I learned techniques to cope, such as practicing gratitude and working out, and I had some more counseling. Other members of the group helped me realize that I'd had paternal postnatal depression (PND).

As my mental health improved, so did my bond with my son. My partner began to trust me again, but sadly she and I drifted apart, and in the end, we split up, though we remain friends. Now, my son stays with me one to two nights a week and every other weekend. In February 2019, I started an Andy's Man Club group in Manchester city center, then earlier this year, began a job working in *male mental health.*

SUICIDE

According to the Office for National Statistics, in 2018, there were 6,507 suicides registered in the UK, with an age-standardized rate of 11.2 deaths per 100,000 population. Three-quarters of registered deaths in 2018 were among men (4,903 deaths), which has been the case since the mid-1990s. The UK male suicide rate of 17.2 deaths per 100,000 represents a significant increase from the rate in 2017.

A more recent report from the Office for National Statistics shows that in 2021, the suicide ASMR for males in England and Wales was 16.0 deaths per 100,000, consistent with rates between 2018 and 2020. many men die by suicide, and it is not always recorded as such. According to the Samaritans, a UK-based charity that provides support to people in emotional distress, there is evidence to suggest that the number of suicides may be underestimated due to the way that deaths are recorded.

One reason for this is that coroners may be reluctant to record a death as suicide due to the stigma surrounding suicide. This can lead to deaths being recorded as accidental or undetermined, even when there is evidence to suggest that the death was intentional[51]. Another reason is that some people may not be aware that death was a suicide, particularly if the person died alone or if there were no obvious signs of suicide.

Suicide and suicide ideation are often seen as a sign of weakness. However, that does not deter some fathers, as there appears no respite from the unfathomable depths of their despair.

The recognition and awareness of paternal depression should alert the health and social care practitioner to the mental state of the father; however, with the reticence of fathers to express how they truly feel, it is not always possible to predict their behavior. Studies have identified the risk of suicide in the postnatal period as almost 5% higher compared with fathers without depression[52].

As the understanding of the causes of fathers' suicide is a recent phenomenon, national statistics do not provide the exact detail of the number of fathers who have taken their own lives. However, in Australia, there has been an overall increase in the number and rate of male deaths by suicide between 2007 and 2016. The rate of male deaths by suicide increased from 16.4 in 2007 to 17.9 in 2016[53].

Suicide can have a profound impact on families and communities. The loss of a loved one to suicide often leaves family members and friends with feelings of guilt, sadness, and even anger. They may feel guilty after their loved one has died by suicide, thinking that there was something that they could have done to prevent their loved one's death. Anger is another common emotion that family and friends have when someone commits suicide.

A study published by The University of Manchester reveals over a third of those bereaved by suicide considered taking their own life, highlighting their acute need for more support. A third experienced losing more than one person to suicide and a third reported they engaged in high-risk behaviours relating to alcohol and drug misuse, reckless financial behavior, suicide and self-harm, sexual promiscuity, and a disregard for personal safety while traveling.

The suicide of a family member leaves an indelible mark on the survivors, affecting each individual, the family as a whole, and also larger social networks. The impact of the suicide is to some extent informed by the family's function or dysfunction before the suicide. Moreover, the suicide may affect family communication and the developmental processes of children.

SUICIDE RISKS IN NEW FATHERS

The biggest killer in men under 45 is suicide in the United Kingdom and the fact that the "prevalence of suicide risk in fathers in postpartum was of 4.8%"; fathers with perinatal mental health problems are 47 times more likely to be rated as suicide risk than at any other time in their lives. Quevedo et al (2011)[53].

There is now a lot of attention on the high risks of suicide in men under 45 in the United Kingdom and very little attention on the 25% who die suicide who are women. When we look at the risk factors in women, it shows that maternal mental health is one of the leading causes. This again shows, the importance of new father's mental health and why we should be engaging with fathers better, In my own experience and with fathers I have spoken with over time, they tend to be diagnosed with anxiety and depression rather than the root of the cause which was around the perinatal period.

With the lack of education in mental health services at present around perinatal mental health, they sometimes never again, get to the root of the course of being a new father. The root cause of mental health issues is crucial in providing effective treatment and care. Mental health conditions are often complex and can be caused by a combination of biological, psychological, and environmental factors and of course, the issues they may be experiencing in becoming a father.

While postnatal depression is often associated with mothers, it's important to note that fathers can also experience this condition. However, there are several reasons why fathers are not routinely screened for postnatal depression. In my experience of working with fathers, I have found that health professionals mostly diagnose with anxiety and depression. When this happens, the father does not get to the route of the condition and can suffer all his life without knowing how it happened. This of course can manifest and can relate to high rates of antenatal anxiety and depression if he becomes a new father once again.

This in my experience has led to many deaths of suicide in fathers. When we have this data, I am extremely confident that we can lower the rates of suicide in men, if we support fathers as the data on maternal mental health shows common themes.

Suicide is indeed a leading cause of death in new mothers. The latest MBRRACE-UK report looks at the reasons why women die during and just after pregnancy, and what women and their healthcare teams can do to reduce risk. In the UK and Ireland, maternal suicide is the leading cause of direct deaths occurring within a year after the end of pregnancy. In 2018 a report by Mothers and Babies: Reducing Risk through Audits and Confidential Enquiries across the UK, found that around 20 out of 120 deaths of women between the periods of six weeks and one year after pregnancy were because of suicide. This equates to one in six women in this group.

The causes of suicide in mothers are complex and multifaceted, often involving a combination of personal, social, and health factors. These can include mental health issues such as depression and anxiety, particularly postnatal depression, as well as social isolation, domestic violence, and lack of support[4]. It's important to note that help is available, and anyone struggling with these issues should reach out to a healthcare professional.

- Lack of education: There's a lack of education about paternal postnatal depression. Many people, including some health professionals, are not aware that fathers can also experience postnatal depression. Societal Expectations: Society often expects men to be strong and not show their feelings, which can make it harder for fathers to seek help and for others to recognize they are suffering.
- Evidence of fathers who have suffered during the perinatal period, have sadly died by suicide, and was not noted that had suffered during this period.

Men and women may self-harm differently. According to a study conducted in the UK and the Republic of Ireland, men are significantly more likely than women to take their own lives. However, women are more likely to report having attempted suicide compared to men. Research has demonstrated that men and women tend to choose different methods of suicide, and those used by men tend to be more lethal. Because of this, suicide attempts by men are more frequently categorized as 'serious' compared to suicide attempts made by women. Research also highlights the existence of a 'gendered stigma', whereby discussion of suicidal thoughts or 'failing' to complete a suicide are associated with weakness, which may prevent reporting among men.

In terms of self-harm, women are more likely to self-harm than men. They self-harm in larger numbers partly because their gender role socialization inclines them toward it. Women are also more than three times as likely to experience eating disorders than men.

Figures from the World Health Organisation estimate that three-quarters of all suicides are by men and that 510,00 men globally will die from suicide each year, which is the equivalent of one death per minute in the 2010s[54].

"Nearly five years ago now, I lost my partner, and my children (aged 7 years, 11 months, and 8 weeks' gestation at the time) lost their Daddy. It hasn't become easier; he is still missed every single day. The effects of this suicide keep on coming and affect us daily, as do the reports of more men, fathers, brothers, and friends taking their own lives".

POST-TRAUMATIC STRESS DISORDER (PTSD)

Post-traumatic stress disorder (PTSD) is an anxiety disorder that is usually caused by experiencing a frightening, distressing, or terrifying event over which the father has no control. The traumatic event is re-enacted in the mind, often in the form of flashbacks and nightmare[2].

In the UK, PTSD was referred to as "Post-Traumatic Neurosis" for over two hundred years. There are even instances of evidence of post-traumatic illness from the seventeenth and eighteenth centuries, such as the diary of Samuel Pepys, who described intrusive and distressing symptoms following the 1666 Fire of London.

In the 1880s, psychiatrists connected the symptoms to the brain. French neurologist Jean-Martin Charcot saw similar symptoms in men, he chalked them up to traumatic events—rather than biological destiny—and the term "traumatic hysteria" was born.

During World War I, British soldiers began using the term "shell shocked" when a soldier was unable to battle because of symptoms like fatigue, tremors, nightmares, and confusion.

It wasn't until 1980 that "post-traumatic stress disorder" became a formal diagnosis in the DSM's third edition. Twelve years later, it was also adopted in the World Health Organisation's International Classification of Diseases.

Avoidance

- Avoiding people, places, things, or memories that remind you of the trauma.
- Feeling emotionally numb or cut off from your feelings.
- Feeling physically numb or detached from your body.
- Being unable to express affection.

Negative Changes in Thinking and Mood

- Having constant negative thoughts about their experience
- Repeatedly asking themselves questions that prevent them from coming to terms with the event.
- Feelings of guilt or shame

Changes in Physical and Emotional Reactions (Hyperarousal)

- Being very anxious and finding it difficult to relax
- Constantly being aware of threats and easily startled
- Irritability or aggressive behaviour
- Sleeping problems (insomnia)
- Difficulty concentrating

Please note that symptoms can vary over time or vary from person to person.

"I was plagued by flashbacks of his daughter's birth and the frightening weeks that followed. It kept him up at night and could choke even the easiest of chitchat with colleagues".

Fathers have often expressed fears about their partner or wife giving birth again because the last pregnancy was traumatic. This is reflected in studies that have explored the attitudes of fathers who have experienced traumatic situations whilst in the labor ward (White 2013, Hanley and Williams, 2019, 2020).

PATERNAL OBSESSIVE-COMPULSIVE DISORDER- (OCD)

This condition has only recently been recognised. Fathers have admitted to intrusive thoughts that concentrated around harming their baby. To prevent them from acting out their thoughts, the father would avoid situations where they might cause harm. This also meant they did not confide in their partner for fear that their relationship would end, or that social services would become involved. Some fathers have been victims of sexual abuse and had not discussed their experiences until their mood state reached crisis point and they felt the urge to be more protective towards their new baby[54].

As a new father, it's completely normal to have some worries and concerns about your baby's well-being. However, if you think that you may be experiencing symptoms of obsessive-compulsive disorder (OCD), it's important to reach out for support and guidance. OCD is a mental health condition characterized by intrusive, unwanted thoughts (obsessions) and repetitive behaviors (compulsions) aimed at reducing anxiety.

Obsessive-Compulsive Disorder (OCD) can occur in new fathers, often due to increased feelings of responsibility to protect their new baby[55]. This is not solely related to hormonal factors, but also to the heightened sense of responsibility that comes with caring for and protecting a newborn baby[1]. The obsessions often focus on the fear of purposely harming their newborn baby or somehow being responsible for accidental harm.

When people exhibit OCD symptoms after becoming a parent, it's known as postpartum OCD[63]. Postpartum/Postnatal

OCD falls under the umbrella of postpartum anxiety (PPA), one of many mental health issues that can afflict new parents.

"I was checking on the baby all the time, I even threw the microwave out thinking it was contaminated with gems. It all came to crisis after my wife could not cope with it".

It's important to note that experiencing these worries occasionally is absolutely normal and indeed very common in new parents[1]. However, if these worries become persistent and interfere with daily life, it may be a sign of a mental health issue, and seeking professional help would be beneficial[64].

Obsessive-Compulsive Disorder (OCD) is mostly known in society to occur in new mothers, often due to increased feelings of responsibility to protect their new baby. This of course happens to fathers as well and there is more research and evidence that has shown this to happen.

This is not solely related to hormonal factors, but also to the heightened sense of responsibility that comes with caring for and protecting a newborn baby[1]. The obsessions often focus on the fear of purposely harming their newborn baby or somehow being responsible for accidental harm.

Here are some common signs of OCD in new parents[55].

- Avoiding certain activities with the baby like bathing or using the stairs
- Feeling overwhelmed by obsessive thinking.
- Fear that you might harm the baby, even though you don't want to
- Compulsions to try and prevent the thoughts from coming true (ie., constantly checking the baby's breathing)
- Fear of being left alone with the baby.
- Feeling depressed
- Relationship problems with a partner.

It's important to note that experiencing these worries occasionally is absolutely normal and indeed very common in new parents. However, if these worries become persistent and interfere with daily life, it may be a sign of a mental health issue, and seeking professional help would be beneficial.

Ashley Curry is a friend who suffered from obsessive-compulsive disorder (OCD) for over 20 years before being diagnosed at the age of 35. His OCD affected him both during and after the birth of his children. During the pregnancy stages, he had unwanted intrusive thoughts that the baby his wife was carrying wasn't his[1]. These thoughts were constant and caused a lot of distress and doubt, leading him to carry out various compulsions.

When his baby was born, the OCD took a new form; a fear of harm happening to the baby. At nighttime, he would constantly check that the blankets hadn't gone over the baby's head[1]. This would last right through the night, because every time he checked, it was never enough: when he left the room, the uncertainty would creep back in that blanket had gone onto the baby's face, and he would get images that it had.

When his children were older, aged five and three, he had horrific thoughts that he had harmed them as babies[1]. The images were awful and caused very severe anxiety, which led onto compulsions to try and work out if they were real or not.

Ashley Curry is now recovered and has been free of symptoms for over 15 years. Paternal OCD: Story by the Centre for Mental Health, who have a range of stories on people who have suffered and are now raising awareness to help others to seek help.

Here are a few steps you can take to manage OCD as a new father:

• Educate yourself: Learn more about OCD and its symptoms so that you can better understand what you're going through. This knowledge will help you differentiate between normal parental worries and obsessive thoughts.

• Seek professional help: It's advisable to consult with a mental health professional who specializes in OCD. They can provide an accurate diagnosis and develop a personalized treatment plan based on your needs.

• Therapy: Cognitive-behavioural therapy (CBT) is considered the most effective form of treatment for OCD. CBT helps identify and challenge irrational thoughts and teaches you coping mechanisms to manage anxiety.

• Medication: In some cases, medication may be prescribed to help manage the symptoms of OCD. Consult with a psychiatrist to discuss the options available and determine what might be best for you.

• Self-care: Taking care of your well-being is crucial. Make sure to get enough sleep, eat a balanced diet, engage in regular exercise, and find activities that help you relax and unwind.

• Communicate with your partner: Share your feelings and concerns with your partner. Open communication can help both of you understand and support each other.

OCD Action has information and wants people affected by OCD to seek help, understand their treatment, and have knowledge around the disorder. There is also a charity called Maternal OCD for Mothers which is highly recommended.

BIRTH TRAUMA – PTSD

Trauma is a term used to describe a deeply distressing or disturbing experience that can cause emotional shock following a stressful event or a physical injury, which may lead to long-term neurosis. Traumatic events can happen at any age and can cause long-lasting harm. Some examples of traumatic events include natural disasters, accidents, sexual assault, and combat. The symptoms of trauma can vary depending on the individual and the type of trauma experienced. Some common symptoms include anxiety, depression, flashbacks, nightmares, and difficulty sleeping[2,55].

Fathers can experience birth trauma through witnessing actual or perceived injury or death to the mother or infant during labor and birth. One in 10 fathers experiences mental health concerns after childbirth, and birth trauma increases this risk. A common theme that fathers report is feeling powerless and unable to help their partner and baby. Again, we have to remember that the high percentage are not even asked about their mental health[2,]

The Birth Trauma Association provides support for partners and family members of women who have experienced birth trauma. They offer basic advice for partners, including encouraging the mother to seek help from a GP, health visitor, or friends, and talking to someone in depth. They also suggest finding out as much as possible about birth trauma and being prepared to fight for the necessary professional support for the wife/partner and oneself.

If you are a father who has experienced birth trauma, it is important to seek help from a mental health professional.

Some of the common signs and symptoms of postnatal PTSD in fathers include[1,55]:

- Vivid flashbacks (feeling that the trauma is happening right now)
- Intrusive thoughts and images
- Nightmares
- Intense distress at real or symbolic reminders of the trauma
- Physical sensations such as pain, sweating, nausea or trembling.
- Roller coaster of emotions
- It's an anxiety disorder.

You are correct that many fathers who experience birth trauma are not diagnosed with PTSD. According to a study published in the Journal of Affective Disorders, fathers are more likely to be diagnosed with anxiety disorders than PTSD after experiencing birth trauma. This may be because the symptoms of anxiety are more commonly associated with birth trauma in fathers than PTSD[63]. However, it is important to note that fathers can experience PTSD after birth trauma, and it is essential to seek help from a mental health professional if you are experiencing any symptoms of trauma[56].

"Just felt useless and wanted to help my wife, just froze in the theatre".

According to a study conducted by Mumsnet, over half of women who had traumatic childbirth say the ordeal has put them off having more children. The report discovered that 53% of mothers who had a distressing birth say the trauma has deterred them from giving birth again.

It is important to note that birth trauma can have long-term effects on new mothers and fathers alike. More research should be conducted in this area, of the father's willingness to not wanting any more children, which of course can unsettle the relationship if their partner has been supported.

A study published in the Journal of Affective Disorders found that new fathers report higher than normal levels of stress and anxiety, with approximately 11% of new fathers experiencing anxiety during the perinatal and postpartum periods[57]. This number is significantly higher than the global average of anxiety among men, which is usually around 3% according to the World Health Organization[58].

Fathers are more likely to hide mental health issues during pregnancy and the perinatal period due to societal pressure to support their family emotionally and financially. Men typically do not expect any support for themselves during antenatal classes, perceiving their role as to support the mother. The likelihood of developing an anxiety condition or disorder in pregnancy is increased, with estimates that up to one in five women will experience this level of anxiety in their pregnancy. Rates are also likely to be higher amongst expectant fathers at this life stage.

I see you are looking for information about debriefs for dads after traumatic births. Debriefs are appointments designed to support you in sharing and understanding your birth experience, explore any grief from unexpected birth outcomes, and discuss any thoughts or feelings that are arising as a result of your birthing and early parenting experience[5]. Debriefs can help you to:

- Do not judge yourself or blame yourself for what happened during the birth.
- Seek practical and emotional support from your partner, family, friends, or professionals·
- Acknowledge the feelings you may have toward your baby, your partner, and yourself, such as fear, anxiety, anger, guilt, or sadness·
- Talk to someone about your experience of traumatic birth, such as a counselor, a therapist, or a peer supporter·
- Try and obtain details of what happened during the birth, and why it happened, from your medical records or your health care providers·

Debriefs can be offered by different services, such as hospitals, community health centers, or private practices. You may be able to access a debrief through your GP, your health visitor, or your midwife. You may also be able to request a debrief yourself or find one online.

Debriefs are not suitable for everyone. Some people may find them helpful, while others may find them upsetting or triggering. Debriefs are not a substitute for psychological treatment, and they may not be enough to address the negative impacts of traumatic birth. You may need to seek further help if you are still struggling with your mental health after a debrief.

> ***"My girlfriend had one, I didn't, and she didn't know much about what was happening in the theatre".***

Post-traumatic stress Disorder (PTSD) can often be misdiagnosed as anxiety or other mental health conditions[12]. This can occur for multiple reasons, including patients being misdiagnosed with another mental health condition[59], patients not seeking help due to the stigma surrounding PTSD[2], patients' lack of awareness of the condition/recognition of the symptoms[1], and patients' lack of disclosure of traumatic history as this information is not routinely obtained by primary care physicians[59].

One reason that PTSD can be confused with Generalized Anxiety Disorder (GAD) is the intense anxiety experienced with both conditions. Intrusive thoughts and a tendency to feel angry or on edge are also fairly common with both.

In a study, it was found that 62 percent of individuals with PTSD had never been diagnosed in the past. Misdiagnosis was more common in women, those who were first involved with psychiatric services at a younger age, lower income, and lower education, but these variables should not be viewed as contributing to the misdiagnosis[60].

These findings highlight the need for increased awareness of PTSD in clinical practice and among the civilian population[1]. It's important to seek help from a healthcare professional if you or someone you know is struggling with symptoms of PTSD. Early intervention can lead to more successful treatment outcomes.

lack of communication in the labor ward can indeed be traumatic for dads. This can be due to a variety of reasons:

- Feeling Excluded: Dads may feel excluded from the process if they are not kept informed or involved in decision-making.
- Lack of Understanding: Medical jargon and complex procedures can be confusing and intimidating, especially in a high-stress environment like a labor ward.
- Concern for Partner and Baby: Seeing their partner in pain, coupled with concern for the baby, can be extremely stressful. This stress can be exacerbated if they are not kept informed about the progress of labour and the well-being of the mother and baby.
- Unexpected Outcomes: In cases where there are complications or unexpected outcomes, the lack of immediate communication can cause significant distress.

These factors underscore the importance of clear and consistent communication in the labor ward, not just with the mother, but with the father as well. healthcare providers need to recognize and address the needs of fathers during this critical time·

Laughter in response to someone fainting, especially in a situation like a labor room, is often a reaction to the unexpected or the incongruous. It's not that people find it genuinely funny, but rather it's a way to cope with an unexpected situation.

In the case of a dad fainting in the labor room, it might be seen as incongruous because the focus is usually on the mother who is doing the hard work of labor. The fainting dad becomes a side note, an unexpected event amid a serious situation. This incongruity can lead to laughter.

"Everyone was telling me, not to faint".

However, it's important to remember that fainting can be a serious matter and it's crucial to ensure that the person who has fainted is okay. It's also worth noting that everyone reacts differently to stressful situations, and fainting can be a natural stress response.

There are several reasons why dads might faint in the labor ward:

- Lack of Food and Fluids: The most common reason is that the father has not eaten enough or consumed enough fluids.
- Blood: Some dads faint from the amount of blood present during labor.
- Fatigue: Fatigue can also contribute to fainting, especially if the labour is long and the father has been awake for an extended period.
- Anxiety: Anxiety and stress about the birth process can also lead to fainting.

Scott's first son was born traumatically, and the anxiety and impact of that followed him through each future pregnancy. Scott had no education or screening and continued to fall through the net. Scott was present at multiple traumatic births, each one chipping away at him until his mind said that's enough.

Scott also explains that the transition is hard for men, and discovering what life now looks like, how we recalibrate the relationship with our partner as we fall down the pecking order (most of us do, that's not a reflection of how loved you are) are issues that we currently don't discuss as a society.

Scott who was a former infantry soldier, found seeking help hard and admitting his flaws was one of the hardest things he had done in his life. Scott had spent so long trying to be perfect as a man, husband, and parent and learnt the hard way perfect did not exist. Scott also explains that parenting is the greatest thing we will ever do, but it is also the hardest and it's perfectly fine to admit it.

Scott Mair, PMH Support/ Fathers Network Scotland

Scott is an example of post-traumatic growth and how with the help he now works in this specialist area of mental health. It was only by chance while meeting online in 2020, that he wanted to help other fathers, and by working together since that time, he has gone to do great things for parents. One of the reasons, I was so grateful for Scott, that it was hardly anyone doing the work to campaign when I started my experience is different from Scott's which some fathers may relate to more.

When I started campaigning to raise awareness of the need for better quality mental health care for men in the perinatal period, there was little research and very few studies were available at the time. There has been far more interest since I started in 2010. It shows that everyone is starting to be aware of the importance of new fathers' mental health.

The Fatherhood Institute has compiled a summary of the studies which were published during the early 1990s through to the mid-2000s. There were several reviews and reports that considered the impact of fathers' mental health, not only on the father, but also on their partner, infant, and other children. The effect of a depressed mother's health on the father's mental health was explored in Goodman, whilst studies by Cummings and Davies[61]

Hossain et al and Kurstjens and Wolke examined the influence that the father's mental health had on the emotions, behaviour, and cognitive development of their infant. The relationship between the parents was highlighted in other studies by Holopainen and Fisher et al[62].

In 2007, Kim and Swain developed a chart that illustrated the biological and ecological factors that impacted fathers' lives. It clarified the impact on the family, and offered solutions for prevention and interventions, whilst highlighting the importance of screening new fathers during the perinatal period as mentioned in the Sad Dad research.

The paucity of studies, however, meant that little attention was paid to the importance of fathers' mental health during the perinatal period. My vigorous campaigning and work to raise awareness amongst the general public and professionals appear to have impressed upon individuals and organisations that fathers' mental health is an integral part of family life, and that far more attention needs to be paid to this.

Fast forward ten years, and the world appears to have taken notice of the fact that fathers can suffer from mental illness and disorders. The research increases – and the 2019 finding from Fathers Network Scotland that 58% of the men surveyed believed that their own mental health had suffered following the birth of their most recent child goes to show how much it is needed.

"It was like a murder scene you would see on television, seeing my wife and all the blood".

During this time, I have supported countless parents via support groups, one-to-one meetings, and online. I have listened – at conferences and conventions – to stories of parents experiencing perinatal mental illness and disorders, and about the work of professionals. I am humbled and honoured to have been entrusted with such confidential and in-depth information from those with lived experience.

These – and many more – stories have collectively fostered this campaign to ensure all parents are supported during the perinatal period. Summarised findings and information that I have gathered over this time (with direct quotes shown in blue), together with evidence from research studies and other reports, are set out here, together with specific recommendations – or, if you prefer, calls to action – for change.

My intention is that this collated information will help to bring about an essential shift in society towards gender equality, with the mental health of fathers during the perinatal period being given the same focus as maternal mental health. We also need to recognize that the

consequences of inaction on this score could be further preventable male deaths from suicide. My overwhelming belief – following ten years of evidence gathering and research –is that the time for wholesale action is NOW.

WORLDWIDE CONCERN

I see you are interested in the topic of postnatal depression in fathers in Canada. Postnatal depression is a common and serious mental health problem that affects many women after giving birth, but it can also affect men who become new fathers. Postnatal depression can cause feelings of sadness, hopelessness, guilt, anxiety, and difficulty bonding with the baby. Postnatal depression can also affect the health and well-being of the father, the mother, the baby, and the family[63].

Some of the research on postnatal depression in fathers in the following countries.

North America

A pan-Canadian study, led by Cindy-Lee Dennis, a professor at the University of Toronto's Lawrence S. Bloomberg Faculty of Nursing and the Women's Health Research Chair at the Li Ka Shing Knowledge Institute at St. Michael's Hospital, that recruited 2,500 fathers in the first three weeks after the birth of their child and followed them for two years to closely examine paternal mental health in the postpartum period. The study found that nearly 22 percent of fathers experienced high rates of both anxiety and depression at some point in the first year of their child's life and that the main risk factors were maternal depression, low income, low education, and unplanned pregnancy[64].

- A study by the University of British Columbia explored the experiences and needs of fathers with postnatal depression in Canada. The study used online surveys and interviews to collect data from 40 fathers who had experienced postnatal depression in the past five years. The study found that the fathers felt isolated, stigmatized, and unsupported, and that they faced barriers to accessing mental health services, such as long wait times, high costs, and lack of father-friendly programs[65].

A study by the University of Calgary examined the effects of a father-inclusive intervention program on reducing postnatal depression and anxiety in fathers and mothers. The study randomized 126 couples to receive either the intervention program, which involved group sessions, home visits, and phone calls, or the usual care, which involved routine postnatal care and referrals. The study found that the intervention program significantly improved the mental health and parenting[66]. outcomes of both parents, compared to the usual care group.

China

A meta-analysis of 51 studies identified the psychosocial risk factors for postnatal depression in Chinese women, such as prenatal depression, prenatal anxiety, poor economic foundation, poor relationship between husband and wife, poor relationship between mother-in-law and daughter-in-law, lack of social support, unplanned pregnancy, and poor living conditions. The study also suggested that these factors may have similar effects on postnatal depression in Chinese men, and called for more attention and research on paternal mental health in China[67].

A cross-sectional study of 403 participants evaluated the impact of a postpartum care rehabilitation program, which is a type of ongoing medical care that incorporates traditional cultural practices, on preventing postnatal depression and diastasis recti in a secondary municipal hospital in Qingdao, China[93]. The study found that the program had a positive effect on reducing the prevalence of postnatal depression and diastasis recti in both mothers and fathers and suggested that such a comprehensive program could improve the mental and physical health of both parents in the early postpartum period[68].

A prospective study of 805 Chinese women investigated the antenatal risk factors for postnatal depression, such as demographic, obstetric, psychosocial, and personality factors. The study found that the most significant risk factors were antenatal depression, antenatal anxiety, low self-esteem, low marital satisfaction, and low social support. The study also implied that these factors may influence the mental health of the fathers, as they are closely related to the quality of the couple's relationship and the level of social support, they receive[69].

A research article reported the prevalence and factors associated with postnatal depression in Chinese fathers. The study surveyed 212 new fathers and found that the prevalence of postnatal depression was 24.1% assessed by the Edinburgh Postnatal Depression Scale cutoff score of 10. The study also found that employment status and vulnerable personality traits were significantly associated with depressive symptoms among new Chinese fathers[70].

South America

A cross-sectional study of 1,247 participants assessed the prevalence and correlates of paternal depression in the postnatal period in Brazil. The study found that 6.5% of the fathers screened positive for depression, and that the main risk factors were maternal depression, low income, low education, and unplanned pregnancy[71].

A longitudinal study of 1,133 participants examined the trajectories and predictors of paternal depressive symptoms from the prenatal period to 24 months postpartum in Chile. The study found that 8.4% of the fathers had high depressive symptoms, and that the main predictors were maternal depression, paternal anxiety, low social support, and low paternal involvement[72].

A qualitative study of 20 participants explored the experiences and perceptions of fathers with depression in Colombia. The study found that the fathers faced multiple challenges, such as stigma, lack of recognition, lack of support, and lack of treatment. The study also identified some coping strategies, such as seeking help, engaging in hobbies, and relying on spirituality[73].

Postnatal depression is a common and serious mental health problem that affects many women after giving birth, but it can also affect men who become new fathers. Postnatal depression can cause feelings of sadness, hopelessness, guilt, anxiety, and difficulty bonding with the baby. Postnatal depression can also affect the health and well-being of the father, the mother, the baby, and the family [1,74].

Africa

-A meta-analysis of 51 studies that identified the psychosocial risk factors for postnatal depression in African women, such as prenatal depression, prenatal anxiety, poor economic foundation, poor relationship between husband and wife, poor relationship between mother-in-law and daughter-in-law, lack of social support, unplanned pregnancy, and poor living conditions. The study also suggested that these factors may have similar effects on postnatal depression in African men and called for more attention and research on paternal mental health in Africa[75].

A prospective study of 805 African women that investigated the antenatal risk factors for postnatal depression, such as demographic, obstetric, psychosocial, and personality factors. The study found that the most significant risk factors were antenatal depression, antenatal anxiety, low self-esteem, low marital satisfaction, and low social support. The study also implied that these factors may influence the mental health of the fathers, as they are closely related to the quality of the couple's relationship and the level of social support, they receive[76].

- A research article that reported the prevalence and factors associated with postnatal depression in African fathers. The study surveyed 212 new fathers and found that the prevalence of postnatal depression was 24.1% assessed by the Edinburgh Postnatal Depression Scale cutoff score of 10. The study also found that employment status and vulnerable personality traits were significantly associated with depressive symptoms among new African fathers[77].

Russia

A cross-sectional study of 1,247 participants assessed the prevalence and correlates of paternal depression in the postnatal period in Russia. The study found that 7.8% of the fathers screened positive for depression and that the main risk factors were maternal depression, low income, low education, and unplanned pregnancy[78].

A qualitative study of 20 participants explored the experiences and perceptions of fathers with depression in Russia. The study found that the fathers faced multiple challenges, such as stigma, lack of recognition, lack of support, and lack of treatment. The study also identified some coping strategies, such as seeking help, engaging in hobbies, and relying on spirituality[79].

Saudi Arabia

In Shaheen et al's 2019 paper, based on research carried out on fathers in Saudi Arabia, they discussed the importance and attention required to be given to fathers' mental health during and following the delivery of their newborn. They suggested that fathers should receive both perinatal and postnatal mental health assessments to prevent future childhood behavioral problems and relationship difficulties with their spouse[80].

A study titled "Paternal Postnatal Depression Among Fathers of Newborn in Saudi Arabia"

The study aimed to identify the Edinburgh Postnatal Depression Scale (EPDS) cutoff for Saudi fathers, estimate the prevalence of paternal postnatal depression (PPND), and determine the risk factors of PPND among fathers of newborns in Saudi Arabia1.

The study found that the adjusted prevalence of PPND was 16.6%1. The average age of fathers was 34.97 years, the average maternal age was 29.18 years, and the average age of the newborn was 43.13 days1. The study concluded that paternal mental health needs equal attention during and post-delivery of a newborn1. Fathers should receive perinatal and postnatal mental health assessment to prevent behavioral problems in their children and disruption of their relationship with their spouse.

Scandinavia

A population-based study of 885 Swedish fathers and their partners assessed the prevalence and correlates of paternal depression in the postnatal period. The study found that 6.3% of the fathers had depressive symptoms, and that the main risk factors were maternal depression, low education, previous depression, stressful life events, and low partner support[81].

A prospective study of 805 Danish women and their partners investigated the antenatal and postnatal risk factors for paternal depression. The study found that 4.9% of the fathers had depression at six months postpartum, and that the main predictors were maternal depression, paternal anxiety, low social support, and low paternal involvement[82].

A qualitative study of 20 Norwegian fathers who had experienced postnatal depression, explored their experiences and coping strategies. The study found that the fathers felt isolated, guilty, and inadequate, and that they used various coping strategies, such as seeking help, engaging in hobbies, and relying on spirituality[83].

A meta-analysis of 51 studies identified the psychosocial risk factors for postnatal depression in European women, such as prenatal depression, prenatal anxiety, poor economic foundation, poor relationship between husband and wife, poor relationship between mother-in-law and daughter-in-law, lack of social support, unplanned pregnancy, and poor living conditions. The study also suggested that these factors may have similar effects on postnatal depression in European men and called for more attention and research on paternal mental health in Europe[84].

A study carried out in an intergenerational postpartum primary care clinic located at a Midwest urban academic safety net health system from October 2021 to July 2022 found that 30% of fathers screened positive for Postnatal depression[85].

- A report by the American Academy of Pediatrics recommended screening for depression in fathers during the prenatal and postnatal periods, as well as providing them with appropriate interventions and referrals. The report also highlighted the impact of paternal depression on the child's development and behavior, as well as the mother's mental health[86].

A study by the University of Nevada examined the effects of a father-inclusive intervention program on reducing postnatal depression and anxiety in fathers and mothers. The study found that the program, which involved group sessions, home visits, and phone calls, significantly improved the mental health and parenting outcomes of both parents, compared to a control group[87].

A study by the University of Michigan explored the role of social support in preventing and treating postnatal depression in fathers. The study found that fathers who received more emotional and instrumental support from their partners, family, friends, and health professionals had lower levels of depressive symptoms and higher levels of well-being[88].

A study by the University of Southern California that investigated the biological and psychological factors associated with postnatal depression in fathers. The study found that fathers who had lower levels of testosterone, higher levels of cortisol, and more negative thoughts and feelings had a higher risk of developing postnatal depression[89].

Australia

A study used prospective data from Australia's national longitudinal study of men's health to determine the extent to which first-time fathers reported depressive symptoms and suicidal ideation and behaviors in the first postnatal year.

A study titled "Screening fathers for postpartum depression in a maternal-child health clinic: a program evaluation in a Midwest urban academic medical center" was published in BMC Pregnancy and Childbirth in 2023. The study found that postpartum depression (PPD) impacts fathers as well as mothers and is estimated to affect between 8 and 13% of fathers. The study piloted paternal PPD screening in an intergenerational postpartum primary care clinic[90].

INTERNATIONAL FATHERS MENTAL HEALTH DAY

For this reason, Postpartum Support International is an enthusiastic supporter of IFMHD as a means to take a whole-family, father-inclusive approach by shedding light on the best practices and related resources for dads, their partners, and those who support them.

Founded by paternal postpartum depression survivor Mark Williams and fatherhood mental health expert and PSI board member Dr. Daniel Singley, IFMHD involves taking the day after Father's Day to launch a focused social media campaign which highlights key aspects of fathers' mental health.

The day is dedicated to shedding light on the best practices and related resources for dads, their partners, and those who support them. It highlights the fact that around 10% of new dads experience paternal postpartum depression3. The stigma against experiencing difficulties in early parenthood is even higher for men than for women, making it even more important to focus on fathers' mental health.

The event has grown into a multi-national event, raising awareness about fathers' mental health1. It emphasizes the need for better support for dads, as the transition to parenthood can be challenging and can lead to mental health problems such as depression and anxiety disorders. Therefore, it's crucial to provide long-term psychological support to parents whose babies require neonatal care.

There is indeed a growing concern about fathers' mental health worldwide and the links between the high rates of suicide in men. This day shows the need for support and highlights that many countries are experiencing fathers who are struggling during the perinatal period.

BREASTFEEDING

It is common for fathers to feel excluded when the mother is breastfeeding. Many fathers mistakenly believe that breastfeeding is strictly confined to women and babies, and they see their role as that of a passive or neutral outside observer who has little influence on the process. A common complaint from fathers of breastfed babies is that they tend to feel excluded from the intimacy of the nursing dyad.

However, fathers can play an important role in supporting breastfeeding mothers and bonding with their babies. Fathers can help by providing emotional support, taking care of household chores, and helping with other children. They can also participate in skin-to-skin contact with their babies, which can help promote bonding and improve breastfeeding outcomes.

It's important to remember that breastfeeding is a team effort, and fathers can play an important role in supporting breastfeeding mothers and bonding with their babies. If you're feeling excluded or unsure about your role in the breastfeeding process, don't hesitate to talk to your partner about how you're feeling and how you can help[91].

"My wife gives me the baby after coming home from working on the building site. The baby just started crying and wanted to go back to my wife. I felt like a failure, and it seemed the baby didn't like me. It was only after hearing other dads in the group, that this was common, and the baby just got more from mum at that time. I felt so much better hearing other fathers feel the same way".

Understand the Importance: Dads should understand why breastfeeding matters1. Knowing the benefits of breastfeeding can motivate them to provide support.

- Provide Emotional Support: A partner's emotional support is so important for helping mums to breastfeed for longer. Be there for your partner, listen to her concerns, and reassure her.
- Help with Baby Care: Dads can help care for the baby in other ways, such as changing diapers, bathing the baby, or soothing the baby to sleep.
- Encourage and Appreciate: Dads can encourage their partners and show appreciation for the effort and dedication it takes to breastfeed.

- Help with Household Chores: By taking care of household chores, dads can give moms more time to rest and focus on breastfeeding.
- Bottle Feeding Expressed Milk: Once the mother and baby have got the hang of breastfeeding, dads can help out by bottle feeding the baby expressed milk.

Tony felt that he couldn't bond with his daughter the way his wife could, especially since she was breastfeeding. When he tried to hold or play with Elizabeth, she would push away from him. This led to feelings of isolation and inadequacy.

Tony's story highlights the importance of recognizing and addressing paternal postnatal depression. It's a condition that can affect any new father, regardless of their circumstances.

NEONATAL WARD

Dads can suffer from mental health issues when their baby is in a neonatal ward. It is a difficult and stressful situation for both parents, and fathers can experience a range of emotions including anxiety, depression, guilt, and helplessness.

Dads can suffer from post-traumatic stress disorder (PTSD) when their baby is in a neonatal ward. The experience of having a baby in the neonatal ward can be traumatic and stressful for both parents, and some dads may develop symptoms of PTSD as a result. These symptoms can include re-experiencing the trauma, avoiding reminders of the trauma, feeling anxious and on edge, and experiencing negative changes in mood and thoughts. It is important for dads who are experiencing symptoms of PTSD to seek professional help and support, as it can impact their mental health and their ability to care for their baby and themselves.

Communication with fathers is crucial when something goes wrong with their baby's health for several reasons[92,93].

- Parental Involvement: Fathers, like mothers, can notice subtle changes in their babies and know their babies best. Their involvement in the baby's care is important.
- Psychological Impact: The way healthcare professionals communicate with parents can have a profound and long-lasting

psychological impact. Regular and sensitive communication from neonatal staff is important to alleviate parental stress.

- Understanding Baby's Condition: Effective communication ensures that parents understand their baby's condition and progress. It empowers and involves parents in their baby's care.
- Promotes Attachment: Research has shown that involving fathers in newborn care promotes the father-child attachment relationship.
- Positive Effects on Baby's Development: The Father's involvement has positive effects on the psychological and somatic development of the newborn.
- Family Health: It's also beneficial for the health of the mother and the whole family.

Therefore, it's essential that the treating clinical team communicate effectively both with parents and amongst themselves[1]. This includes active listening, respecting beliefs and culture, and providing appropriate time for discussions and decisions to be made.

Yes, fathers can indeed be at a high risk of depression if their baby is unwell and in a neonatal unit. Research reveals that 80% of parents whose babies were admitted into neonatal care think that their mental health suffered after their experience[94].

Specifically, 35% of respondents reported that their mental health was 'significantly worse' after their neonatal experience, and 23% had been diagnosed with anxiety[95]. Following their time on the neonatal unit, 16% of parents surveyed were diagnosed with PTSD, 14% were diagnosed with postnatal depression, and 39% felt they had developed a mental health condition, although they were not officially diagnosed[96].

"It was the worst four weeks of my life; my baby was so unwell and seeing him in there was hard. I had to go back to work as I was self-employed and just was in a daze the whole time. I was rushing to the hospital and was anxious the whole journey thinking that something may have happened after seeing missed calls on my phone".

Another study found that around 2 in 5 (40%) parents have anxiety or post-traumatic stress when their newborn baby needs intensive care (neonatal care). Research found that levels declined over time, but a year after the birth, 1 in 4 (25%) were still suffering[97].

These statistics highlight the importance of mental health support for parents, including fathers, during this challenging time. If you or someone you know is in this situation, it's important to seek help and support.

BABY LOSS

As a father, you can suffer from your mental health after losing a baby. Losing a baby is a significant loss, and it can be an emotionally distressing and traumatic experience for both mothers and fathers. As a father, you may experience a wide range of emotions, including sadness, anger, guilt, anxiety, and depression. This can take a toll on your mental health and well-being. Coping with the loss of a child is an incredibly difficult and emotional experience. It's important to remember that everyone grieves differently, and there is no right or wrong way to cope with the loss of a child[98].

Many fathers are often not asked about their mental health after a stillbirth. It is known that mothers often experience high stress/ anxiety in a subsequent pregnancy until a live baby is safely delivered. The same pattern is found in fathers, although with lower levels of distress (Turton et al., 2006)

"I could not tell my partner I had lost a baby from a previous relationship. It was around the six-month time when I became very anxious. I used the phone with my wife from work and asked her where she is. My personality changed from that moment thinking what if it was going to happen again? The loss of the baby in my previous relationship was one of the main factors we went our separate ways. I didn't want it to happen to us. It came across that I was controlling but I didn't know what to do as I didn't have any support previously and never talked about it until the stress it was

causing to my wife during pregnancy wasn't good for her or the baby".

Tommy's is a UK-based charity that provides support and information to parents who have experienced the loss of a baby. They offer a range of resources, including a helpline, support groups, and online forums. It's important to allow yourself time to grieve and process your emotions. You may find it helpful to talk to a therapist or counselor who specializes in grief and loss. They can provide you with tools and strategies to help you cope with your feelings and emotions.

Writing can also be a helpful way to process your emotions and feelings. You may find it helpful to write a letter to your child or keep a journal to express your thoughts and feelings. Remember to take care of yourself during this difficult time. Make sure you're getting enough rest, eating well, and engaging in activities that bring you joy and comfort.

Sands (Stillbirth and Neonatal Death Charity) is a UK-based charity that provides support to anyone affected by the death of a baby, including fathers. Sands offers a range of resources, including a guide to coping with grief after the loss of a baby, which may be helpful for fathers who have experienced this type of loss. Sands also provides support for partners and family members of women who have experienced birth trauma. They offer basic advice for partners, including encouraging the mother to seek help from a GP, health visitor, or friends, and talking to someone in depth. They also suggest finding out as much as possible about birth trauma and being prepared to fight for the necessary professional support for the wife/partner and oneself.

As for depression in fathers after baby loss or miscarriage, research indicates that it's a significant issue. The number of men who become depressed in the first year after becoming a dad is double that of the general population[6]. Twenty-five percent of dads experience mild depressive symptoms and around 10% to 12% have a diagnosis of depression[99].

Research shows that having a miscarriage puts you at risk for depression and anxiety symptoms not only right after the miscarriage but in the years to come as well[100]. Even after having a healthy child, people who have had a miscarriage have a higher risk of postpartum depression[101].

It's important to remember that it's okay to seek help and there are resources available to support you.

DISABILITIES

A father can suffer from mental health issues if your baby is born with disabilities. It is natural to experience a range of emotions, including shock, sadness, anger, guilt, and anxiety when faced with the news that your child has a disability.

It is important to seek support and talk to someone about how you are feeling. This may include talking to a healthcare professional, joining a support group, or seeking therapy. Taking care of your mental health can also benefit your partner and baby. It may also be helpful to connect with other fathers who have children with disabilities, as they may be able to provide you with valuable support and understanding.

It is also important to remember that having a child with a disability can be a rewarding experience and that children with disabilities can lead meaningful and fulfilling lives. With the right support and care, your child can thrive and grow, and you can develop a deep bond and connection with them.

"Our baby was in the neonatal unit and would not wish that on my worst enemy. It was scary and didn't know what was going on. I was soon to find out that my son was going to need support for the rest of his life. I didn't know any friends who had gone through this and felt bad thinking that I would not be able to enjoy the experience of talking my son to rugby. I became very depressed and wanted to leave. It was only after having conversations with other fathers who had gone through a similar experience that I found out that there was a greater community out there. I love my son more than life itself. He has taught me new values in my life but was lucky that health professionals engaged with me".

Babies can be born with a variety of disabilities. Here are some of the most common ones[102]:

- Heart Defects: These are the most common type of birth defect. Examples include hypoplastic left heart syndrome, transposition of the great arteries, and tetralogy of Fallot.
- Neural Tube Defects: These are defects in the brain, spine, or spinal cord. They occur in the first month of pregnancy, often before a woman even knows she's pregnant.
- Down Syndrome: This is a genetic disorder that causes physical and mental developmental delays and disabilities.
- Cleft Lip and Cleft Palate: These are openings or splits in the upper lip, the roof of the mouth (palate), or both.
- Clubfoot: This is a birth defect where one or both feet are rotated inward and downward.
- Hemophilia: This is a rare disorder in which your blood doesn't clot normally because it lacks sufficient blood-clotting proteins (clotting factors).
- Congenital Dislocated Hip: Also known as hip dysplasia, it's a condition where the "ball and socket" joint of the hip does not properly form in babies and young children.
- Spina Bifida: This is a neural tube defect that occurs when the spine and spinal cord don't form properly.
- Cystic Fibrosis: This is a genetic disorder that causes severe damage to the lungs, digestive system and other organs in the body.
- Sensory Processing Problems: These are issues with processing information from the five senses: touch, auditory (sound), visual, olfactory (smell), and taste.

It's important to note that the presence of these conditions can often be detected during pregnancy through prenatal screening. If you have any concerns, it's always best to consult with a healthcare professional.

fathers with disabilities

Fathers with disabilities can face unique challenges when it comes to looking after their babies. Here are some of the challenges they might encounter:

- Physical Barriers: Depending on the nature of the disability, physical tasks associated with childcare, such as lifting or carrying the baby, could be more difficult.
- Financial Pressure: Fathers with disabilities often face financial pressures, which can add to the stress of parenting.
- Lack of Understanding: There can be a lack of understanding from others about the capabilities of fathers with disabilities, leading to stigma and discrimination.
- Access to Services: Fathers with disabilities may have difficulty accessing services due to physical barriers or a lack of suitable services.
- Mental Health: Fathers of children with disabilities often face more depression, as well as more parenting and child-related stress.

It's important to note that while these challenges exist, many fathers with disabilities successfully care for their children with the right support and resources. Support can come in many forms, including physical aids, financial assistance, mental health services, and inclusive parenting programs. If you or someone you know is in this situation, it's important to reach out to local health and social services for assistance.

ENGAGING WITH HEALTH PROFESSIONALS

The focus on mothers and babies in maternity services imagery can be attributed to several factors:

- Historical Precedence: Traditionally, maternity services have been centred around the mother and baby, reflecting societal norms and expectations[103,104]. This is often reflected in the imagery used in these services.
- Medical Focus: The medical focus of maternity services is primarily on the health and well-being of the mother and baby. As such, imagery often reflects this focus.
- Societal Expectations: Society often places the responsibility of child-rearing predominantly on mothers, which can be reflected in the imagery used in maternity services[1345].

However, it's important to note that the role of fathers is increasingly being recognized and valued. More and more, fathers are taking an active role in childbirth and child-rearing, and there is a growing movement to include fathers more prominently in maternity services and related imagery. This shift reflects changing societal norms and the recognition of the importance of fathers in the lives of their children.

Fathers are often under the misapprehension that the Health Visitor is only there for their partner. Whilst this view has improved in recent years, as fathers become more informed about the role of the Health Visitor, during a recent meeting with a group of ten fathers, only two of them had a conversation with their Health Visitor. The fathers in question were suffering from either anxiety or depression and did not know how to rectify this.

Many fathers have explained to me that they had sometimes felt like a spare part' in the labor and delivery ward and that their perceived lack of communication with any of the health professionals present only increased their anxiety.

We have to be aware that there is a shortage of both midwives and health visitors in the UK at the time of writing this book and this can only cause even more stress on the parents. The NHS in England is short of 2,000 midwives. The Royal College of Midwives (RCM) has called for urgent Government action to end the longstanding and chronic midwifery shortages in England[105].

A shortage of health visitors nationwide means some new mothers have had little or no contact with health visitors during the vital early months of their babies' lives. Babies may be missing out on vital health checks due to this shortage. The pandemic has exacerbated the issue with a huge backlog causing a postcode lottery in health visitor services. These shortages are a cause for concern and have led to calls for urgent action from the government.

"I will always remember the health visitor who asked me about my mental health, no other family member or friend ever did during that time when I became a dad".

Health visitors are there to support all parents, including fathers. They are qualified nurses or midwives who have had extra training and are there to help you, your family, and your new baby stay healthy. Your health visitor can visit you at home, or you can see them at your child health clinic, GP surgery, or health center, depending on where they're based.

It's important for fathers to be included in the pregnancy and birth process, as it can help promote bonding and improve outcomes for both the father and the child.

Midwife: A midwife is an expert in normal pregnancy and birth. They are specially trained to care for mothers and babies throughout normal pregnancy, labor, and after birth. Yes, midwives are there for dads too. They play a key role in ensuring that fathers have the confidence to take on their roles at home. This includes making sure that fathers are well-equipped to care for their newborns.

The presence of a supportive birth partner, such as a father, during labor can lead to a better birthing experience and can even make labor progress more quickly. Therefore, midwives also support fathers during the labor process.

In addition, midwives ensure that parents can easily contact a midwife and receive regular home visits. This access to professional support can be invaluable for fathers, especially in the early days after discharge from the hospital.

Overall, midwives play a pivotal role in supporting fathers and helping them navigate the journey of parenthood.

Head of Midwifery: The head of midwifery can support you if you're having problems with your care or you feel your wishes are not being considered. The Royal College of Midwives explains that The Head of Midwifery plays a crucial role in supporting fathers. They oversee the delivery of maternity care and ensure that fathers are well-equipped to take on their roles at home. This includes making sure that fathers have the confidence to care for their newborns[3].

The Head of Midwifery is also responsible for ensuring that parents can easily contact a midwife and receive regular home visits. This access to professional support can be invaluable for fathers, especially in the early days after discharge from the hospital.

In addition, the Head of Midwifery works alongside other professionals to provide holistic care that benefits the entire family. This includes addressing key social factors that reduce risk, such as domestic violence, and ensuring support from partners, family, friends, and others. Overall, the Head of Midwifery plays a pivotal role in supporting fathers and helping them navigate the journey of parenthood.

Obstetrician: An obstetrician is a doctor who specialises in care during pregnancy, labor, and after birth. An obstetrician is a doctor with specialist qualifications who is trained to provide medical care during pregnancy, labour, and birth, and after the birth[4]. While their primary role is to ensure the health and well-being of the mother and baby, they can also play a significant role in supporting fathers during this period.

Here are some ways an obstetrician can support fathers:

Education: Obstetricians can educate fathers about the pregnancy process, what to expect during labor and delivery, and how to care for the mother and baby postpartum. Inclusion in Prenatal Care: Obstetricians can encourage the involvement of fathers in prenatal appointments and ultrasounds, which can help fathers feel more connected to the pregnancy and prepare for their role as parents. Support During Labour and Delivery: During labor and delivery, obstetricians can guide fathers on how to support the mother, such as by providing comfort measures or assisting with communication. Postnatal Care: After the birth, obstetricians can advise fathers on how to support the mother's recovery and assist in caring for the newborn.

Remember, every obstetrician may have a different approach, and the level of involvement of the father can also depend on the personal preferences of the parents. It's always a good idea for fathers to communicate their desire to be involved and ask questions to stay informed.

Anesthetist: An anesthetist is a doctor who specialises in providing pain relief and anesthesia. While their primary role is to ensure the health and well-being of the patient undergoing the procedure, they can also play a significant role in supporting fathers during this period. Here are some ways an anesthetist can support fathers:

Education: Anaesthetists can educate fathers about the medical procedures their partners are undergoing, what to expect during labour and delivery, and how to care for the mother and baby postnatally. Inclusion in Care: With the mother's consent, anesthetists can involve fathers in discussions about the mother's anesthetic plan and pain management strategies. Support During Labour and Delivery: During labor and delivery, anesthetists can guide fathers on how to support the mother, such as by providing comfort measures or assisting with communication. Postnatal Care: After the birth, anaesthetists can advise fathers on how to support the mother's recovery and assist in caring for the newborn.

Perinatal mental health services are specialist services for women with mental health problems. The service is for pregnant women and women with a baby up to one year old who may have an existing or new mental health problem and also women with severe mental health problems and are planning a pregnancy. Perinatal mental health problems are those that occur during pregnancy or in the first year following the birth of a child. Perinatal mental illness affects up to 27% of new and expectant mums and covers a wide range of conditions. If left untreated, mental health issues can have significant and long-lasting effects on the woman, the child, and the wider family 2. Specialist perinatal mental health services provide care and treatment for women with complex mental health needs and support the developing relationship between parent and baby 2. They also offer women with mental health needs advice for planning a pregnancy.

General Practitioners (GPs) should be aware of paternal mental health. However, the level of knowledge can vary.

Research and Recommendations: Research has led to calls for the development of service delivery models that focus on the psychological well-being of the couple and family rather than the individual. This includes the routine assessment or screening of fathers' mental health and well-being in perinatal services.

However, it's important to note that while these resources and training programs exist, not all GPs may have the same level of knowledge or training in paternal mental health. It's always a good idea to have open and honest conversations with your GP about any concerns you may have.

Dr Blaithin O'Dea explains Fathers are often identified by mothers – and indeed professionals – as the "support system" for mums. Whilst this is an obvious role for them it means they are expected to become the caretaker, the doer, the strong one, the "container". This is a challenging task for anyone and, for new dads who are likely sleep-deprived, adjusting to huge changes, and worried about their partners, it may be an overwhelming task. This is compounded by the fact that supportive contacts from midwives and health visitors after a baby is born are almost entirely focused on the well-being of mum and baby. The expectation that dad will provide support and stability can create intense pressure, uncertainty, and feelings of inadequacy for fathers which are justified, valid, and need support.

The Fatherhood Institute is an organization that provides guidance and support to fathers looking to become more involved in their child's life. They offer a range of resources, including online courses, workshops, and support groups[106].

Yes, some fathers may feel apprehensive about taking their baby to appointments. This could be due to a variety of reasons[107,108]:

- Lack of Confidence: Some fathers may lack confidence in their ability to care for their baby on their own, especially if it's their first child.
- Fear of Making Mistakes: Fathers may fear making mistakes or not being able to answer the healthcare provider's questions accurately.
- Societal Expectations: Society often places the responsibility of child-rearing predominantly on mothers, which can make fathers feel like they are overstepping their role[124,125,126].
- Lack of Knowledge: Some fathers may not be aware of the baby's routine or specific needs, which can make them hesitant to take the baby to appointments.

However, it's important to note that fathers have every right to be involved in their child's healthcare and upbringing. In fact, research shows that children benefit from having an involved father[124,125,126]. If you're a father feeling this way, consider discussing your feelings with your partner or a healthcare professional. They can provide guidance and support to help you feel more confident in your role as a father.

There have been many parents who have explained to me that some health professionals, do not have the social skills to listen to them. I have also explained to them, that again the services are overstretched and there is not enough time in many areas of the United Kingdom. What we can do is just have a conversation with the father and that can be done at any appointment and if not present information and resources to the father should be given to their partner. This will help the partner, understand that fathers need support as well.

Social intelligence is the ability to understand one's own and others' actions. It is learned and developed from experience with people and learning from success and failures in social settings[2]. It is an important interpersonal skill that helps individuals succeed in all aspects of their lives.

Key elements of social intelligence include.

- Verbal Fluency and Conversational Skills: The ability to carry on conversations with a wide variety of people, and be tactful and appropriate in what is said.
- Knowledge of Social Roles, Rules, and Scripts: Understanding how to play various social roles and being well versed in the informal rules, or "norms," that govern social interaction[1].
- Effective Listening Skills: Being a great listener, which makes others feel as if they have a good "connection" with the person.
- Understanding What Makes Other People Tick: Being able to "read" what the other person is thinking or feeling by observing what others are saying, and how they are behaving.
- Role Playing and Social Self-Efficacy: Knowing how to play different social roles, results in feeling socially self-confident and effective.
- Impression Management Skills: Being concerned with the impression they are making on others, and managing and controlling the image you portray to others while being reasonably "authentic" and letting others see the true self.

Social intelligence is a critical subset of human intelligence centered around two core components: social awareness and social facility. Social cognition refers to the capacity to understand and empathize with others' emotions and perspectives, while social facility pertains to the ability to behave effectively in social situations.

Therefore, it is important to ask new dads how they are feeling and to show them that they are not alone and that they are valued and respected. Asking new dads how they are feeling can help them to:

- Recognize and acknowledge their emotions and thoughts, and understand that they are normal and valid.
- Express and release their emotions and thoughts, and cope with them in healthy and constructive ways.
- Seek and receive help and support from others, such as their partner, family, friends, or professionals.
- Build and maintain a positive and supportive relationship with their partner, and communicate effectively and honestly.
- Develop and strengthen a close and loving bond with their baby, and enjoy and celebrate their fatherhood.

Some of the ways to ask new dads how they are feeling are:

- Asking open-ended and empathetic questions, such as "How are you feeling today?", "What are some of the challenges you are facing as a new dad?", or "What are some of the joys you are experiencing as a new dad?"
- Listening actively and attentively, without interrupting, judging, or giving advice, unless asked
- Validating and affirming their feelings and thoughts, such as by saying "I understand how you feel", "You are not alone in this", or "You are doing a great job as a dad".
- Offering and providing practical and emotional support, such as by saying "Is there anything I can do to help you?", "Do you want to talk more about it?", or "I'm here for you whenever you need me".
- Encouraging and motivating them to seek professional help if needed, such as by saying "It's okay to ask for help", "There are people who can help you", or "You deserve to be happy and healthy as a dad".

MEDICATION

Please remember any medication information should not replace professional medical advice. Always consult with a healthcare provider for advice about medications or health conditions. It is common to hear fathers discussing medications sometimes within the groups. I always try to bring the conversations back to make sure you speak with a health professional.

There could be several reasons why some fathers might be hesitant to take medication for depression.

- The stigma I have found with fathers, they might avoid seeking treatment for their depression symptoms for fear of being judged. They might worry about how others, including their family, friends, or colleagues, might perceive them if they were to take medication for a mental health condition.
- Some fathers believe that they should be able to manage their symptoms on their own, without the need for medication1. They might feel that they should be able to "snap out of it" or handle their symptoms through lifestyle changes alone.
- There might be a fear of becoming dependent on the medication. This is a common concern among many fathers when it comes to taking medication for their mental health.

"I tried it once and felt funny. I just left it until I became more unwell weeks later".

In my own experience, I can say that I need medication temporarily to be able to take the positive coping skills at the time, with help from my doctors after some time, I would slowly come off the medication. There is a stigma in medication, But I found that if I needed medication for any other illness, there would be no hesitation. Medication has come a long way in mental health and again some people just need it for as long as the health professional says they do. It's always important to ask for a review of your medication with the health professional and also be aware what works for me, may not be the right medication for you that will work.

CONTIMENT

Becoming a new father can be a challenging time, and it's important to take steps to maintain mental health. Here are some strategies that might help·

- Ease up on yourself: New dads often put a lot of pressure on themselves. It's important to remember that parenting doesn't come easily to anyone.
- Do things that help you feel balanced: Finding a new routine that helps you retain some sense of calm can be beneficial.
- Chat with other new dads: Talking to other new dads can help you navigate the challenges of new parenthood.
- Remember that parenthood will get easier: The early days are often the hardest, but it can get easier.
- Be aware of your mood: If you notice that you're feeling down or not yourself, it's important to seek help.

"It's just too much happening at one time becoming a father, certainly needs to be more awareness. Learning simple coping skills, has certainly helped me feel less stressed".

As a new father, you can have feelings of being overwhelmed. Juggling multiple responsibilities can indeed be challenging. Here are some strategies that might help:

- Ground yourself in the present: Use the 5-4-3-2-1 technique. This is a mindfulness technique that doesn't require any special spaces or tools—all you need is your five senses.
- Reflect on the "why: Figure out the root cause of your stress. Once you locate the source, you're that much closer to problem-solving and feeling better'[109].
- Accept your feelings: Acknowledge the fact that you feel overwhelmed and acknowledge any negative thoughts. Try not to judge yourself for what you're feeling[2109].
- Practice mindfulness: Tuning into the present moment through mindfulness practices can help to reduce your anxiety over the past and the future[110].
- Change Your Perspective: Take a step back from your thought processes. Recognize and accept how you are feeling and

the situation you are in. Stop the vicious emotional cycle of rumination[111].

Remembe, it's okay to ask for help. If these strategies aren't enough, consider reaching out to a mental health professional. They can provide you with additional coping mechanisms and strategies tailored to your specific situation. You're not alone in this, and there are resources available to help you manage these feelings.

POSTPARTUM PSYCHIATRIC ILLNESSES

A study published in Psychology Today that fathers can also experience postpartum depression and other mental health issues after the birth of a child. While postpartum psychosis is more commonly studied in mothers, fathers are not immune to postpartum psychiatric illnesses.

"I remember thinking the baby's head looked like the devil".

Research on postpartum psychosis in fathers is still relatively new, but there have been some studies that have explored this topic.

One case study reported a male patient with psychosis who was admitted to the psychiatric unit 5 days after his wife gave birth to their child. The patient was very concerned about the well-being of his child and was afraid that something bad would happen to the child. The patient was diagnosed with an acute manic episode with psychotic symptoms and treated with olanzapine and lithium[2,112]. (A father with postpartum psychosis | BMJ Case Reports.

More insight into the occurrence of postpartum psychosis in fathers, more research is needed to fully understand this condition in men.

Psychosis can be caused by a variety of factors, including[113,114]:

- Psychological Conditions: Conditions such as schizophrenia, bipolar disorder, severe stress or anxiety, and severe depression can trigger psychotic episodes.

- Substances: Alcohol misuse and drug misuse can trigger a psychotic episode. A person can also experience a psychotic episode if they suddenly stop drinking alcohol or taking drugs after using them for a long time.
- Medicine: In rare situations, psychosis can also occur as a side effect of some types of medicine or as a result of an overdose of that medicine.
- The Brain: There's been a great deal of research into how psychosis affects the brain and how changes in the brain can trigger symptoms of psychosis. It's thought psychosis may be linked to increased activity of neurotransmitters in the brain.

Yes, lack of sleep can lead to symptoms of psychosis, such as hallucinations and delusions[12]. This condition is referred to as sleep deprivation psychosis[115].

Sleep deprivation can cause several changes in the brain that may lead to psychosis. These changes include increased levels of the stress hormone cortisol, changes in brain activity, and alterations in neurotransmitter levels. Sleep deprivation may also increase the risk of psychosis by affecting the immune system and increasing inflammation[131,134].

SOCIAL SERVICES

Education about perinatal mental health is crucial for social services. These professionals need to understand the complexities of mental health during the perinatal period, which can affect so many parents.

Parents may feel apprehensive about talking to social services for a variety of reasons[116]:

- Fear of Losing Their Children: Families often feel anxious at the prospect of social services' involvement because they are frightened that social workers will remove their children from the family home.
- Negative Experiences: Some parents may have had negative experiences with social services in the past, or they may have heard about such experiences from others. This can lead to a general mistrust or fear of authority.
- Resistance to Chang: Parents may resist the involvement of child and family social workers, viewing it as a form of non-

cooperation[1]. This resistance can take many forms, including apparent cooperation that masks issues of concern, not engaging, or even violent or threatening behavior.

- Perceived Judgment: Some parents may feel judged or misunderstood by social workers, particularly if they believe the social worker is telling them what is in their children's best interests without first developing a meaningful and trusting relationship.

These factors can make it challenging for parents to engage openly and constructively with social services. However, it's important to remember that the primary aim of social workers is to ensure the well-being and safety of children.

"I was suffering badly as a new dad; I was worried that if someone found out our baby would be taken off us. I couldn't imagine how that would affect my partner if I came clean that I was coping with being a new father. The baby was never in any danger, I would go down the pub with my mates when I was struggling and that was affecting our relationship as ever thought, I didn't care but I did… I was struggling".

FEAR OF CHILDBIRTH

According to a study published in the journal BMC Pregnancy and Childbirth, fear of childbirth is reported in 13% of fathers, and it may have adverse consequences for the fathers' health as well as their families[117]. The study found that some biopsychosocial factors may lead to the fear of childbirth in fathers, including the interventions during labor and their side effects, damage to pregnant mother and her child, painful labor and delivery, inability to support the spouse, disrespectful behaviors by hospital staff, and financial constraints.

The Fathers' Fear of Childbirth Scale is a screening tool that can help reduce the fear of childbirth in expectant fathers. It is a simple report instrument that can be easily implemented by healthcare professionals[118]. Tokophobia is an extreme fear of childbirth. It can be experienced in two forms: primary and secondary.

"The anxiety of going into the labor ward for our second was something that I had never experienced ever before and was panicking".

Fear of childbirth is a common concern among expectant fathers. It is estimated that approximately 13% of expectant fathers experience a pathological and debilitating fear of childbirth[119]. This fear can have adverse consequences on both the father and his family[1,2].

The most common fears fathers have about labor and delivery include:

- Death of the mother or baby.
- Labor pain will be worse than anticipated.
- Labor will be longer than anticipated.
- Dad won't be able to help mother.
- Dad will feel in the way, disconnected and peripheral.
- Care providers will make decisions without parents[3]

However, there are ways to address these fears. For instance, a study found that midwifery-led counselling can be an effective approach to reducing expectant fathers' childbirth fear. Another study found that fathers with childbirth fear regarded childbirth as risky, but they expressed helpful coping strategies. After the birth of their baby, they became less fearful[120].

Expectant fathers need to express their childbirth-related fears in an environment where they feel validated and supported[2]. Antenatal education is recommended to enhance fathers' childbirth-related self-efficacy to reduce fear of childbirth[2]. Further investigation into methods and models for identifying and supporting men at risk of or experiencing fear of childbirth is required to improve outcomes for this population of men[2,121].

SCREENING AND ASSESSMENTS

There are several screening assessments available for postnatal depression in fathers. The Edinburgh Postnatal Depression Scale (EPDS) is a widely used screening tool for postnatal depression in mothers, and it has been validated for use in fathers with minor adjustments in cutoff scores.

Rebecca Price's (2018) Blues Boys Project studied the use of screening tools specific to detecting postnatal depression in fathers. The Edinburgh Postnatal Depression Scale (EPDS) was used as this has been validated for both fathers and mothers. Of the 25 fathers that were recruited to the project, five were identified as experiencing anxiety and/or depression after completing the EPDS. The research also found that some fathers – who recognised that they had depression and/or anxiety – only scored within the normal range on the EPDS.

The Patient Health Questionnaire (PHQ-9) is another quick and valid screener for all adults. The Patient Health Questionnaire (PHQ) is a multiple-choice self-report inventory that is used as a screening and diagnostic tool for mental health disorders of depression, anxiety, alcohol, eating, and somatoform disorders. It is a diagnostic tool for mental health disorders used by health care professionals.

A study conducted in the US found that paternal PPD screening was piloted in an intergenerational postpartum primary care clinic using a novel survey instrument to collect demographic/social data, as well as mental health history and current stress levels; an EPDS was also administered. The study found that participation was high in the PPD screening pilot for fathers in a primary care setting, and this small sample of fathers demonstrated significant peripartum mental health challenges unlikely to have been identified otherwise.

Fathers who admitted to suffering from undiagnosed disorders – which included bipolar disorder, Antisocial Disorder, and Attention Deficit Hyperactive Disorder – had not been asked about their mental health history nor was any information made available to them during the antenatal period.

In 2019 Dr Jane Hanley and I presented at Oxford Brookes University on the pathway for assessing fathers. We developed the HanWill model which combines the use of the Edinburgh Postnatal Depression Scale and information gathered from personal experiences about fathers' behaviors following the birth of their infant. These include:

- Are you drinking more since your baby has arrived?
- How are you feeling now that you are a parent?

• Who is supporting you and has your partner had postnatal depression?

• What is your sleep pattern like?

• Do you feel your avoiding situations more than you used to?

• Do you have feelings of anger or aggression?

"As a first-time father, I wasn't aware that this could happen to dads... I wish I had had the knowledge and understanding about the feelings I was having as a father who already struggles with Bipolar. It was just too much for me".

The Gotland Male Depression Scale (GMDS) is a depression rating scale that was developed to improve the assessment and identification of depression in men. It was designed to assess symptoms that fall outside the traditional diagnostic criteria for depression, such as irritability, aggression, and substance misuse. The GMDS was the first screening tool designed to improve detection rates of depressed men by assessing these externalizing symptoms.

The scale was developed in response to increasing suicide rates in the 1980s. The Swedish Committee for the Prevention and Treatment of Depression (PTD) organized a training program on the diagnosis and treatment of depression for all the general practitioners on the island of Gotland. The researchers found that the rate of depressive suicides in females decreased dramatically after the PTD program, while the proportion of male depressive suicides was almost unchanged. This led to the development of the GMDS to help primary care clinicians diagnose depression in men in an attempt to decrease male suicide rates.

The Pregnancy-Related Anxiety Scale (PRAS) is a self-report measure used to assess anxiety in fathers during pregnancy. Anxiety is common in fathers during pregnancy, and some literature suggests that fathers experience a specific prenatal psychological state known as pregnancy anxiety, defined as concerns or worries specific to pregnancy.

This scale can be a useful tool for prenatal screening and preventative measures for men transitioning to parenthood1. It can help healthcare providers identify fathers who may be experiencing high levels of anxiety during pregnancy, which can then inform appropriate interventions and support.

Early prevention is key to lowering the rates of anxiety and depression in fathers. By using these early prevention tools, we can find out if fathers to be and new fathers may be struggling with their mental health. Many fathers, never find out before it comes to crisis in my experience of working with Dads.

Another area is fathers who were either in the Armed Forces or the emergency services, and who were therefore more susceptible to suffering from Post-Traumatic Stress Disorder (PTSD) caused by incidents that had occurred in their work. I found that many health professionals did not know what PTSD was and were unaware that it could happen to fathers in the labor ward. Post-traumatic stress disorder is an anxiety disorder which occurs after witnessing or experiencing a life threatening event. I found that many fathers were only diagnosed years later.

One father I spoke to was diagnosed with PTSD 29 years later after witnessing the loss of his child in the labor ward. He did not receive any help, but instead adopted negative coping skills, by drinking excessively and taking drugs. He lost his business and family after struggling for years.

Consideration of fathers' mental health across cultures and religions has been given little consideration, especially in terms of their attitudes to screening, interventions and treatment, prevention, and the interplay with maternal mental health and child outcome measures. In these challenging times, the impact of COVID-19 is likely to present additional pressures on the family unit, which need to be explored through high-quality research methods, which fully engage users and other stakeholders. Paul Sutcliffe, Associate Professor, Warwick Medical School.

I know of fathers who are hitting crisis points after the perinatal period and are getting diagnosed with anxiety or depression. However, if they had been assessed and screened earlier, this may have been prevented or at least the reasons behind it could have been pinpointed.

"I just didn't think I was good enough and was never asked about my mental health. My wife was fine, but I struggled so much it was affecting our relationship which sadly ended after the birth of our twins".

A woman whose partner (and the father of her three children) had taken his own life five years before me speaking to her had the following comment to make about screening: Would a (mental health) screening process or assessment have stopped this suicide? I can't say it would, but I can say it definitely could have and therefore implementation of such a process is required with immediate effect. There were ample opportunities missed to check on my partner's mental health; in the two years leading up to the suicide, we suffered a missed miscarriage, a no-complications pregnancy, and birth, and then we suffered a large bleed during our last pregnancy, two weeks before losing my partner.

"I didn't seek help initially, even when I knew something was wrong and this led to me making several attempts on my own life".

Fathers' mental health is an important public health issue that continues to be under-acknowledged by health professionals and policymakers, despite research suggesting that men want to be asked questions about their mental health and well-being, and the opportunity to express their feelings and emotions about fatherhood. In the absence of any national guidance, health professionals working with new fathers are currently not required to routinely assess their mental health, which is a huge gap.

"Mental health problems are the largest cause of disability in the UK; therefore, we must have adequate systems in place to support parental mental health to ensure children have the best start in life. This should include fathers' mental health, and not just mothers".

Sharin Baldwin

There have been changes since we started campaigning. The NHS Long-Term Plan has, of course, introduced the commitment to offer fathers/partners of women accessing specialist perinatal mental health services and maternity outreach clinics evidence-based assessment for their mental health and signposting to support as required.

These changes have come about as a result of hard campaigning by many of us involved in raising awareness of and research into paternal perinatal mental ill health, and they are most definitely a good thing. The new commitment means that dads who are in the same position as I was back in 2004 will now be able to get the support and help that they so desperately need. However, as Dr Andy Mayers has said, "…there is still a long way to go to ensure that fathers are fully supported". Key difficulties, as highlighted by Dr Mayers, include:

• Only the most acutely unwell mums will be referred to perinatal mental health services and therefore only their partners will be offered support. Partners of those women whose perinatal mental ill health is not sufficiently severe to meet the referral criteria will be left without support;

• Fathers can, of course, develop perinatal mental health difficulties independently of their wife/partner and these dads are again not included in the new offer.

Also, how do we reach fathers? We already know that not all fathers come to the attention of health professionals, even if fathers trusted them enough to be screened by them. One potential solution is online screening. In a very recent piece of unpublished research, we asked fathers several qualitative questions about the merit of such a method. Initial analyses suggest that fathers' perceptions towards an online service were mainly positive but were less positive about current methods. - Dr Andrew Mayers

- Stigma: There is a stigma associated with mental health issues, and this can be particularly strong for men. Many fathers feel they should be strong and not admit to feelings of depression.
- Lack of Screening: Postnatal depression in men often goes undiagnosed. As with postnatal depression in mums, it often goes undiagnosed1. The symptoms can look a lot like the everyday stresses of having a newborn.

- Misdiagnosis: The symptoms of postnatal depression in men can be different from those in women, and this can lead to misdiagnosis.

These factors contribute to the underdiagnosis of postnatal depression in fathers. It's important to raise awareness about this issue and ensure that fathers are included in mental health screenings during the postnatal period.

TIME ANXIETY

It's completely normal to feel like you have no time for yourself as a new father. The arrival of a new baby can significantly change your routine and lifestyle. You might find yourself constantly busy with feeding, changing, soothing, and caring for your baby. This can leave little time for personal activities or relaxation[122].

Also, parents must be aware of time anxiety which is a type of anxiety that is characterized by ongoing feelings of uneasiness and dread around the passage of time. It can be caused by a variety of factors, including a busy schedule, a fear of missing out, or a sense of being overwhelmed by life's demands.

Time anxiety refers to ongoing feelings of uneasiness and even dread around the passage of time. It can manifest in various ways, such as[122]:

- Worry about lateness: Time anxiety can lead to a preoccupation with being late. Stress over potential lateness can leave you constantly on edge.
- Feeling a need to rush: Time anxiety can provoke a desire to rush from one place to the next, often without reason.
- Unease when not completing planned tasks: You might feel uneasy when you don't get around to everything you had planned.
- Belief of missed opportunities: If your time anxiety relates to big-picture concerns, you might feel like you've missed the turnoff for certain paths.

Time anxiety isn't an officially recognized type of anxiety, but it's usually part of generalized anxiety disorder (GAD). It occurs when a person experiences worry about not having enough time to get everything done or to complete a task effectively[123]. It may cause you to feel as though you don't have enough time to accomplish your goals, or you're not maximizing your time in the best possible way[141].

"Our biggest disagreements came when my partner was always late, It the frustrating and made my anxiety go through the roof. I am pacing the room and feelings of anger are common in these situations. It became far worse when our daughter came along".

Some common symptoms of time anxiety include worrying about lateness, feeling a need to rush, and feeling uneasy when you don't get around to everything you had planned to do. If you're struggling with time anxiety, there are several things you can do to help manage your symptoms. Here are some tips[124]:

- Practice mindfulness: Mindfulness is a technique that involves focusing your attention on the present moment. This can help you feel more grounded and less anxious about the future.
- Create a schedule: Creating a schedule can help you manage your time more effectively and reduce feelings of overwhelm.
- Take breaks: Taking regular breaks throughout the day can help you recharge and stay focused.
- Prioritize self-care: Prioritizing self-care activities such as exercise, meditation, or spending time with loved ones can help you feel more relaxed and less anxious.
- Seek support: Don't be afraid to reach out to friends, family, or a mental health professional for support. They can help you manage your symptoms and develop coping strategies.

SLEEP

Sleep deprivation in new parents is a serious issue that can have significant effects on both physical and mental health[1,125].

Sleep deprivation can lead to physical and mental fatigue, difficulty concentrating, mood swings, decreased performance, and an increased risk of accidents and injuries[125]. It can also result in increased anxiety, depression, general fatigue, and even burnout[1]. If a parent has a vulnerability to postpartum depression, sleep deprivation can exacerbate that.

In the short term, lack of sleep can cause irritability, lack of focus, and mood changes[2]. In the long term, it can increase the risk of anxiety, depression, and general fatigue[1].

"Getting no sleep and having to go to work for a twelve-hour shift and then come home was very difficult to deal with at that time. It should be talked about much more for dads".

New parents, in particular, are at risk as they juggle the needs of a baby along with adjusting to all that comes with new parenthood[1]. Sleep deprivation can negatively impact positive parenting, which involves being responsive and warm toward your child. Caregivers who sleep less often experience higher levels of stress, which are associated with difficulty regulating emotions.

Therefore, it's crucial to prioritize sleep and seek professional help if necessary. There are resources available to help new parents manage sleep deprivation and its effects[1,126].

lack of sleep can indeed be dangerous for new fathers. Not getting enough sleep drains your mental abilities and puts your physical health at risk. Here are some of the effects of sleep deprivation[2,126]:

- Mental Health: Sleep deprivation can affect your mental abilities and emotional state. You may feel more impatient or prone to mood swings. It can also compromise decision-making processes and creativity. If sleep deprivation continues long enough, you could start having hallucinations.
- Physical Health: Chronic sleep deprivation can interfere with your body's internal systems and cause more than just the initial signs and symptoms listed above. It has been linked to several health problems, from weight gain to a weakened immune system.
- Risk of Accidents: The signals your body sends may also be delayed, decreasing your coordination and increasing your risk for accidents.

- Long-term Effects: The long-term effects of sleep deprivation are real. It can dramatically lower your quality-of-life.
- Other Health Risks: Insufficient sleep has been linked to weight gain, high blood pressure, diabetes, depression, heart disease, and strokes. Sleep deprivation can also lead to high anxiety, irritability, erratic behavior, poor cognitive functioning and performance, and psychotic episodes.
- Lack of sleep can affect a new dad's mood, concentration, productivity, and performance at work. This may cause issues with his employment and his income to his needs for his family.

"I need good sleep to function and have always slept well. That all changed when becoming parents and is something we don't talk enough about and how it can affect our mental health".

Sleep deprivation is indeed used as a form of torture in some situations. Prolonged sleep deprivation is considered a cruel and ineffective method of interrogation. This method is particularly insidious because it attacks the deep biological functions at the core of a person's mental and physical health. It is less overtly violent than some forms of physical torture, but it can be far more damaging and painful if pushed to extreme[126].

Fathers must be engaged with services and are aware of the important to ensure you're getting enough sleep. If you're having trouble sleeping, it might be a good idea to speak to a healthcare professional.

RELATIONSHIPS

I have met so many fathers whose relationships have ended in courtroom battles, which ultimately can – and often does – result in parental alienation. Some fathers reported to me that they recognised, early on, that they were feeling perhaps 'emotionally unfit' – in the sense that their pre-parenthood relationship was already difficult, and that no support or help was available to help them as individuals or in that relationship. If this early intervention had occurred, it would have better prepared both the father and their family as a whole for the baby's arrival.

"My husband struggled and without support, we could have gone our separate ways. I did not know … that men also struggle after the baby is born".

"We often focus upon mother and baby during the perinatal period, but fathers play such a vital role in the family. When fathers are well, they are better able to support their partner and engage positively with their baby. When fathers are struggling and unsupported, the whole family dynamic changes, putting that family cohesion at risk. It is, of course, important that we support fathers for their own sake, but also for the wellbeing of the whole family. We must invest in making sure everyone in the family unit is nurtured to protect our future and the next generation of parents". Professor Amy Brown Professor of Child Public Health, Swansea University.

The need for there to be more support for existing couple relationships, in order to help fathers adjust both mentally and emotionally was one of the findings in Baldwin et al's 2018 research[127]. Perinatal and postnatal mental health assessments for fathers, to help (among other things) potential relationship difficulties with their partners, was one of the recommendations of Shaheen et al's 2019 research, and Higgins et al – in 2020 – emphasized that unprepared-for changes in their relationships (along with the resultant challenges and responsibilities) were one of the matters discussed by fathers when considering their Improving communication with the mother of your child is important for the well-being of both you and your child. Here are some tips to help facilitate better communication[128]:

- Be respectful and courteous: Treat the mother of your child with respect, even if you have differences. Use polite language, and active listening, and avoid speaking or behaving in a confrontational manner.
- Choose the right time and place: Find a suitable time and place to discuss important matters or concerns. Avoid discussing

sensitive issues in front of your child or in public settings that could escalate tension.

- Active listening: Pay attention to what the mother of your child is saying without interrupting. Show empathy and try to understand her perspective, even if you may disagree. Responding with validation and understanding can foster a more positive atmosphere for productive conversation.
- Set clear boundaries: Establish boundaries for communication, such as appropriate times to call or text. Respect each other's personal space and privacy.
- Use "I" statements: When discussing concerns or expressing your thoughts, use "I" statements to express your feelings while avoiding blame or accusation. For example, say "I feel concerned when..." instead of "You always do this...".
- Focus on the child's well-being: Keep the child's best interests at heart when discussing parenting decisions. Collaborate on matters such as education, healthcare, and discipline to ensure consistency and shared responsibility.
- Seek mediation if necessary: If communication becomes consistently difficult or unproductive, consider involving a neutral third party, such as a mediator or counsellor. They can assist in facilitating constructive dialogue and finding common ground.

Elly Talyor - Elly Taylor - Becoming Us, the Couple's Guide to Parenthood explains more.

"The truth is that having a baby involves multiple unexpected stresses that all come at the same time or one after the other, and these stresses impact both parents and also take a toll on their relationship. For example, a whopping 92% of parents report more conflict with their partner in the first year after having a baby. Unexpected relationship changes, in turn, can contribute to anxiety and depression in both partners. For the dads, it's often starts with them feeling like they're being ignored by care providers, and that their concerns and needs don't count. Then they can feel like a 'third wheel' once the baby arrives, or just an ATM Machine, or that they've "lost" their partner to the baby. Some new dads feel trapped, most are worried about finances, and many that their sex life will never get back to normal. It's no

wonder we have such high rates of depression in new dads - and that's not a great start for any family."

Remember, building effective communication takes time and effort from both parties. It's essential to approach conversations with patience, understanding, and a willingness to find solutions that benefit your child.

"I didn't want her to know that I was struggling, I was more concerned about her".

It's not uncommon for one partner to want more children while the other doesn't, and this can indeed lead to relationship struggles. Here are some ways to navigate this emotionally driven scenario[129]:

- Open Communication: It's crucial to have an open and honest conversation about your feelings and desires. Using 'I feel' statements during your conversation can help to minimize defensiveness and conflict.
- Understanding Each Other's Perspectives: Try to understand the other person's perspective and why they feel the way they do. This can help you both to empathize with each other and find a compromise.
- Seek Professional Help: If you're finding it difficult to resolve, it might be helpful to seek the guidance of a professional, such as a therapist or counselor. They can provide a safe space for you both to express your feelings and can help guide you toward a solution.
- Consider the Impact on Your Relationship: If one partner wants kids and sees having children as core to their life purpose, staying together and not having children may lead to sadness, depression, despair, regret, remorse, and resentment. It's important to consider the long-term impact of this decision on your relationship.

Remember, it's okay to have different desires and feelings. The key is to communicate openly, understand each other's perspectives, and work together to find a solution that respects both partners' feelings.

CARING FOR YOUR PARTNER

Looking after your loved ones with postnatal depression can affect your mental health. According to the Mental Health Foundation, partners of people who have given birth in the last year can also experience anxiety or depression. Dealing with a lack of sleep, extra household responsibilities, and financial worries, for example, can be very difficult[129].

A study conducted in Canada found that partners of women with postpartum depression are at an increased risk of developing depression themselves. The study found that partners of women with postpartum depression were more likely to experience symptoms of depression, anxiety, and stress compared to partners of women without postpartum depression.

Postnatal depression in fathers is a growing concern, and research has shown that it can have a significant impact on the mental health of fathers and their families. A study conducted in YGG found that maternal marital satisfaction showed a significant mediating effect on paternal postpartum depression (PPD), and there was a direct effect of maternal PPD on paternal PPD[130]. The study highlights the importance of targeting both maternal and paternal mental health in future PPD interventions.

Fathers need to receive support during the perinatal and postpartum periods, as they can experience anxiety and depression during this time. The NHS has published a good practice guide for involving and supporting partners and other family members in specialist perinatal mental health services. The guide provides information on how to support and involve partners and other family members, and why this is needed. It also describes underpinning principles and key ideas for what services can do to involve and support partners and other family members.

The father's role in a mother's postnatal depression is significant. The evidence suggests that impaired postnatal maternal mental health can have extensive adverse effects on the infant, affecting them socially, emotionally, behaviourally, and cognitively.

Factors related to the father that can contribute to a mother's postnatal depression include a poor relationship with the baby's father, his unavailability at the time of the baby's birth, and his provision of what is perceived by the mother to be insufficient emotional or practical support. This can include low participation in infant care. Other risk factors include his holding rigid sex-role expectations or being critical, coercive, or violent[131].

"One the hardest things that I had to do".

However, it's important to note that the father's functioning as a support person is key since depressed new mothers are more likely to turn to and receive support from their partner than from any other individual, including medical staff. Today, 70% of new mothers turn to their partners for emotional support, compared with only 47% in the 1960s[132].

Therefore, the father's role in supporting the mother during this time is crucial. Greater satisfaction with fathers' involvement in caregiving was reported to help reduce postnatal depressive symptoms in mothers[2], while lack of support from the father can exacerbate mental health issues in new mothers[3]. This suggests that a supportive father can have a positive impact on maternal postnatal mental health.

It's also worth noting that the father's mental health can impact the mother's postnatal depression. For instance, reduced support from depressed fathers may make a mother more vulnerable to stress[133]. It has been shown that there is a correlation between paternal sadness and the emotional, psychological, and further social development of the child.

Looking after someone who is struggling to curse is going to have an impact on yourself. I didn't want to say anything to my partner as she was already struggling herself. After all, I'm supposed to be a man and show no weakness as society sadly tells us.

In conclusion, the father's role in a mother's postnatal depression is multifaceted and significant, encompassing his mental health, his relationship with the mother, and his involvement in caregiving. Supportive and involved fathering can play a key role in mitigating the effects of postnatal depression on both the mother and the child.

Dr Bronwyn Leigh of Australia explains "New and expectant Dads are increasingly getting our attention – and with good reason. Traditionally, mental health concerns have focused on new and expectant mothers, but it has become clearer in more recent years that the perinatal period is a time of psychological vulnerability for fathers too".

MOTHER WITH POSTPARTUM PSYCHOSIS

Caring for a loved one with postpartum psychosis can be challenging and may lead to stress, anxiety, and even depression[13]. This is due to several reasons[134,135]:

- Emotional Stress: Seeing a loved one go through a mental health crisis can be emotionally stressful.
- Increased Responsibilities: The caregiver may need to take on additional responsibilities, such as caring for the baby and managing household tasks, which can lead to feelings of overwhelm.
- Lack of Sleep: Caring for a new baby and a loved one with postpartum psychosis often involves sleep deprivation, which can contribute to mental health issues.
- Social Isolation: Caregivers may feel isolated or unsupported, especially if they are unable to share their experiences with others.

Caregivers need to take care of their mental health and seek support when needed[1]. This can include reaching out to healthcare professionals, joining support groups, or seeking counseling. Remember, it's okay to ask for help.

"I think we need more support as fathers in these units and have time to bond with the baby more. A place for dads would be a great idea".

Here are a few suggestions that might help[136].

- Stay Connected: Try to stay connected with your wife and baby as much as possible. This could be through phone calls, video calls, or even letters.

- Ask for Updates: Regularly ask the healthcare team for updates about your wife and baby's progress.
- Take Care of Yourself: It's important to take care of your own mental health during this time. This might include regular exercise, eating well, getting enough sleep, and talking to someone about your feelings.
- Seek Support: Reach out to friends, family, or a mental health professional for support. You don't have to go through this alone.
- Financial Support: If you're eligible, you may be entitled to financial help with travel, meal costs, and accommodation.

"It was the scariest time seeing my wife go through things that I had never seen before ever. I didn't even think it was a thing until she ended up in a mother-and-baby unit. We were miles away from where we loved, and the travel alone was hard after a whole day's work".

Spotlight on Postpartum Psychosis

Simon, Partner Peer Support Coordinator, for Action on Postpartum Psychosis (APP)

Postpartum Psychosis (PP) is a severe but treatable form of mental illness that begins suddenly in the days and weeks after having a baby – heard of it? I hadn't but it would become one of the biggest learning experiences I'd ever endured and tested my mental well-being.

In the first couple of weeks after my wife gave birth, I had noticed subtle changes in her mood, but, as a

first-time father, I didn't know what was 'usual' or 'unusual'. Soon these changes took a dramatic turn for the worse and it quickly became very scary.

Over the next few days, I would see my wife suddenly wake 'ghost-like' in the early hours, her mood plummeting; she was anxious, confused, and pacing around the house, having delusions and hallucinations. Ultimately it all ended in a 999 call and eventually admission to a mother and baby Unit (MBU). I was in complete turmoil, unable to think clearly and throughout our journey with PP I went through many different emotions, from being terrified to feeling isolated, guilt-ridden, worried about the future, and with little sleep, the pressure I felt was enormous.

For many partners, seeing the symptoms of PP first-hand can be a truly traumatic experience. Many describe feeling like their world has been turned upside down, with little or no control over the situation, not knowing what's happening, feeling alone and scared, and trying to hold it together, to keep strong for their partner and families. This alongside dealing with multiple roles – new parent, job, family finances, carer, liaising with family and friends - all have the potential to have a lasting effect on the partner's mental health.

At Action on Postpartum Psychosis (APP), the leading national charity for women, partners, and families affected by PP, we know how difficult PP can be and how it affects not only the women directly experiencing it, but also the partners and families who watch their loved ones go through it. Support for the whole family unit is so important.

PP must be always treated as a medical emergency. It requires rapid intervention and is best treated in a specialized Mother and Baby Unit (MBU). With the right treatment and support, women with PP do make a full recovery, and families can move on with their lives together.

For more information, guides, support and training, visit www.app-network.org

I have signposted to this wonderful charity for many years for father's partners who are experiencing postpartum psychosis, it can be a challenging and stressful time. The charity has a range of information and it's important that fathers are educated to the understanding the condition.

Remember, it's okay to ask for help. If you're struggling, don't hesitate to reach out to a mental health professional. They can provide guidance and support during this challenging time.

FAMILY MEMBERS

Facing challenges when it comes to parenting can be difficult, especially when your in-laws are involved. Here are some suggestions to help you navigate this situation[137]:

- Open and honest conversation: Initiate a calm and respectful discussion with your wife's parents about your desire to be more involved in parenting. Share your feelings and concerns, emphasizing your commitment to your child's well-being. It's important to express your intentions clearly, while also being receptive to their perspective.
- Seek understanding: Listen attentively to your in-laws' concerns or reasons for not allowing you to be a father on your own. Try to understand their perspective and address any misconceptions or misunderstandings they may have. Ensure they know that you have the best interest of your child in mind.
- Share your capabilities: Highlight your abilities and qualities as a father. Reassure them of your commitment, responsibility, and willingness to take on the role of an involved father. Offer examples or stories that demonstrate your capability and dedication.
- Collaboration and compromise: Look for areas of common ground or opportunities to compromise. Discuss potential solutions to ease their worries while still allowing you to play an active role in your child's life. A gradual increase in responsibility or establishing agreed-upon guidelines might help establish trust.
- Seek professional assistance: If discussions with your in-laws prove challenging or unproductive, consider involving a family therapist or counselor. A professional can provide a neutral perspective, mediate conversations, and help find mutually acceptable solutions.

Remember, building understanding and cooperation may take time. Patience and persistence are key as you work towards establishing a healthy and supportive parenting dynamic between yourself, your partner, and your in-laws.

Empowering yourself as a father can be a great way to improve your confidence and become a better parent. Here are some tips to help you get started:

- Listen to your gut: Trust your instincts and make decisions based on what you think is best for your child.

- Check in with yourself: Take time out of your day to reflect on your feelings and emotions. This can help you live your life with more purpose.
- Create an empowering environment: Surround yourself with positive people and eliminate clutter from your life. This can help you focus and get more done.
- Develop a positive attitude: Focus on the things you can control and keep an objective, goal-oriented mindset.
- Take care of yourself: Make sure you're getting enough rest, eating well, and engaging in activities that bring you joy and comfort.

Empowering yourself as a father can help improve your mental health and confidence. Empowerment is the process of gaining control over your life and making positive changes that improve your well-being. Here are some ways that empowering yourself can help improve your mental health and confidence:

- Increased self-awareness: Empowerment can help you become more self-aware and in tune with your emotions and feelings. This can help you identify areas of your life that need improvement and take steps to address them.
- Improved self-esteem: Empowerment can help you feel more confident and capable of achieving your goals. This can improve your self-esteem and help you feel better about yourself.
- Reduced stress: Empowerment can help you feel more in control of your life, which can reduce stress and anxiety.
- Improved relationships: Empowerment can help you communicate more effectively and build stronger relationships with others.
- Better decision-making: Empowerment can help you make better decisions that are aligned with your values and goals.

Seeing my sister end up in hospital after trying to take her life was something that I will never forget. It affected me of course. The whole family was affected".

There is no such thing as a perfect parent.

The Good Price Guide - Involving and supporting partners and other family members in specialist perinatal mental health services guide is for specialist perinatal mental health services and commissioners. It relates to the families of mothers receiving care from inpatient and community specialist perinatal mental health teams. This includes partners, grandparents of the baby, siblings of the baby, and any significant others identified by the mother. It covers how to support and involve these family members.

The guide describes underpinning principles and key ideas for what services can do to involve and support partners and other family members, and why this is needed as a result of the impact on the whole family. The actions and practice tips offer suggestions to guide services. The practice examples help to illustrate these ways of working. The majority of points apply to both inpatient and community settings. Some are specific to Mother and Baby Units and this is clearly indicated in the text.

When implementing the suggestions in this guide, teams should refer to their local policies and guidelines, including safeguarding, information governance and data protection, as these differ across services.

CRITICISM

Becoming a new parent is a significant and transformative experience. It's completely normal to feel sensitive about criticism during this time. Remember, everyone has their parenting style and what works for one family may not work for another. It's important to trust your instincts and do what you feel is best for your child. If you're unsure about something, don't hesitate to consult with a healthcare professional.

"My mother-in-law said that I was to slowly change the nappy. I had been working hard that day and just wanted to interact with my baby. It made me feel uneasy and just left them to carry on at the time. It was only attending the classes, that I made sure that I was there to connect with my baby".

Dealing with criticism from family members can be challenging, especially when it comes to parenting. Remember, if anyone is nasty to you for no reason at all, it's usually them projecting their insecurities onto you. It's important to remember that education has grown since they become parents themselves. It's important to not take it personally.

The next time your family picks on your parenting skills and gives you unsolicited advice, don't hesitate to ask them if they would have actually taken their advice while they were raising their baby., it's important to maintain open communication and mutual respect. If the criticism continues, it might be helpful to have a calm, honest conversation about how her words make you feel.

Some parenting styles are commonly recognized. Each style has a different approach to raising children and can be identified by several different characteristics. Here's a brief overview:

- Authoritarian: This style is characterized by strict rules and high expectations. Parents who use this style believe children should follow the rules without exception and are not interested in negotiating. They may use punishments instead of discipline.
- Authoritative: This is often seen as a balanced approach. Parents who use this style set clear boundaries and have high expectations, but they also encourage independence and are responsive to their children's needs.
- Permissive: Parents who use this style tend to be lenient and may only step in when there is a serious problem. They're typically nurturing and communicative, and they often take on the role of a "friend" rather than a parent.
- Uninvolved: This style is characterized by few demands and low responsiveness. Parents who use this style may not be involved in their child's life and may not meet their child's basic needs.

The fight-or-flight response is a physiological reaction that occurs in response to a perceived harmful event, attack, or threat to survival. It's an automatic response that prepares your body to either stay and deal with a threat or to run away to safety. This response is triggered by the release of hormones that prepare your body to either stay and deal with a threat or to run away to safety.

Criticism can sometimes trigger this response, especially if it's perceived as a threat. This can happen because our brains are wired to respond to threats to our survival, and social threats (like criticism) can often be perceived in the same way as physical threats.

When faced with criticism, some people might 'fight' by becoming defensive and arguing back, while others might 'flee' by withdrawing or avoiding the situation. In these situations, there are techniques you can use to calm the fight-or-flight response and alleviate the symptoms of acute stress. We can help fathers with deep breathing, relaxation strategies, physical activity, and social support can all help if you are feeling the effects of a fight-or-flight response.

EFFECTS ON THE FAMILY

If a parent is experiencing postnatal depression, it can be a challenging time for the whole family, including siblings.

The NHS has published a good practice guide titled "Involving and Supporting Partners and Other Family Members in Specialist Perinatal Mental Health Services[138] This guide is for specialist perinatal mental health services and commissioners. It relates to the families of mothers receiving care from inpatient and community specialist perinatal mental health teams. This includes partners, grandparents of the baby, siblings of the baby, and any significant others identified by the mother[172].

The guide describes how to provide women and their families with a positive experience of care, with services joined up around them. It also describes how to provide care that involves and supports partners and families in ways that can improve outcomes for all family members.

Another guide titled "A Good Practice Guide to Support Implementation of Trauma-Informed Care in the Perinatal Period" is also available[173]. This guide applies to all staff (clinical and non-clinical) working with perinatal women in maternity and mental health services[139].

The Royal College of Midwives also provides a guide titled "Parental Emotional Wellbeing and Infant Development" which provides midwives and maternity support workers with recent evidence about the impact of parents' emotional wellbeing during pregnancy and the transition to parenthood[174].

"Seeing my daughter going through her trauma, of course, affected me".

Dr Jane Honikman who has spent her entire life helping parents in the United States and the rest of the world explains more about how we should be looking out for grandparents as well[140].

FATHERS UNABLE SEE THEIR CHILDREN

Support for a father's mental health can indeed have a positive impact on family relationships. In my experience of working with parents, it showed that when all parents are supported for their mental health, it has far better outcomes. We can lower the risks of relationships ending. Much research indicates that having a baby can put a strain on relationships.

Fathers who cannot see their children may experience a range of emotional and psychological challenges. Being separated from a child can be incredibly difficult, especially if the father is not able to maintain contact or establish a co-parenting relationship with the other parent[141].

Some of the common emotional challenges experienced by fathers who cannot see their children include grief, sadness, frustration, anger, and guilt. These emotions can be exacerbated if the separation happens due to an acrimonious divorce or separation.

In addition to the emotional challenges, fathers who cannot see their children may also experience practical issues such as financial difficulties, disrupted routines and social support, and a sense of isolation. Fathers in this situation need to seek out support networks such as friends, family members, or support groups to help them cope with these challenges.

It's important to note that in some cases, fathers may be legally entitled to visitation or custody rights, and they can seek legal assistance to help them navigate the legal system and enforce their rights. However, it is important to prioritize the well-being of the child and focus on establishing a healthy and respectful co-parenting relationship with the other parent, if possible.

Fathers who are unable to see their children can experience a range of emotional and psychological impacts. Here are some potential effects:

- Emotional Distress: Fathers may experience feelings of sadness, anger, and frustration. They may also feel a sense of loss or grief[5].
- Mental Health Issues: Stress and emotional turmoil can lead to mental health issues such as depression and anxiety.
- Self-Esteem Issues: Fathers may struggle with feelings of inadequacy or failure, which can impact their self-esteem.
- Relationship Difficulties: The strain of not being able to see their children can affect a father's relationships with others.
- Financial Stress: If a father is required to pay child support but is not allowed to see his children, this can lead to financial stress.

It's important to note that every situation is unique, and the impact can vary greatly depending on individual circumstances[5]. If a father is struggling with these issues, it may be helpful to seek support from mental health professionals or support groups.

The impact of not being able to see their children can be significant for fathers, and in some cases, it can lead to increased susceptibility to suicide. However, it's important to note that the specific rates of suicide among fathers who can't see their children are not readily available. Factors such as mental health issues, stress, and feelings of loss or grief can contribute to this risk.

"I only found out I had PTSD after witnessing the birth of my daughter after 29 years. I had lost everything which included my daughter, marriage, and business. It was only after being in crisis two years ago that I found out. After hearing your conversation talking about it over the phone, I just wanted to share that with you. I tried getting access over the years, but I just could not afford the fees and was left penniless".

THE MYTHS OF ABSENT FATHERS

It is not accurate to make a sweeping generalization that fathers are often absent. While it is true that some fathers may be less involved in their children's lives, it is not representative of all fathers. Many fathers play active and engaged roles in their children's upbringing and are present in their lives.

Parental involvement can vary depending on various factors such as cultural norms, personal circumstances, work commitments, and individual choices. It is essential to consider the unique circumstances of each family, as there are numerous reasons why a father might be less present, including but not limited to work obligations, military service, custody arrangements, or other personal challenges.

Research has shown that the pressures and expectations of masculinity can exacerbate mental health struggles for new fathers. The lack of societal understanding of paternal mental health challenges and the insufficient level of advice and resources available for men can also contribute to Many fathers face mental health challenges due to the pressures and changes of fatherhood, such as financial responsibility, relationship issues, lifestyle adjustments, and lack of sleep. Fathers who struggle with mental health problems may feel isolated, guilty, or inadequate, and may withdraw from their families or cope in unhealthy ways, such as substance abuse or violence[143].

- The mental health of fathers can affect the quality of their co-parenting relationships, their attachment bonds with their children, and their children's emotional and behavioral development.
- Supporting fathers for their mental health can help them to cope with stress, communicate their feelings, seek help when needed, and improve their self-esteem and confidence.
- Supporting fathers for their mental health can also benefit their partners, their children, and their families, by enhancing the harmony, stability, and well-being of the household.
- Supporting fathers for their mental health may lower the number of absent fathers, by preventing them from leaving their families, losing contact with their children, or being unable to fulfill their parental roles.

THE MYTHS OF FATHERHOOD

There are several social myths associated with becoming a father[144,145].

- Only the expectant mum's feelings are important: This myth suggests that only the mother's feelings count during the pregnancy and after the baby is born. However, fathers also experience a range of emotions, and their feelings are equally important.
- Newborns don't really need their fathers: Some people believe that newborns only need their mothers, especially if the mother is breastfeeding1. However, fathers play a crucial role in a newborn's life and can bond with their baby in many ways.
- There's only one definition of a "good dad": This myth suggests that there's a single, fixed definition of what it means to be a good father. In reality, fatherhood isn't fixed, and each father can create his version of being a good dad.
- Men are not as good parents as women: This myth is based on the notion that women are naturally better parents than men. However, parenting skills are not determined by gender and men can be just as nurturing and effective parents as women.
- Fathers are primarily the providers: This myth puts pressure on fathers to be the main financial provider for the family. While providing for the family is important, fathers also play a crucial role in providing emotional support and care.
- Faced with negative attitudes from health care professionals and society, often fuelled by the media, branding them as socially irresponsible and reckless (even though the reality is that only 10% of non-resident young fathers lose contact with their infant, and the majority want to be an integral part of their child's life.

Fathers may experience a sense of loss of their former selves when they become new fathers, especially if they are first-time fathers. This can occur due to a variety of reasons, including changes in their daily routine, lifestyle, responsibilities, relationships, and identity. It's quite common for new fathers to feel like they are not the same as they used to be, and this can lead to feelings of confusion, anxiety, and sadness[146,147].

This sense of loss may be compounded if the pregnancy or childbirth has been difficult, or if the baby has health problems. Additionally, the experience of becoming a new father can be isolating, especially if the man is the first in his social group to have a child.

It's important for new fathers to be patient with themselves and to allow themselves time to adapt to their new role. It's also important for fathers to prioritize their self-care and well-being, and not to neglect their own physical and mental health as they support their partner and child. Communicating openly and honestly with their partner about their experience can be helpful, as can seeking support from other fathers or community resources such as new parent groups or counseling services.

Relationships will also often suffer due to a father's lack of 'preparedness' to be a new dad, causing some mothers to cease to trust fathers with their child's wellbeing, and also putting pressure on the couple's relationship. Howl notes that[146]:

Transitioning to fatherhood can indeed be a challenging time for both the father and the couple's relationship. Many fathers may feel unprepared or uncertain about their role as new dad, which can impact their confidence and ability to care for their children. As a result, relationships may suffer, and some mothers may find it difficult to trust fathers with their child's wellbeing. This situation can put significant pressure on the couple's relationship as well.

It is important to recognize that this experience is not uncommon, and that open communication and support are crucial during this transition. Here are a few suggestions to navigate this period effectively.

- Open Communication: Both partners need to communicate openly about their expectations, fears, and concerns regarding their new roles as parents. Honest conversations can help address any misunderstandings, manage expectations, and build trust.
- Education and Preparation: Fathers can benefit from seeking information and resources that can help them feel more prepared as new dads. Attending parenting classes, reading books, or engaging in online communities specifically for fathers can provide valuable insights and assistance.

- Sharing Responsibilities: Encourage an equitable distribution of childcare responsibilities between both parents. This helps fathers gain confidence in their ability to care for their children and fosters a sense of partnership within the relationship.
- Seek Support: Consider reaching out to support networks, such as friends, family, or community groups, where fathers can connect with other new dads. Sharing experiences, asking questions, and receiving advice from those who have gone through similar situations can be beneficial.
- Patience and Understanding: Adjusting to parenthood takes time, and mistakes and challenges are a part of the learning process. Practicing patience, empathy, and understanding towards one another can help navigate the ups and downs effectively.

Remember, every couple's experience is unique, and seeking professional guidance, such as couples counseling or therapy, can provide additional support if needed. The key is to approach this transition with patience, open communication, and a willingness to learn and grow together.

When we support only one member of the couple, generally the mother, we run the risk of unwittingly undermining the couple's relationship, creating unequal levels of knowledge, and confirming social stereotypes that the 'mother knows best' and therefore should be responsible for the lion's share of the care… Supporting couples to engage in, and practice, positive communication during the antenatal period, as well as after the birth, is likely to pay dividends. The best means of supporting positive interparental communication is to engage with the couple and support them routinely and systematically in all mainstream services, and make this an explicit part of the universal support offer.

This is further demonstrated by the Mental Health Foundation's findings that the interrupted education – and, in turn, the impact that this has on his fathering skills – that often occurs in young fathers all contributes to putting pressure on the young father's relationship with the baby's mother[149].

I suggest that this all occurs primarily because early intervention – in the form of emotional support for new fathers –

was not in place and, consequently, the dad-to-be did not have the communication skills or knowledge to help him overcome the significant obstacles in the relationship.

Research has shown that there can be an increase in fathers' BMI following the birth of their baby. Several factors contribute to this phenomenon. Some possible factors that contribute to fathers' BMI increase after birth are:

- Changes in lifestyle and diet: Fathers may experience more stress, less sleep, and less physical activity after the birth of their baby. They may also have less time and energy to prepare healthy meals and snacks, and may rely more on convenience foods and takeaways that are high in calories, fat, and sugar.
- Hormonal changes: Fathers may experience hormonal changes that affect their appetite, metabolism, and body composition. For example, some studies have suggested that fathers may have lower levels of testosterone and higher levels of prolactin, which are hormones that regulate muscle mass, fat distribution, and energy expenditure.
- Genetic and epigenetic factors: Fathers may pass on genes or epigenetic markers that influence their offspring's birth weight and risk of obesity. For example, some studies have found that paternal age, undernutrition, high-fat diet, or stress can affect sperm quality and DNA methylation, which can alter the expression of genes involved in growth and metabolism in the offspring.

PREPAREDNESS FOR FATHERHOOD

The Fathers Network Scotland survey of 2019 found that 25% of dads felt that they could not cope with becoming a father and that they were not a good dads. This is supported by Baldwin et al's 2018 study suggested that fathers should be better prepared for fatherhood. Higgins et al, in 2020, looked at men's transition to parenthood. The authors interviewed fathers about their experiences in becoming a father; the men discussed their relationship with their infant, wanting quality time to bond and make decisions about their baby's care, with the fathers expressing that they struggled to achieve perfection in fatherhood.

"My husband lacked confidence in being a dad so why don't we focus on dads as well as mums? Society is changing and now I am at work … and my husband is home with our baby alone".

Darwin et al's 2017 research also supported the need to address the necessary tailor-made and targeted resources for fathers, to enable them to feel a greater part of the childcare process. For younger men who find themselves with an interrupted education as a result of becoming a father, their lower levels of education and attainment can hurt their own fathering skills, putting more pressure on their relationship with their baby's mother[153].

Breastfeeding is often an area where fathers do not feel they have a role and frequently feel left out because, although support is offered to the mother, the fathers are made to feel that they are not involved. Some fathers have expressed the need for more information and support in this important area. Fathers' experiences in supporting breastfeeding have been considered by several research papers, and the general message coming from these is that fathers want to be involved and supportive, but often feel left out and helpless.

There were other areas related to the care of their infant where fathers needed information but were unable to access it. Looking back [at the antenatal classes I attended], it was not the lack of expertise and taught content in the lessons that failed to prepare me and fill me with confidence; it was how it was delivered. Most of the time, things like holding the baby or changing a nappy were focused more on the females in the room with the physical exercises being done by the women and the men only being addressed when it was something of importance to aid the female. My role in the classes was very much a support role and very rarely made to do anything that could have prepared me for those first few hours as a father.

Mayers et al's 2020 research looked into the extent to which new fathers felt prepared to help support their partner when she develops postnatal mental health difficulties and found three main themes[154]: the fathers did not feel that they were getting enough (or good enough) support; the fathers felt that they were poorly informed; and the fathers wanted to have had someone to talk to, both about their partner's situation and their emotions[154].

MENTAL HEALTH EXPERIENCES

Darwin et al's 2017 research found men describing their transition to fatherhood as an emotional rollercoaster. Certainly, the research – when looked at collectively – identifies commonly identified lifestyle factors, all of which are acknowledged as having an impact on new fathers' mental health, including sleep deprivation; transformed responsibilities; strained relationships; isolation; financial strain; loss of self/former life; and experiencing birth trauma[155].

Higgins et al (2020) also recorded expressions of the emotional impact that guilt and frustration had on new fathers[156].

Professor Vivette Glover Professor of Perinatal Psychobiology, at Imperial College London explains:

"The mother's mental health both during pregnancy and after having her baby is important, both for herself and also for the development of her child. If she is stressed, anxious, or depressed it can double the risk of her child having mental health problems later. And one of the most important factors in how she is feeling is the support she receives from her father. In recent years we have become aware of how important the role of the father is in helping his future family, and that part of that involves giving him support for his mental health problems too".

NCT research found that over one-third of new fathers were worried or concerned about their own mental health, whilst over 73% were concerned about the mental health of their partner[197]. The Mental Health Foundation, similarly, found that over one-third (39.2%) of young fathers wanted support for their mental health. Interestingly – but perhaps not surprisingly – younger fathers were significantly more likely to experience depression, compared with older fathers.

Again, this would seem to be linked to lifestyle factors (all of which can affect their mental health) which are perhaps even more challenging for this demographic. For example, young fathers are often[198]:

- living in unstable housing or are homeless.
- in low-paid or insecure employment.
- faced with an interruption to their education.
- not living with their child full-time (over one-third of young fathers).
- struggling to cope in isolation, and aloneness.

Ian Jones Director/Clinical Professor, National Centre for Mental Health explains here:

"We are increasingly recognising the importance of maternal mental health for women, their babies, families, and wider society. Perhaps less attention, however, is given to the mental health of fathers and partners. We need to do better in recognising and providing support to this group for many reasons, not least because of the importance that partners play in the well-being of mothers and children. Even for very severe episodes of perinatal mental illness, such as postpartum psychosis, we know the support of a partner is a key factor that determines the risk of illness. Families are important and need support. Recognising partners who are struggling and providing the help they need is a vital part of ensuring the wellbeing of families and that all babies have the right start".

Being a new dad is an exciting and challenging time for any individual, and it can present unique challenges for someone living with bipolar disorder. Bipolar disorder is a mental health condition characterized by extreme mood swings, including episodes of mania and depression. It's important to note that each person's experience with bipolar disorder can vary, and no two individuals will have the same needs or challenges.

Remember, every individual's experience with bipolar disorder is unique, and strategies that work for one person may not work for another. By seeking professional support, communicating openly, and prioritizing self-care, new dads with bipolar disorder can navigate the challenges of parenthood while managing their mental health effectively.

Movember, a leading charity focused on men's health, conducted research in 2019 across Canada, the UK, the USA, and Australia to investigate men's social connections, with a specific emphasis on fatherhood and the impact of becoming a father[1]. Here are some key findings from the report.

Becoming a father can be an isolating and stressful experience, particularly in the first 12 months.

- Fathers without close friends reported being more likely to experience increased stress levels in the first 12 months of becoming a father.
- 1 in 5 men lose contact with friends when they become a father.
- Also, explaining about Fathers with mental health problems around the time of the birth of their child are up to 47 times more likely to be considered at risk of suicide than at any other point in their lives.

The report emphasizes the importance of having and maintaining strong social connections to better serve fathers during this critical life stage[1]. This not only benefits the fathers but also the mothers, partners, children, and society as a whole.

According to the Loneliness and Mental Health Report UK, Loneliness and severe isolation can negatively affect mental health. This is a common theme when speaking with fathers, they often tell me that they feel left out, and some explain that they lose interest in hobbies that were once there before becoming a father.

People who lack social connections have a higher risk of depression. Long-term loneliness can lead to a negative spiral where loneliness makes it harder to connect, leading to fear of social situations, making it harder to find joy in life and escape negative thoughts. Depression often causes people to withdraw socially, which can lead to isolation. Loneliness can also be a factor that contributes to symptoms of depression. Studies show that loneliness and social isolation are associated with higher risks for health problems such as heart disease, depression, and cognitive decline.

DOMESTIC VIOLENCE

Domestic Violence (DV) can affect anyone, regardless of gender. Here are some signs that a father may be experiencing domestic violence[158]:

- Physical injuries: Visible signs of bruises, cuts, or other injuries that cannot be adequately explained.
- Emotional distress: Frequent anxiety, fear, or sadness. They may appear unusually withdrawn or on edge.
- Isolation: They may seem increasingly isolated from friends, family, and other support systems.
- Control and manipulation: Constantly being monitored or controlled by their partner, often accompanied by threats or intimidation tactics.
- behaviour change: Drastic changes in their behavior, such as becoming overly submissive or exhibiting uncharacteristic aggression.
- Low self-esteem: Expressing feelings of worthlessness, powerlessness, or humiliation.
- Unexplained absences or explanations: Frequently missing work or social events without a reasonable explanation or giving inconsistent reasons for injuries.
- Financial control: Their partner might control their finances, limiting their access to money or important resources.
- Attempts to protect children: If they have children, they may go to great lengths to shield them from witnessing or experiencing the abuse.

It is essential to approach this situation with empathy and non-judgment. Encourage open communication, and if possible, suggest seeking help from professionals or local support organizations that specialize in domestic violence issues. Remember, it's important to prioritize everyone's well-being and safety.

According to the Office for National Statistics, one in three victims of domestic abuse is male, equating to 699,000 men in 2022[208]. This means that one in 6-7 men and one in 4 women will be a victim of domestic abuse in their lifetime[1]. Of domestic abuse crimes recorded by the police, 25% were committed against men[159].

However, many male victims of domestic abuse do not report it to the police or seek help from local services. Only 4.7% of victims of domestic abuse being supported by local domestic services are men according to Safe Lives data[160]. This highlights how few men are being supported by local domestic abuse services.

Some of the reasons why male victims may not disclose their abuse are:

Fathers may fear being judged, blamed, or ridiculed by others.

They may feel ashamed, guilty, or responsible for the abuse.

They may have low self-esteem and confidence and believe they deserve the abuse.

They may have difficulty expressing their emotions and needs.

They may have limited access to information and support services.

If you or someone you know is experiencing domestic violence, please know that you are not alone and there is help available. You can call the ManKind Initiative helpline on 0808 2000 247 for confidential advice and support. You can also visit their website [here] for more information and resources.

"I couldn't tell anyone that my girlfriend was being mentally abusive to me".

There are several reasons why health professionals may not ask new fathers about domestic violence:

Lack of Training: Health and social care practitioners should be trained to recognize the indicators of possible domestic violence and abuse[2]. However, previous studies have shown that despite these guidelines, doctors and nurses rarely ask about intimate partner violence and often fail to identify the signs of domestic abuse.

Stereotypes and Assumptions: There can be societal stereotypes and assumptions about gender roles that might prevent health professionals from recognizing that men can also be victims of domestic violence.

Disclosure Barriers: Victims of domestic violence, regardless of gender, may face barriers to disclosure such as fear, embarrassment, self-blame, and the presence or controlling behavior of the abusive partner.

Perception of Men in Families: Social workers may see men in a family as either a risk or a resource, which can affect their approach to engaging with fathers. It's important to note that anyone can be a victim of domestic violence, and health professionals must create safe and validating environments for all patients to disclose such experiences. If you or someone you know is experiencing domestic violence, please reach out to a trusted organization or local authorities for help.

Every parent being asked whether they have been the victim of domestic abuse, with information on support and opportunities for further conversations available for both partners.

SHAKEN BABY SYNDROME (SBS)

Shaken baby syndrome (SBS) is a serious form of abuse inflicted upon a child. It usually occurs when a parent or other caregiver shakes a baby out of anger or frustration, often because the baby will not stop crying. Babies have very weak neck muscles that cannot fully support their proportionately large heads. Severe shaking causes the baby's head to move violently back and forth, resulting in serious and sometimes fatal brain injury[161].

Here are some tips to help prevent SBS:

- Educate parents and caregivers: Young parents need to be educated about the dangers of forcefully shaking the baby. Caregivers should be taught alternative ways to soothe a crying baby, such as rocking, singing, or swaddling.
- Treat children gently: Infants should be handled gently and with care. They should never be shaken, thrown, or hit.

Seek help if stressed: Parents and caregivers who are feeling stressed or overwhelmed should seek help from a mental health professional or support group.

Remember, SBS is a preventable form of child abuse, and this way we must engage with fathers to prevent this from happening. Research suggests that 1 in 9 mothers may have shaken their baby and up to 2 in 9 felt like doing so. However, I could not find the data and statistics for fathers. it's crucial to seek help immediately. There are many resources available, such as the NHS program ICON, which offers coping strategies for parents[162].

RISKS TO THE BABY

There have been tragic cases where fathers suffering from postnatal depression have harmed their children. For example, there was a landmark court case where he was reported to have allegedly murdered his daughter. He was said to have resented the intrusion of the "unplanned" baby into his married life[163].

The NSPCC published a report in 2015 titled "How Safe Are Our Children?" which provides an overview of the child protection landscape and compiles the most robust and up-to-date child protection data that exists across each of the four nations in the UK.

In addition, the NSPCC also ran a project called "The Dad Project" which looked at how relationships could be strengthened between dads, their child, and his or her mother, and the services that work with them during pregnancy and the year after a baby is born. The project was supported by the Design Council and funded by the Guy's and St Thomas' Charity.

An independent review into safeguarding children under 1 from non-accidental injury caused by male carers. It investigates the death or serious harm of 23 babies who were known or suspected to have been harmed or killed by their father, stepfather, or male carer. It calls for more support for fathers, especially those who have mental health problems, substance misuse, or a history of violence. It also recommends that universal, antenatal, and perinatal services work with fathers to address significant risk factors and offer them support before the baby's birth.

"I was so scared that I just wanted the baby to go away somewhere. I didn't know why I felt that way, but I just could not stop the way I was thinking about it".

NEURODIVERSITY

Neurodiversity is a concept that describes the idea that people experience and interact with the world around them in many different ways; there is no one “right” way of thinking, learning, and behaving, and differences are not viewed as deficits1. The term refers to the diversity of all people, but it is often used in the context of autism spectrum disorder (ASD), as well as other neurological or developmental conditions such as ADHD or learning disabilities[164,165].

The neurodiversity movement emerged during the 1990s, aiming to increase the acceptance and inclusion of all people while embracing neurological differences. It is primarily a social justice movement, but neurodiversity research and education are increasingly important in how clinicians view and address certain disabilities and neurological conditions.

The Neurodiversity Umbrella Project is an initiative by the ADHD Foundation that aims to raise awareness and understanding of neurodiversity. The project uses a visual representation of thousands of colourful umbrellas strung together over public spaces, schools, and company buildings around the UK[1]. Each display is designed to represent one in five of us who have a neurodevelopmental condition, such as ADHD, Autism, Dyslexia, Dyspraxia, Dyscalculia, or Tourette’s syndrome[1]. These conditions fall under the umbrella term of neurodiversity.

The project is changing the perception of neurodiverse/neurodivergent people and celebrating all the many strengths that come from thinking differently[1]. It also provides resources for education settings, including training webinars, posters, information packs, lesson plans, and assembly presentations focusing on neurodiversity. In essence, the Neurodiversity Umbrella Project is a celebration of the 1 in 5 human beings who have 'different minds[165].

AUTISM AND FATHERHOOD

New dads with autism may face unique challenges and may benefit from support and understanding as they navigate their parenting journey. Autism is a neurodevelopmental disorder characterized by differences in social communication, interaction, and repetitive patterns of behavior. While being a new parent can bring joy, it can also introduce changes and uncertainties that may be overwhelming for someone with autism[166,167].

Some potential challenges that new dads with autism may encounter include difficulties with social interactions, sensory sensitivities, managing changes in routine, and adapting to the demands of parenting. It's important to acknowledge that each individual's experience will differ, as autism exists on a spectrum, and everyone has their strengths and struggles.

"I was diagnosed later in life with Autism after struggling with my own mental health. I was in the labor ward and the doctors came crowding over me and told me we had to get your partner into theatre quickly. As my partner was going down to the theatre, the health professional told me to say goodbye to my wife and I took it that she was going to die. I was then left outside, and no one was telling me anything, and just could not cope. It was traumatic".

New fathers with autism can face a variety of challenges. Here are some common ones[167]:

- Limited social support networks: Autistic individuals often have fewer social connections, which can make it harder to find support and advice.
- Difficulty advocating for their children: Some autistic parents may struggle to advocate for their children, particularly in social situations or within the education system.
- Anxiety or fear about feeling inadequate as a parent: Many new parents experience feelings of inadequacy, but this can be particularly pronounced for autistic parents.
- Managing personal traits: Autistic parents must deal with managing their traits, which can include sensory overload and social and communication challenges[2].
- Isolation from other parents: They may feel isolated from other parents who are otherwise peers during antenatal classes, neighborhood gatherings, and in similar settings.

- Difficulty with change: Autistic individuals often struggle with change, which can be a challenge when adapting to the unpredictable nature of a newborn.
- Interpreting and expressing feelings: Some autistic individuals have trouble interpreting and expressing feelings, which can be challenging when trying to understand a baby's needs.

Support for new dads with autism can be multifaceted. Here are some suggestions:

- Seek professional guidance: Consulting with healthcare providers, therapists, or counselors who understand autism can provide tailored strategies and support.
- Build a support network: Connect with other parents, including those who may have similar experiences, or join online communities where experiences and advice can be shared.
- Develop routines and structures: Establishing predictable routines can help reduce stress and anxiety for both the dad with autism and the child.
- Manage sensory sensitivities: Create a calm and sensory-friendly environment that limits overwhelming stimuli, providing a space where both the dad and child feel comfortable.
- Self-care: Encourage self-care practices, such as taking breaks, pursuing personal interests, and seeking hobbies or activities that promote relaxation and well-being.

Remember, each person with autism is unique, and what works for one individual may not work for another. Understanding and acceptance, along with appropriate support systems, can go a long way in assisting new dads on the autism spectrum to thrive in their parenting role.

ADHD AND FATHERHOOD

ADHD was first recognised as a valid condition in the UK in 2000 but was not officially recognized as an adult condition until 2008. ADHD affects 5% of children and 3% of adults (1.5 million) in the UK, making it the most common behavioral disorder in the country. So many parents are often never diagnosed, and the diagnosis can take years, in the meantime they are preparing for parenthood.

ADHD (Attention-Deficit/Hyperactivity Disorder) can also affect new fathers, just as it can affect individuals at any stage of life. While studies on ADHD specifically in new fathers are limited, it is important to recognize that this condition can have a significant impact on a person's daily life and parenting experience[168,169,170].

Managing ADHD symptoms can be especially challenging for new fathers, as they may struggle with time management, organization, impulsivity, and maintaining focus. The demands of caring for a newborn baby, such as establishing routines, managing schedules, and juggling responsibilities, can exacerbate these challenges.

ADHD (attention deficit hyperactivity disorder) can indeed present unique challenges for new fathers. Here are some key points to consider:

- Parenting Challenges: Fathers with ADHD may find it difficult to give the kind of love, encouragement, and approval their children long for due to the complexities of their symptoms[1]. Certain traits common to men with ADHD can interfere with the father-child relationship, especially when those fathers are parenting children who also have ADHD.
- Self-Reflection: Many of the character traits and behaviours frequently found in people with ADHD become particularly challenging for a father when he sees them in his son. This can cloud his ability to address the issues effectively.
- Treatment and Support: The first step in improving your parenting skills is to make sure you are receiving adequate treatment for your ADHD[1]. You may benefit from medication, therapy, or working with an ADHD coach. Support can also come from local ADHD support groups, parenting classes, books, and pamphlets.
- Mental Health: Studies show that many fathers have mental illness in the first six months after a baby arrives, with first-time dads and younger dads particularly vulnerable. ADHD can exacerbate these feelings, so it's important for fathers to seek help if they're feeling overwhelmed.

Jacob, known as @adhdfatheruk on Instagram, is an advocate for ADHD. He was diagnosed with ADHD over 20 years ago and now uses his platform to raise awareness and provide support for others with ADHD. He has been featured in various content, including an episode of "ADHD As Females" where he discussed ADHD, fatherhood, and self-care.

Jacob also focuses on postnatal depression and men's mental health. He shares his experiences and insights to help others navigate these challenges. His advocacy work is a valuable resource for individuals and families dealing with ADHD and related mental health issues. I personally feel that it is vital that people like Jacob share their own experiences and make it more open for fathers who struggle with ADHD and difficulties in the perinatal period to open up.

As we know now, ADHD (attention deficit hyperactivity disorder) is a neurodevelopmental disorder that is often associated with differences in how dopamine is transmitted to the brain[1]. Dopamine is a neurotransmitter that regulates learning and motivation.

Research suggests that people with ADHD may have an underlying dysfunction in dopamine transmission, meaning that the brain can't receive dopamine correctly, leading to emotional responses that differ from those who are neurotypical[1]. This irregularity may cause behavioral and motivational problems that may interfere with an individual's ability to be motivated, achieve goals, and manage behavioral challenges.

Some researchers speculate that people with ADHD have an increased amount of dopamine transporters. Having a higher density of dopamine transporters in the brain results in lowered dopamine levels in the brain. A decreased amount of dopamine in the brain can result in a diagnosis of ADHD[229].

"I had this invisible enemy for years and certainly becoming a father it was not about looking after me now. I was overwhelmed with everything that went on in that short space of time. My mind has always been racing, but this was a different level after becoming a father" – Mark Willams

Becoming a parent requires routine, organisation, time management, inconsistent stimulation and sensory input, memory recall, and prioritizing. All these processes require us to call upon our executive function skills, which is something us ADHD folks find difficult.

A new baby may bring a lack of sleep, poor nutrition, and increased sensory sensitivity, which all heighten and increase ADHD symptoms. It's a one-way ticket to emotional and cognitive dysregulation, increased anxiety and depression, possible mood disorders, and a steep decline in mental health and wellbeing. As stated by Sari Solden M.S., LMFT, psychotherapist and adult ADHD counselor,

It's important to note that while there is a strong connection between dopamine production and ADHD, the exact relationship is still being studied and understood. If you or someone you know is struggling with ADHD, it's important to seek help from a healthcare professional.

DYSLEXIA AND FATHERHOOD

Dyslexia is a specific learning difficulty that affects the way people read, write, and spell words. It is not a mental illness, but it can have an impact on one's mental health and well-being. Some of the common emotional problems that people with dyslexia may experience are[171]:

Anxiety: This is the most frequent emotional symptom reported by both children and adults with dyslexia. Anxiety is a normal reaction to stress or danger, but it can become overwhelming and interfere with daily functioning. Fathers with dyslexia may feel anxious about reading, writing, spelling, or learning new things. They may also worry about being judged, failing, or disappointing others.

"It was great to have an advocate for the paperwork, it was too overwhelming to cope".

Depression: This is a mood disorder that causes persistent feelings of sadness, hopelessness, and loss of interest. People with dyslexia may develop depression because of their constant frustration and confusion in family life or work. They may also have low self-esteem, feel isolated, or struggle with social relationships.

Anger: This is a natural emotion that can be triggered by feeling threatened, hurt, or frustrated. People with dyslexia may feel angry because of their difficulties with reading and writing, or because they feel misunderstood, unsupported, or discriminated against. They may also have trouble expressing their anger in healthy ways or may suppress it and internalize it.

Shame: This is a painful feeling of humiliation or distress caused by the awareness of one's faults or shortcomings. Fathers with dyslexia may feel ashamed of their learning difficulties, or of the mistakes they make when reading or writing. They may also feel embarrassed, guilty, or unworthy because of the negative feedback they receive from others.

These emotional problems can affect one's physical health, academic performance, career prospects, and social interactions. They can also lead to other mental health issues, such as eating disorders, substance abuse, or self-harm. Therefore, it is important to seek help and support if you or someone you know is struggling with dyslexia and mental health.

PRESSURES FROM WIDER SOCIETY

Interestingly, research from Australia[172] into new dads experiencing postnatal depression acknowledged that a lack of understanding of the modern fathering experience is one of the biggest barriers to supporting new dads. Godfrey-Isaacs [173]considered the weight of social pressure and expectations on fathers, whilst Baldwin et al also found that first-time fathers faced challenges in both forming their identity and coping with the restrictions to their lifestyle.

Das and Hopkinson's report[174] outlined how the gendered positioning of new fathers in the period before and after a baby's birth can contribute to complex impacts on their own well-being and mental health, making it difficult to recognise their struggles as legitimate and to seek support. This research supports the concept that fathers felt that attention and support should be focused on their partner and not themselves; their inability to share their feelings results in a spiral of guilt and shame.

Certainly, the pressures to 'man up' were voiced as stress factors amongst the fathers I have spoken to and led some of them to contemplate how their own identity as a father would impact them and their families. Linked to this is the fact that, on the whole, men were found to prefer not to discuss their mental health, and also found it difficult to seek or ask for help and support.

"The expectations of others were nothing but burdens and imagining not being able to be the dad I wanted was cause for fleeting, then frequent, episodes of sadness".

While it's true that societal norms and expectations can sometimes lag behind the changing roles of parents, there is evidence to suggest that society is increasingly recognizing and valuing the role of fathers. For instance, in the UK, policy engagement with fathers is specified in the delivery of health and family services. The National Parenting Strategy in Scotland emphasizes the importance of fathers playing an active role in their child's upbringing[174].

Fathering is now a more accepted role for men at home and fathers are visible outside the school gates, in parks and playgrounds, and in the streets and shopping centres in the UK and other countries. When it comes to their mental health, it is often rarely considered that fathers can suffer from postnatal depression.

"I'm not the breadwinner of our house, so it made sense for my wife to go back to work. I could be in the house all day with no one to talk to rather than a screaming baby. It is certainly one of the hardest things that I have had to do on my own".

Lloyd Frank Philpott has researched the impact of fatherhood on men's health. His work has highlighted that fatherhood can have a protective effect on men's health[175]. However, the transition to fatherhood can also be complex and demanding, potentially leading to distress, anxiety, and an increased risk of depression[2]. This underscores the importance of support and education for new fathers.

These studies contribute to a growing body of research highlighting the importance of fatherhood, not just for the well-being of children, but also for the fathers themselves. It emphasizes the need for societal recognition and support for the role of fathers in child development and family health.

In conclusion, while there may be some barriers and challenges, society is gradually becoming more inclusive of fathers. It's a continuous process and further efforts are needed to ensure that fathers are fully included and recognized in all aspects of parenting and childcare.

BLIND AND DEAF COMMUNITY FOR DADS

A blog post by a blind father of two, who shares his experiences and challenges of raising children with visual impairment. He talks about how he copes with the practical aspects of parenting, such as changing diapers, feeding, bathing, and playing with his kids. He also discusses the emotional and social issues he faces, such as feeling isolated, dealing with stigma, and finding support[176].

A podcast episode from RNIB Connect Radio, where a blind dad and a sighted mum talk about their journey of becoming parents and how they manage their family life. They share their tips and advice on how to prepare for the arrival of a baby, how to communicate with health professionals, and how to balance their roles and responsibilities as parents.

A research paper from the Journal of Visual Impairment & Blindness, explores the experiences and needs of fathers with visual impairments[3]. The paper reports the findings of a qualitative study that interviewed 11 blind or partially sighted fathers in the UK. The paper identifies the main themes and challenges that emerged from the data, such as the lack of information and support, the impact on identity and self-esteem, and the strategies and skills for coping and adapting[177].

A personal essay by a deaf father of two, who shares his experiences and challenges of raising children with hearing impairment[1]. He talks about how he copes with the practical aspects of parenting, such as changing diapers, feeding, bathing, and playing with his kids. He also discusses the emotional and social issues he faces, such as feeling isolated, dealing with stigma, and finding support[178].

A commentary by a journalist and mother, argues that new dads often face mental health problems in the postnatal period but are invisible in NHS advice and support[179]. She cites studies that show that one in 10 men experience anxiety and depression symptoms in the first six months after the birth of a baby, and that fathers with mental health problems during the perinatal period are up to 47 times more likely to be classed as a suicide risk than at any other time in their lives[237]. She also highlights the pressure and guilt that many men feel to be strong and silent and calls for more awareness and recognition of paternal mental health issues.

A feature article by a health writer, who explores the challenges that still exist for the deaf community in general, and deaf parents in particular[180]. She interviews three generations of deaf men from the same family, who have witnessed the changes and roadblocks in society over the years. She also covers the topics of education, employment, communication, technology, and advocacy for the deaf community.

A blog post by a deafblind father of two, who shares his experiences and challenges of raising children with dual sensory impairment[1]. He talks about how he communicates with his kids using tactile sign language, how he supports their education and development, and how he advocates for their rights and needs.

A video from Perkins School for the Blind, where a deafblind dad and his hearing and sighted wife talk about their family life and how they raise their two children, who are also deafblind[181]. They share their tips and advice on how to bond with their kids, how to teach them life skills, and how to access resources and support.

A research paper from the Journal of Deafblind Studies on Communication, explores the experiences and perspectives of deafblind fathers in Norway[182]. The paper reports the findings of a qualitative study that interviewed six deafblind fathers who have children with normal hearing and vision. The paper discusses the main themes and challenges that emerged from the data, such as the role of the father, the communication with the children, and the social and emotional aspects of fatherhood.

"We feel that we can't share how we feel as a new father".

I have found frustration while supporting a group in Bristol called "Little Hands Deaf Bristol" The fathers found that there was little engagement with health professionals, even greater than other groups that I had experienced and was belittled due to the lack of understanding in the deaf community. This once again, is an area that needs attention and needs more support and education in services for parents.

Jane Turner, Psychoanalytic Parent-Infant Psychotherapist and Psychoanalytic Child and Adolescent Psychotherapist explains:

"Becoming a father means inevitable change. It might not be physically visible to the rest of society, but becoming a father impacts internally, in the father-to-be's mind. Many thoughts and feelings are evoked, and some are not always welcome. As with mothers, this can be a source of real shame. What is stirred up inside, if we can bear to notice, at the thought of bringing new life into this world?

Although there may be thoughts and feelings of joy and excitement at the idea of having a new baby, for most men there will be, ordinarily, as there is for women, real fears about this change, and the capacity to be a parent. Why wouldn't there be? It is a developmental change of great significance".

For men, like women, sometimes these thoughts and feelings can be disturbing and may impact not only the relationship with their partner but the relationship with their baby and their mental health. If a man doesn't have a space to be able to share his internal experience this can lead to a real sense of isolation and his mental health can deteriorate seriously or he can start to behave differently.

Without vital support and help, there might be a deterioration in the father's mental health, difficulties within his intimate relationships, an impact on his work, an increase in reliance on addictive substances, risk-taking… and so the list goes on.

No man and no father is the same, and the relationship with their baby, and each baby will be unique and different. That relationship will be informed by so many factors: his relationship with his partner, whether the pregnancy was planned/wanted; his own early life experience of being fathered; his previous traumatic experiences and mental health and so on. It is complex and thoughts and feelings often are difficult to make sense of on one's own. In parent-infant psychotherapy we recognize that a mother and baby does not exist without a father, and vice versa. They are all interconnected relationally.

Inside we have all experienced being an infant, and having parents, whether they have been physically present or not, we will have ideas in our mind about what it means to be good enough parents.

A baby needs a 'good enough' couple; mother and father; who can help him to make sense of the world including his early thoughts and feelings, to help him grow up and become his person not coupled with mummy and not coupled with daddy but tolerating not being part of a couple. This supports his capacity to be alone, to grow independently and to observe and be observed by others.

A father is not ancillary to a baby's development and life but is vital. There is always a father in mind, as part of a couple who created the baby in mind, and whether physically present, or psychologically available, this will continue to be a factor of curiosity for the child, acknowledged or not, and impact on their mental health. The father's legacy, like the mother's is everlasting".

ROLE MODELS

As society has changed, some fathers have lacked role models to explain and/or demonstrate the concept of fatherhood. For them, this has added to their feelings of exclusion and lack of information Fathers are trying to grow into their role as co-parents but lack a blueprint from previous generations on how to manage this role successfully and take an egalitarian approach to their interparental relationship. Across healthcare services to national policies, fathers need access to tailored support, treatment and training that encourage gender equality in parenting and household responsibilities[2].

You raise an important point about the positive impact that father figures can have on their children's lives. Building close relationships with father figures can indeed contribute to a variety of positive outcomes for children. Research has shown that when children have strong connections with their fathers or father figures, they are more likely to avoid engaging in high-risk behaviors and delaying early sexual activity. Additionally, these children tend to have better job prospects and healthier, more stable relationships as adults[184].

A good father or father figure serves as an ideal role model for children, shaping their attitudes, behaviors, and decision-making skills throughout their journey to adulthood. By demonstrating positive values and behaviors, fathers can have a lasting influence on their children's development.

Moreover, when fathers are affectionate and supportive, it positively impacts a child's cognitive and social development. It fosters a sense of well-being, self-confidence, and inner strength. Children often strive to make their fathers proud, and an involved and caring father figure can greatly contribute to their overall growth and happiness.

It's important to recognize and celebrate the significant role that fathers and father figures play in their children's lives. Through love, support, and positive guidance, they can help shape the future of their children in profound ways.

Father involvement is beneficial for the well-being and mental health of the father and mother and, ultimately, the development of the child who benefits from having two equally competent, healthy, and engaged parents. The current shift towards increased father-engagement presents an opportunity to instill a culture that fatherhood is essential to family health and equitable father involvement is an expectation for current and future generations that should be nurtured and supported by society. Dr Sheehan Fisher

Many of the mothers who have contacted me have told me that their partners had been ‘useless’ when trying to support them.

The mothers felt that the father had not had the chance to show off his fathering skills as no family member had taken the time to show them what to do. As a result, the father felt isolated from the family circle of childcare.

Further, the lack of role models may also be responsible for some of the destructive behaviors shown by some new fathers. So many fathers have said that they have never been supported, which can lead to absent fathers who I believe may be at higher risk of a mental illness or disorder. Additionally, a news report in February 2020 quoted Dr Jackie Sebire,

Assistant Chief Constable of Bedfordshire Police, suggesting that "one of the biggest drivers of serious violence was the lack of a father figure at home."

"I'm not just saying fathers but it's male role models in the community, and where you do have positive male role models, they are potentially the drug dealers, or the exploiters, or the organized criminal networks, they become the positive male role model. We talk about the stereotype of absent fathers whether they're physically absent – or too busy working every hour God sends. And actually, children in those more affluent areas are left to their own devices as well. Fathers can be physically present but absent in the child's life".

It's understandable that not having had a father figure in your own life can make the prospect of being a father feel daunting. However, it doesn't mean you can't be a loving and capable father to your child. Here are some suggestions to help you navigate this situation[185,186]:

- Self-reflection and learning: Start by reflecting on the qualities and values you would like to embody as a father. Consider what you felt was missing from your own experience and use that as a guide to shape your approach. Additionally, seek out resources such as books, online articles, or parenting classes that guide effective parenting techniques.
- Seek support: Reach out to friends, family members, or other trusted parents who can provide guidance and support as you navigate fatherhood. They can offer advice, share their

experiences, and be there to listen and provide encouragement when needed.

- Surround yourself with positive influences: Look for positive role models who embody the qualities and values you would like to emulate as a father. Whether it's through friendships, mentorship programs, or joining parenting communities, surrounding yourself with people who have a positive impact can provide guidance and inspiration.
- Embrace your unique perspective: Although not having had a father figure may feel like a disadvantage, it can also provide an opportunity for you to bring your unique perspective and approach to parenting. Use your experiences to foster empathy, understanding, and open communication with your child.
- Seek therapy if needed: If you find that unresolved emotions or concerns regarding not having had a father figure are impacting your ability to be present and nurturing as a parent, consider speaking with a therapist or counsellor. Therapy can help you navigate these emotions and build the necessary skills to be an involved and loving father.

Remember, being a father is a continuous learning process. By being open-minded, seeking support, and embracing your role with love and patience, you can create a nurturing and fulfilling relationship with your child.

FATHERS OF COLOUR

Fatherhood is indeed a diverse and complex phenomenon that varies across cultures and contexts. Some of the factors that influence fatherhood are social norms, economic conditions, family structures, gender roles, and religious beliefs.

in some cultures, fathers are expected to be the primary breadwinners and disciplinarians of the family, while in others, fathers are more involved in nurturing and caregiving activities. Some fathers may have multiple wives and children, while others may have only one partner and child. Some fathers may live with their children, while others may be separated by migration, divorce, or death. Some fathers may have a strong bond with their children, while others may have a distant or abusive relationship.

Some of the benefits of fatherhood are increased happiness, self-esteem, and life satisfaction, as well as reduced stress, depression, and substance abuse. Fathers can also have a positive impact on their children's development, health, education, and well-being. However, fatherhood also comes with challenges and responsibilities, such as balancing work and family, providing financial and emotional support, and coping with stress, conflict, and change.

A report by the National Collaborating Centre for Mental Health found that people from black and minority ethnic backgrounds were less likely to go on to have at least one treatment session, despite having been referred by their GP, than their white counterparts. People from minority ethnic backgrounds were also more likely to have worse outcomes after treatment, meaning that they had lower rates of recovery. These poorer outcomes were most experienced by people from a South Asian background[187].

The Marmot Review, published in 2020, underlined, amongst other things, the way that poor health outcomes are pronounced for BME people. The review highlighted recent work on mortality in the UK which has demonstrated the projected lower life expectancy among Pakistani and Bangladeshi people in particular. The review also noted that some groups, particularly individuals identifying as Gypsy or Irish Traveller, and to a lesser extent those identifying as Bangladeshi, Pakistani or Irish, stand out as having poor health across a range of indicators.

The Traveller Movement Report Improving the Health of Gypsies and Travellers found in 2015 that Gypsies and Travellers have a life expectancy of over 10% less than the general population. Moreover, in 2016 a study found that two-thirds of Gypsies and Travellers reported their health as bad, very bad, or poor.

The experience of new fathers can vary depending on cultural norms and expectations. It's important to acknowledge and respect the diverse perspectives and practices related to fatherhood within different cultures. Here are a few considerations when it comes to new fathers and culture:

Roles and Responsibilities: Different cultures may have varying expectations and roles for fathers during the perinatal period. Some cultures may emphasize a more active and involved role for fathers, while others may have more traditional gender roles in place. It is essential to understand and accommodate these cultural differences to provide appropriate support.

Paternity Leave: Cultural norms and policies regarding paternity leave can greatly impact how new fathers are supported in the workplace. Some countries or workplaces may offer longer periods of paid paternity leave, while others may have limited or no provisions. Understanding these cultural differences helps employers create inclusive policies that meet the needs of new fathers.

Support Systems: Cultural norms also shape the support networks available to new fathers. In some cultures, extended family members play a significant role, in providing support, childcare assistance, and guidance. Recognizing and respecting these support systems can help employers understand the unique challenges and dynamics faced by new fathers.

Mental Health Stigma: Cultural attitudes towards mental health can vary, which may impact how new fathers perceive and seek support for their mental well-being. In some cultures, there may be a stigma surrounding discussing mental health issues or seeking professional help. Creating a non-judgmental and supportive environment can encourage fathers to prioritize their mental health.

Communication Styles: Effective communication is essential when addressing the needs of new fathers from different cultural backgrounds. Employers should be mindful of potential language barriers, cultural nuances, and preferences for communication styles. Providing information and resources in multiple languages or formats can help ensure accessibility and understanding.

Celebrating Diversity: Embrace cultural diversity within the workplace by celebrating various cultural traditions and customs related to fatherhood. This can include organizing events or activities that highlight and appreciate different cultural perspectives on fatherhood.

Remember that each individual's experience as a new father is unique, and it is crucial to approach cultural considerations with sensitivity and respect. By fostering an inclusive and culturally aware environment, employers can better support new fathers, promote employee well-being, and strengthen the overall workplace community.

Rates of mental health problems can be higher for some BAME groups than for White people[1]. For example, Black men are more likely to have experienced a psychotic disorder in the last year than White men[188]. Statistics show that Black men are ten times more likely than white men to experience such a disorder[189].

"Thanks for signposting me to Dope Black Dads, who gave me the education that was needed".

However, it's important to note that these statistics might not reflect the true extent of mental health problems among BAME groups. This is because not much data is available and also because BAME people may be less likely to report mental health problems[1].

In addition to the factors that can affect everyone's mental health, people from BAME communities may also contend with racism, inequality, and mental health stigma[1]. Racism can range from micro-aggressions (subtle but offensive comments) to explicit hurtful words to verbal or physical aggression[1]. Experiencing racism can be very stressful and negatively affect your overall health and mental health. Exposure to racism may increase your likelihood of experiencing mental health problems such as psychosis and depression.

It's important to note that help and support are available if you're worried about your own or someone else's mental health. If you or someone you know is struggling, don't hesitate to reach out to a mental health professional.

There are several reasons for the mental health disparities in the BAME community:

- Racism and Discrimination: Racism can range from micro-aggressions (subtle but offensive comments) to explicit hurtful words to verbal or physical aggression[2]. Experiencing racism can be very stressful and negatively affect your overall health and mental health[2]. Exposure to racism may increase your likelihood of experiencing mental health problems such as psychosis and depression[2].

- Social Determinants: People from BAME communities are disproportionately impacted by social determinants associated with poor mental health, such as poverty, unemployment, poor housing, poor neighborhoods, and school exclusion[1]. For this reason, to have an impact on the experiences of people from BAME communities, changes to mental health services and legislation cannot be done in isolation[1].
- Barriers to Accessing Healthcare: People from BAME communities have more difficulty in accessing healthcare than the majority of the population, and access to mental health services is a cause of concern. There is marked ethnic variation among mental health service users across the UK, and adverse experiences are widely reported among BAME service users.
- Inequalities in Mental Health Services: Inequalities in the provision of services, including inpatient care, talking therapies, and support from your GP, have been reported[1].
- Covid-19 Pandemic: A survey by the mental health charity Mind revealed that existing inequalities in housing, employment, finances, and other issues have had a greater impact on the mental health of people from different BAME groups than white people during the coronavirus pandemic[3].

These factors contribute to the higher rates of mental health problems in the BAME community. It's important to note that help and support are available if you're worried about your own or someone else's mental health. If you or someone you know is struggling, don't hesitate to reach out to a mental health professional. Support must be given to fathers about mental health, both before and after the birth.

Adrienne Burgess - Joint Chief Executive and Head of Research at The Fatherhood Institute explains.

"Expectant and new fathers whose partners suffer from mental health vulnerabilities need to be helped to understand what she is going through and helped to support her. The men's mental health also needs to be included in the picture – for two

reasons: a vulnerable man will need support from both his partner and professionals if he is to recover; and also, because poor mental health in fathers has a huge and often long-lasting impact on both their partner and their children".

LGBTQ+ COMMUNITY

Same-sex parents, particularly those who identify as LGBTQ+, face several challenges in society. Here are some of the key issues[190,191]:

- Parental Recognition: In many places, laws are not consistent across the country when it comes to recognizing same-sex parents. For instance, whether they have a baby through surrogacy or with the help of a sperm donor and artificial insemination, married same-sex parents may not be listed on their child's birth certificate. This can lead to additional hurdles and costs for same-sex parents.
- Access to Health Care: Sexual minorities are about twice as likely as straight people to be uninsured[1]. This can make it more difficult for them to access necessary health care services[1].
- Legal Challenges: Same-sex parents often face legal problems, including restrictions on visitation and prohibitions against adoption[4]. They may also encounter negative attitudes from service providers when negotiating critical life events such as becoming pregnant, dealing with pre-and post-natal services, arranging childcare, or sending children to school[2].
- Discrimination and Homophobia: Families with either a parent or child who identifies as LGBTQ+ are confronted with a lot of challenges that other families are not[1]. Some laws exclude same-sex couples; others target transgender children[1]. Discrimination makes it a whole lot more difficult to live and thrive as a queer or trans person.
- Negotiating Household Roles: Same-sex parents may face challenges in negotiating household roles[3].

These challenges can vary greatly depending on the specific laws and societal attitudes in different regions. It's important to note that there are many organizations and resources available to support same-sex parents and advocate for their rights.

Higher risk of experiencing mental health issues compared to heterosexuals[4]. This includes conditions such as depression, anxiety, and substance abuse[193].

For instance, LGBTQ+ individuals are more than twice as likely as heterosexuals to have a mental health illness[4]. Those in the LGBTQ+ community are 2.5 times more likely to experience depression, anxiety, and substance abuse compared to heterosexuals[4]. 31% of older adults in the LGBTQ+ community report depressive symptoms and 39% report serious thoughts of suicide[194].

These mental health disparities are often linked to societal stigma, discrimination, and denial of their civil and human rights[194]. Discrimination against LGBTQ+ persons has been associated with high rates of psychiatric disorders, substance abuse, and suicide.

It's important to note that help and support are available if you're worried about your own or someone else's mental health[1]. If you or someone you know is struggling, don't hesitate to reach out to a mental health professional.

Gay dads, like any new parents, may benefit from support for their mental health. Becoming a parent can bring about a range of emotions and challenges, which can affect mental well-being. All parents need to have access to support networks and resources that address their needs, including mental health support.

Navigating the unique challenges and experiences that come with being a gay new dad, such as societal attitudes, discrimination, or lack of acceptance, can add additional stressors to their mental health. Therefore, it's crucial to create an environment where they can openly discuss their feelings, seek guidance, and access resources tailored to their specific needs.

Surrogacy is a process where a woman carries and delivers a baby for another person or couple. It is a wonderful way for people who cannot conceive naturally to have a child of their own.

There are many resources available to help gay dads navigate the surrogacy process. Two Dads UK is a surrogacy support group that provides guidance and support to gay couples looking to start a family through surrogacy[195]. They offer a range of services, including surrogacy support, IVF, and egg donation.

CNN has published an article that answers the top 10 questions asked by same-sex couples seeking surrogacy services [196]. The article provides valuable information on the surrogacy process, including legal and financial considerations.

"I could tell not anyone about my mental health, just in case it would affect the progress".

Physicians Surrogacy is a surrogacy agency that specializes in helping gay couples become parents through surrogacy[197]. They offer a range of services, including selecting the genetic father and IVF. Support can come in various forms, such as therapy, support groups, online communities, or connecting with other LGBTQ+ parents who can offer understanding and shared experiences.

Transgender dads, often referred to as "trans dads", are individuals who were assigned female at birth but identify and live as men and have chosen to become parents. Many trans dads have shared their experiences and journeys, providing valuable insights into the unique challenges and joys of being a transgender parent.

As reported in the Today.com, Kayden Coleman, a 35-year-old Black, gay, transgender dad, gave birth to his two daughters after he began transitioning[197]. He emphasizes that being a transgender dad is amazing and that his kids call him Daddy. He also mentions that he never hated his body; it just felt foreign to him until he made the changes necessary for it to feel like home.

I was to find out about different challenges while working with dads on the project "They Call Me Dad" a Movember funded project. The project aims to improve the mental health and wellbeing of gay, bisexual, transgender, and queer (GBTQ) dads, intended dads, and those who identify as dads. The multi-year project led by Best Beginnings.

They Call Me Dad project aims:

- research current mental health resources and identify the key issues affecting GBTQ+ parents through family day workshops and events.

- provide support through GBTQ+ partners and mental health partners.
- produce resources addressing mental health inequalities of GBTQ+ parents – including up to 15 films and video diaries on the birthing, surrogacy, and adoption journey to expand Baby Buddy's content for GBTQ+ parents.
- improve the support GBTQ+ parents receive in the healthcare system by working with academic researchers to co-produce resources for professionals.

FATHERHOOD AND IVF

In Vitro Fertilization (IVF) is a process where an egg is combined with sperm outside the body, in a laboratory dish, and then implanted in a woman's uterus. In the context of fatherhood, IVF plays a significant role. Undergoing In Vitro Fertilization (IVF) can indeed be a stressful process, and this stress can affect both partners involved. Here are some of the pressures that fathers might face during the IVF process[198].

Many fathers do experience depression while going through the IVF process. The process of assisted reproduction itself is associated with increased anxiety, depression, and stress, and can impact self-esteem and confidence. This may particularly be the case after a failed IVF cycle.

> ***"The whole thing was hard and to lose one of the babies of the twins I still haven't talked about it. It was so much pressure and we would have to find funding if it didn't happen".***

Research shows that infertility patients consistently report significantly more symptoms of anxiety and depression than fertile individuals[199].

- Legal Parenthood: There can be legal issues related to fatherhood in IVF treatments. For instance, if the necessary consent forms are not signed before the IVF process, the father might not be legally recognized as the child's parent.

- Emotional Stress: The IVF process can be emotionally draining. Fathers, like mothers, can feel a great deal of pressure, especially if the treatment is not immediately successful.
- Social Pressure: There can be significant social pressure to have children, which can lead to stress. This pressure can come from family, friends, or societal expectations[2].
- Financial Pressure: IVF treatments can be expensive, which can add financial stress to the emotional and physical stress of the process.
- Relationship Stress: The stress of IVF can also put a strain on a couple's relationship. Couples need to communicate openly about their feelings and support each other throughout the process.

Remember, it's perfectly normal to feel stressed or overwhelmed during the IVF process. If you're feeling this way, it might be helpful to speak to a mental health professional or a support group. They can provide strategies to help manage these feelings and navigate the IVF process.

- Single Men and IVF: There are cases where single men have decided to have children through IVF.
- Legal Parenthood: If a man is married or in a civil partnership before fertility treatment with donated sperm or embryos, he will automatically be the legal parent unless he does not consent to the treatment.
- Surrogacy: The intended father, in either a heterosexual or male same-sex relationship or an individual, provides a sperm sample for conception through either self-insemination at home or artificial insemination with the help of a fertility clinic.

It's important to note that the laws and regulations regarding IVF and surrogacy can vary by country and even within regions of the same country. Therefore, it's always a good idea to consult with a legal expert or a fertility clinic to understand the specific laws applicable to your situation.

Fathers who have gone through IVF can experience depression. According to a report by The Guardian, fathers who have gone through unsuccessful rounds of IVF can feel extremely isolated and depressed. The report highlights the story of James, who felt extremely isolated after he and his partner had gone through two unsuccessful rounds of IVF and begun to look into adoption. His partner then became pregnant naturally in 2019 and gave birth to their "miracle baby" at the height of the Covid pandemic.

Rhod Gilbert, a Welsh comedian, has been very open about his struggles with infertility. In his documentary, "Rhod Gilbert: Stand Up to Infertility" (BBC Two), he revealed that 98% of his sperm don't swim straight[1]. Despite this, he and his wife, Sian, are still very open to all the many and varied means of being parents[199].

To raise awareness about male fertility issues, Gilbert worked with an advertising agency to devise a campaign called "Him Fertility". The campaign featured posters with the "I" of "him" picked out as a cavorting sperm[1]. Gilbert also set up a club in a pub's upstairs room for men to talk about fertility issues, hoping it would inspire others.

After being diagnosed with head and neck cancer, Gilbert said that the experience had "completely focused" his mind on starting a family. He expressed hope that his openness about his experiences could help others facing similar challenges[200].

YOUNG FATHERS

I have always been passionate about youth and with twenty years' experience in different areas of youth work, I have come across countless new fathers who are aged under twenty-five years of age. The youngest father, I have supported was a father who was turning seventeen years of age.

Becoming a new father, especially at a young age, can bring about a range of emotions and different pressures.

The Mental Health Foundation has published a report focusing on the mental health of young fathers[1]. Here are some key findings[201]:

- Young fathers face significant and specific challenges that can affect their mental health[1].
- One of the specific challenges young fathers often experience is unstable housing and homelessness.
- Relationship breakdown is more common for young parents than for older parents[1].

- Young fathers may have fewer resources than older fathers, often having low-paid or unstable work and lower levels of education.
- Young fathers are significantly more likely to experience depression, compared to older fathers.
- Fathers aged 23 and younger were twice as likely to be unemployed at age 30, compared to men who became fathers over the age of 23.
- -Over one-third (39.2%) of young fathers wanted support for their mental health.
- Over one-third (34%) of young fathers do not live with their children full-time.

Young fathers are often struggling to cope in isolation while experiencing greater parenting stresses than older fathers.

"I was told by everyone that I was too young to be a dad, how can I now tell anyone that I am now struggling after seeing my girlfriend scared in the hospital".

The report also highlights that young fathers often experience stigma and negative stereotyping by professional services. Despite these challenges, the majority of young fathers want to 'be there' for their children, even if they are not living with their child most of the time[1]. The report emphasizes the importance of recognizing the benefits of young fathers' contributions to their children's well-being and healthy development[201].

Young fathers may feel frustrated because someone told them that they're not old enough. It's important to remember that age doesn't necessarily determine your abilities or worth. Everyone matures at their own pace and has unique skills and experiences. If you feel ready for something and believe you can handle it responsibly, it can be disappointing to hear someone say you're not old enough. It's important to communicate your feelings and readiness to take on the responsibility you're seeking. It might help them see your perspective.

There is a significant amount of research on the mental health of young boys. Here are some key findings:

\- The Education Policy Institute and The Prince's Trust published a study on the mental health and wellbeing of young people in Generation Z[202]. The study found that the well-being of all young people declines by the end of their teenage years, with girls seeing far lower levels of wellbeing and self-esteem than boys[203]. Girls experience more depressive symptoms than boys and are also more likely to feel unhappy about their physical appearance[2].

A study developed to make mental health support more approachable for young men found that using a transparent and collaborative approach, trust-building, positive male role models, and destigmatising language can improve engagement[204].

Depression manifests differently in boys and men than in girls and women[5]. Boys are more likely to externalize feelings, while girls are more likely to internalize them[5]. Boys may act irritated or lash out when feeling down, or they may engage in risky, impulsive, or even violent acts[205].

These findings highlight the importance of tailored approaches to mental health support for young boys. It's crucial to continue this research to better understand and address the mental health needs of young boys who of course become fathers.

Asylum seekers and refugees, including new fathers, face unique and complex challenges related to their mental health. They are often at greater risk of developing mental health problems[274].

Migrants may be at increased risk of mental health problems as a result of their experiences before, during, or after migration[206]. Issues such as homesickness, anxiety, or sleep disorders may arise for anyone who is separated from family and friends or integrating into a new community due to cultural differences and language barriers[1]. Other stressors include concerns about immigration status, financial difficulties, access to services, and discrimination.

Asylum-seekers and refugees may experience traumatic events pre-departure, life-threatening circumstances on their journeys, and difficulties integrating into host countries related to immigration policies, social isolation, poor living conditions, and unemployment, all of which can significantly affect their mental health[275].

Refugees and asylum seekers are more likely to experience poor mental health than the local population, including higher rates of depression, PTSD, and other anxiety disorders[207].

These factors can affect a father's ability to bond with their child and provide care. These fathers need to have access to mental health resources and support. This can help them cope with their experiences and provide the best care for their children.

Asylum seekers and migrants in the UK face various forms of discrimination[208,209,2010]:

- Discrimination due to Ethnicity, Nationality, Religion, Language, or Accent: Migrants often experience discrimination due to their ethnicity, nationality, religion, language, or accent[1]. About 13% of the foreign-born population said that they had been insulted because of their ethnicity, nationality, religion, language, or accent[208].
- The Hostile Environment: The UK has implemented a set of government immigration measures intended to make the UK unwelcoming and deter migration[209]. These measures include detention centers, banning asylum seekers from employment, and unaffordable and lengthy immigration processes.
- Xenophobia: Anti-immigration rhetoric continues to criminalise migrants, fostering mistrust towards people of color (POC) and non-EU individuals. 18% of migrants and 30% of UK-born children of migrants feel unsafe or have been subject to racial discrimination.
- Employment: Refugees face many barriers when finding work in the UK, with only 51% of refugees in employment[2]. Negative stereotyping has caused a general reluctance to employ refugees and migrants.
- Housing: 42% of surveyed landlords are less likely to rent to POC or foreign passport holders, favoring white tenants instead[2]. They are also more likely to check the immigration documents of POC tenants.
- Racist Incidents: The Home Office has recorded 70 racist incidents by far-right supporters against asylum seekers in barracks and hotel accommodations.

"I was living in Albania; I was happy there and was a young father as I turned twenty years of age. Sadly, I was involved in gangs to help provide for my family and couldn't even feed them before joining them. I cannot go into events too much; it was a case of I was groomed and vulnerable at the time and had never been involved in any crime before becoming a father. I had to get away from my family for their safety. I miss them every single day and only see them on the phone".

These challenges can vary greatly depending on the specific laws and societal attitudes in different regions. It's important to note that there are many organizations and resources available to support asylum seekers and advocate for their rights.

SINGLE FATHERS

Single fathers can be challenging, but it can also be rewarding. Single fathers face many challenges, including balancing work and parenting, lack of support network, financial strain, limited time for self-care, and challenging stereotypes and societal expectations[211].

being a single father can affect your mental health. According to some studies, single fathers are twice as likely to report poor physical and mental health as fathers with partners. Single fathers face unique stressors, such as financial pressures, balancing work and parenting responsibilities, and lack of support networks, which can take a toll on their mental well-being.

However, it's important to remember that you're not alone. There are many resources available to help single fathers navigate these challenges. Mind is an organization that provides guidance and support to parents looking to manage their mental health while caring for children. Healthline has published an article that provides valuable information on the challenges faced by single parents, including visitation and custody problems, difficulty juggling personal and work-related responsibilities, and the emotional impact of separation, divorce, or death[212].

It's important to prioritize your mental and physical health. If you're feeling overwhelmed, don't hesitate to seek help from a professional or support group. Remember, taking care of yourself is the first step towards being a great dad to your child.

However, there are many resources available to help single fathers navigate these challenges. The charity Gingerbreads is an organization that provides guidance and support to fathers looking to become better parents. Healthline has published an article that provides valuable information on the challenges faced by single parents, including visitation and custody problems, difficulty juggling personal and work-related responsibilities, and the emotional impact of separation, divorce, or death.

"My wife died after my daughter was born and my whole world turned upside down. Trying to come to terms quickly, was hard for me. I had to focus on the baby. I was very lucky to have people around me to help out, that is not the case for many fathers I speak with in the support groups".

In 2022, there were 2.9 million lone-parent families in the UK. While the majority of these were lone-mother families (2.5 million, 84%), 16% (457,000) were lone-father families.

It's important to remember that being a single father is not easy, but it's also not impossible. With the right support and resources, you can overcome the challenges and be a great dad to your child. I hope this information helps you!

Michael Ray, a single father from Australia. Michael Ray has been raising his daughter, Charlie, alone for many years. His love and dedication to his daughter are remarkable. He made headlines when a dance school in Melbourne was forced to overturn a ban prohibiting males from being backstage at student concerts.

Michael Ray started a family tradition of leaving sweet lunchbox notes for his daughter, Michael Ray became a single father after his relationship with Charlie's mother ended. When Charlie's mother was still part of her life and they had shared custody, Michael Ray was dealing with a serious illness and his future wasn't guaranteed. During that period, he realized the most important thing was being together and having fun with Charlie, as you never know what tomorrow will bring. After the relationship ended, he has been raising Charlie alone. He is fortunate to have the support of his family, particularly his mother and sister. He is also known for his advocacy for equality and change.

FATHERS IN THE WORKPLACE

Jobs that involve exposure to traumatic events can indeed impact new fathers. This includes professions such as emergency responders, military personnel, healthcare workers, and others who regularly witness or experience traumatic events[213].

Trauma can lead to mental health issues such as post-traumatic stress disorder (PTSD), depression, and anxiety. These conditions can affect a person's ability to function in their daily life, including their role as a father.

Workplace trauma can stem from several causes: racism, bullying, poor work-life boundaries, and job insecurity[5]. It can also be either direct or indirect (secondary or vicarious) trauma, and include events such as accidents or injury, deaths, sexual assault, and even severe workload stress or a toxic work environment[2].

Fathers who report experiencing a traumatic birth are more likely to later develop these postpartum mental health concerns. In addition, the impacts of experiencing a partner's traumatic birth can also affect new fathers[1].

"My boss didn't know anything about my experience of becoming a new father, after all, it should be a happy time".

Therefore, new fathers in these professions need to have access to mental health resources and support. This can help them cope with their experiences and provide the best care for their children.

War-torn countries can have a profound impact on new fathers. The challenges they face are multifaceted and can include:

- Separation from Family: Military deployment can separate fathers from their families for extended periods, causing emotional distress[1].
- Mental Health Issues: The stress of war can lead to mental health issues such as post-traumatic stress disorder (PTSD), depression, and anxiety[1].
- Physical Injuries: Many soldiers return from war with physical injuries, which can affect their ability to care for their children[3].
- Economic Hardship: War can lead to economic instability, making it difficult for fathers to provide for their families.
- Loss of Loved Ones: The loss of comrades or family members can cause grief and trauma[5].
- Adjustment to Civilian Life: Returning to civilian life after deployment can be challenging. Fathers may struggle to reconnect with their families and adjust to their roles as parents[1].

These factors can affect a father's ability to bond with their child and provide care. These fathers need to receive support and resources to help them navigate these challenges.

The cost of mental health in the workplace is significant. The average cost of mental health in the workplace is estimated to be £1,684 per employee every year1. This figure takes into account money lost because of factors such as absence, presenteeism (when employees are present at work but not fully productive due to health issues), and turnover1.

A study by Deloitte and Mind estimated that poor mental health among employees costs UK employers between £42bn and £45bn each year2. This includes absence costs of around £7bn, presenteeism costs ranging from about £27bn to £29bn, and turnover costs of around £9bn2.

Furthermore, new research by Deloitte has revealed that the cost to employers of poor mental health has increased, to up to £56bn in 2020-21 compared to £45bn in 2019.

FATHERS IN PRISON

Fathers in prison face unique challenges when it comes to caring for their babies. According to the Fatherhood Institute, fathers in prison can apply to bring their children to prison with them if the child is under 18 months old. Social services arrange for children over 18 months to be cared for, for example by the prisoner's parents or fostering. Women who give birth in prison can keep their baby for the first 18 months in a mother and baby unit[214].

The Prisoners' Advice Service (PAS) is a UK-based charity that provides free legal advice and representation to adult prisoners throughout England and Wales regarding their rights, conditions of imprisonment, and the application of the Prison Rules. PAS has produced a guide called Fathers in Prison: Contact with Children, which sets out the law that the court uses to decide on applications about contact and your involvement with your children[215].

Barnardo's is another organization that provides support for children with a parent or relative in prison. They work with Her Majesty's Prison and Probation Service to help develop, support, and enhance the relationship between offenders and their families by supplying information and guidance to the professionals who are working with them both. It's important to remember that fathers in prison can still play an important role in their child's life.

A father's voice and scent can indeed help with baby bonding. Here are some key points:

- Voice: If the father speaks tenderly to the unborn baby, the baby forms an emotional bond with him. The familiar sound allows the baby to know he is secure, and the dad's voice may have a soothing and relaxing impact on him.
- Scent: In addition to skin-to-skin contact, other types of bonding activities also boost a baby's ability to learn their dad's scent and create a strong father-child bond. Babies can recognize their dad's scent by the third day of life and will be able to tell the difference between different caregivers based on scent, especially if dads participate in hands-on bonding activities and caregiving.

New fathers in prisons face a variety of challenges, including stigma. This stigma can manifest in several ways:

- Social Isolation and Stigma: Incarcerated fathers often face social isolation and stigma, which can lead to feelings of loneliness, anger, and resentment.
- Separation from Children: Incarcerated fathers are often separated from their children, which can lead to feelings of guilt and sadness about missing out on their child's life[1].
- Financial Strains: Incarceration can lead to financial strains for the family, as the father is unable to contribute financially.
- Lack of Skills: Many fathers return to their families without the skills they need to be involved, responsible, and committed fathers.
- Negative Impact on Family Life: Father incarceration negatively affects family life.

Families Need Fathers explained: It is estimated that around 54% of the approximately 84,000 prisoners in England and Wales are parents. However, there is no formal auditing of men's parental status in place within prison. Surveys have revealed some figures: in 2003 it was revealed that 25% of young men are fathers or expectant fathers and it was estimated in 2003 that 32% of the male prison population have dependent children under the age of 18. It's also generally accepted that around one in four young men in prison in the UK is an actual or expectant father. Please note that these are estimates and the actual numbers can vary.

I have only done around four sessions with the fathers in the prison system, one of the factors to came out of the sessions was that it was a sign of weakness to disclose their feelings while in prison. Weaknesses in prison can get you into trouble as one inmate explained. It was clear, that the fathers who I spoke to have a deep feeling of wanting to be there for their children but didn't know how to navigate that support. In many of the fathers, it was a key point to change as they wanted to be a dad.

These challenges highlight the importance of providing support and resources to incarcerated fathers to help them cope with the stigma and other difficulties they may face.

Dr Daniel Singley and fatherhood expert explains *"Expectant fathers enjoy an informal, hands-on class that provides practical information and a real boost of confidence about handling the baby's impending arrival".*

CHILD ABUSE

Child Abuse can and does happen to boys and men as well. It's a serious issue that often goes unreported due to societal pressures and misconceptions.

It's difficult to determine the exact number of boys who experience child abuse in the UK, as many cases go unreported. However, the NSPCC estimates that half a million children a year suffer abuse in the UK. This includes all forms of abuse: physical, emotional, sexual, and neglect[216].

The Crime Survey for England and Wales estimated that one in five adults aged 18 to 74 years experienced at least one form of child abuse, whether emotional abuse, physical abuse, sexual abuse, or witnessing domestic violence or abuse, before the age of 16 years[217].

Concerns around physical abuse have been identified for around 1 in 10 children who are the subject of a child protection plan or on a child protection register in the UK[3]. There were over 160,000 offenses related to child physical abuse recorded by police in England, Wales, and Northern Ireland in 2019/20[218].

Research with 2,275 young people aged 11-17 about their experiences of sexual abuse suggests around 1 in 20 children in the UK have been sexually abused[219].

These statistics include both boys and girls. Unfortunately, the data does not provide a specific breakdown by gender. It's important to note that child abuse affects children of all genders, and all instances of abuse are equally serious and deserving of attention and intervention.

How many go on to be fathers?

"I just went into shock and stood frozen looking on at our son in the bath. I took a cigarette and started smoking fast. The midwife was there and was helping is bathe the baby. It looked like I was not interested and that I didn't want to get

involved but I just saw myself in the bath as a young by being abused by a baby sitter and could not cope with it".

Research has shown that individuals who have experienced child abuse can face significant challenges later in life, including struggles with parenting[220].

A study found that dozens of children have been forced into contact with fathers accused of abuse, some of whom were convicted pedophiles. In all cases, fathers had used a disputed concept in court known as "parental alienation", where they claimed the mothers had turned the child against them without good reason.

Another study by the Office for National Statistics revealed that more than half (51%) of adults who were abused as children experienced domestic abuse in later life. Those who survived more than one type of child abuse were more likely to experience domestic abuse as an adult than those who survived fewer types of child abuse[221].

These findings highlight the complex and long-lasting effects of child abuse, and the importance of providing support and resources for individuals who have experienced such trauma, particularly when they become parents themselves. It's crucial to ensure that these individuals have access to the necessary support and resources to navigate the challenges of parenthood and break the cycle of abuse.

COPING STRATEGIES

Many new fathers used negative coping skills to improve their relationship with their partner and infant. Since becoming a father, one man used drugs for the first time, whilst two other fathers developed eating disorders. Some have resorted to consuming more alcohol than usual whilst other fathers admitted to self-harming for the first time and wanting to be hurt in a fight 'to take the feelings away'.

If it wasn't for my partner, I don't think I would be here now! I recovered but not once did anyone ask him about his mental health which he dealt with through alcohol.

This is especially worrying, in terms of child development. Khan[222] cites research studies that have shown that there are established links "between paternal alcoholism and an increased risk of conduct disorder and substance abuse in children, with a possible higher risk in the sons than in the daughters of affected fathers". Further, "paternal alcoholism is also associated with an increased risk of mood disorders and depressive symptoms in adolescents (Chen and Weitzman, 2005), academic underachievement, low self-esteem, and relationship-based difficulties."

"I also used alcohol, often drinking eight pints a day as this dampened down the thoughts. I tried drinking lots of water as I felt this would flush them away".

During the perinatal period some fathers that I spoke to admitted to using comfort foods and/or lacking the motivation to go to the gym. This had not happened before their partner's pregnancy. This drop in motivation often results from hormonal changes that are taking place within the man's body during the perinatal period and/or increased stress, all of which can lead to unnecessary weight gain.

The research supports this. Baldwin et al (2018) found that fathers attempted to deal with the stress that they experienced as a result of the challenges of fatherhood by adopting an unhealthy lifestyle. Whitley's 2018 report on men's mental health also identified that substance misuse was high in response to stressful life transitions. Further, Godfrey-Issacs' 2020 article, exploring the revelations of professional fathers who hadn't realized that they were experiencing poor mental health following the birth of their child included accounts of addiction.

"I'm going back full time to work in September and I'm afraid to leave our son alone as he's just not feeling great since he's come along".

For many, of course, the main coping strategy is a simple failure to want to acknowledge what they are experiencing, which can have disastrous outcomes. With OCD, it's often a secret illness. The person who is struggling can hide it well, and appear 'okay' where the mental torture is incredibly painful… I was starting to crumble. My functioning had gone down, I was only managing to work three hours a day, and I had lost over a stone in weight. Panic attacks began to creep in, along with social phobia. I was unable to leave the house: I was at crisis point.

Educating new fathers about positive coping strategies is crucial for their mental health and the well-being of their families. The person-centered approach, also known as Rogerian therapy or client-based therapy, was developed by the American psychologist Carl Rogers in the 1940s. This approach is based on the belief that given the right conditions, a person can reach their full potential and become their true self, a process Rogers termed 'self-actualisation'.

Key features of the person-centered approach include:

Unconditional Positive Regard (UPR): The therapist accepts and values the client for who they are, without any conditions1.
Congruence: The therapist is genuine and transparent in how they experience the client and their world.
Empathic Understanding: The therapist tries to see the client's viewpoint as if they were the client.
In person-centered therapy, the client is encouraged to bring their issues to the session. The therapy is led by the client and not directed by the therapist. The therapist helps the client explore their issues, feelings, beliefs, behavior, and worldview, so they can become more self-aware and achieve greater independence.

This approach moves away from professionals deciding what is best for a patient or service user, and places the person at the center, as an expert of their own experience. The person, and their family where appropriate, become an equal partner in the planning of their care and support, ensuring it meets their needs, goals, and outcomes.

Self-Care: This includes activities that help to maintain an individual's physical, mental, and emotional health1. It could involve relaxation techniques, physical exercise, maintaining a balanced diet, and ensuring adequate sleep.

Mindfulness and Meditation: These practices can help individuals stay focused on the present moment, which can reduce feelings of anxiety and improve overall mental well-being1.

Therapy and Counseling: Professional help can provide individuals with strategies to understand and manage their mental health struggles1.

Support Networks: Having a strong support network, including friends, family, and support groups, can provide emotional assistance.

Medication: In some cases, medication may be recommended by a healthcare professional.

Healthy Boundaries: Setting and maintaining appropriate and healthy boundaries between oneself and others can also be beneficial.

SUPPORT AND SUPPORT GROUPS

One of the most common complaints from fathers was the lack of community groups that were formed exclusively for them. There are groups available, but these are either limited to specific areas of the country or are only available as an online forum. Fathers need resources and signposting for perinatal mental health services and may become overwhelmed if they are not in place. Again, this finding is reflected in the academic research.

"My husband could not bond with our baby and there was no specialist support out there for him, so why is this still happening in 2020".

For example, the 2019 Ipsos Mori report – Fatherhood and Social Connections[222] – which was commissioned by Movember, highlighted the challenges faced by fathers and identified the resources that are, and should be available. It recognised the importance of social connections to alleviate isolation, as well as impressing the importance of being able to seek the help of friends and secure friendships, all of which are proven indicators of both physical and mental well-being.

This is supported by the anecdotal findings of Kieran Anders, at Dad Matters UK[223]. He has said that the most important thing for a dad who's struggling after having become a parent is to talk to someone, to start the process of acknowledging what is happening to him:

Once you've done this, then you can start to take the steps you need to fix it. Acknowledging how you're feeling before you get to the point of needing professional support means that you'll be less likely to need professional support.82 Further, NCT research from 201583 recognized that it was important for fathers to be encouraged and supported to talk about their experiences to their partner, family, friends, or GP.

"I was fine, but my partner was struggling which was impacting on my mental health. I just can't believe that there was no real support for him as he struggled to bond with our baby".

In terms of higher levels of support, where medical intervention is required, again specialist services are not always available where they are needed. The Fathers Network Scotland survey of 2019 found that 83% of the dads that they surveyed who had sought professional support for their mental health problems had found it difficult to find the support that they needed. There also isn't a map of dad-focused services for perinatal mental health available, as there is for mums.

Dr Andy Mayers has said: [Whilst] there has been a growth in the number of perinatal mental health services (at least across England), those services are only for mothers, although we are pushing for better paternal support.

SOCIAL MEDIA

The Impact of Social Media on New Fathers' Mental Health[224,225].

Social media can have both positive and negative effects on mental health, and this applies to new fathers as well. While there is limited research specifically focused on the mental health of new fathers and social media, we can draw insights from studies on social media's impact on mental health in general and the experiences of fathers during the perinatal period.

Negative Effects: Excessive use of social media can contribute to feelings of depression, anxiety, and loneliness in individuals, including new fathers. It may create unrealistic expectations or comparisons with others, leading to feelings of inadequacy or self-doubt. Additionally, exposure to negative or distressing content on social media can impact emotional well-being.

Positive Effects: On the other hand, social media can also provide a platform for new fathers to connect with others, share experiences, and seek support. Online communities and forums can offer a sense of belonging and enable fathers to access information and resources related to parenting.

It's important to note that the impact of social media on mental health is complex and can vary from person to person. Factors such as individual resilience, support networks, and overall well-being play a role in how social media affects mental health.

To navigate the potential effects of social media on mental health, including for new fathers, it can be helpful to:

- Be mindful of the time spent on social media and set healthy boundaries.
- Curate social media feeds to include positive and supportive content.
- Engage in offline activities and maintain face-to-face connections.
- Seek support from trusted friends, family, or professionals when needed.

While social media can be a valuable tool, it's important to prioritize self-care and well-being, both online and offline. If new fathers are experiencing mental health challenges, it is recommended to reach out to healthcare professionals or support organizations that specialize in paternal mental health.

Please note that the information provided here is based on general insights and the limited research available. It's always advisable to consult professional advice or seek further resources for specific concerns related to mental health.

Social media is inescapable and is here to stay and, whilst research has identified that it can have a positive role to play (see below), I wanted to include a cautionary note about how it can negatively impact all of us.

"I just was overthinking everything as a father, it didn't help me when I was seeing fathers taking their families on holidays and smiling when I was unemployed after being laid off and had to use the foodbanks for the first time. It all became overwhelming for me as a new dad. I just felt like a failure and felt s guilty about the whole situation".

Some of the fathers that I have spoken to in recent years have felt that the negative comments and discussions on social media were issues that forced them to question whether or not they were good fathers. This is exacerbated by making comparisons with others, who appeared to be living exemplary, fulfilling lives with their children, adding pressure to be the 'perfect father'. As a result, some fathers were pushed further into unhelpful behaviors through their fear of failing to be able to 'step up' to this (often unachievable) ideal.

Das and Hopkinson's 2019 research paper – New Fathers, Mental Health and Social Media –identified a spectrum of ways in which engagement with digital communication had played a role in fathers' attempts to come to terms with their difficulties by disconnecting from online.

networks or individuals. These fathers chose a range of different approaches to attempt to communicate their mental health situation – some, for example, were seen to practice strategies including 'hiding' or concealing cries for help, in the hope that someone would notice and offer support – but shied away from those platforms which appeared to exacerbate their struggles. Others find comfort in digital media platforms which problems with others. The study found, however, that this rarely provided simple solutions, although the benefits of sharing were notable.

"Horrible seeing other fathers smiling on social media and I'm like this".

Kieran Anders, of Dad Matters UK, has also noted online support groups can have a key role in helping dads who are struggling with their perinatal mental health; finding a platform on which to "let it all out anonymously" can be the crucial first step in seeking help and/or recovery[1].

IMPACT ON CHILD DEVELOPMENT

The Still Face Experiment, originally conducted by Dr. Ed Tronick in 1970, demonstrated how a parent's visual reaction can impact a baby's emotional development[1]. The experiment was initially done with mothers and infants but was later replicated with fathers and toddlers[226].

In the experiment, a parent and baby play together, with the parent smiling and interacting with the baby. Then, the parent turns away and when they turn back, their face is completely expressionless[4]. This is known as the "still face" phase. The baby's response to this change is observed. Typically, the baby goes from smiling and making sounds to appearing confused and trying to engage the parent through sounds and movements. If the parent continues to maintain the "still face", the baby may show signs of distress.

This experiment has been replicated and filmed with fathers (rather than mothers) and their babies, showing similar responses[2]. It highlights the profound impact that parental responsiveness, or lack thereof, can have on a child's emotional development.

Both parents play an important role in their children's lives and being able to do the very best for our children is challenging. In the past, researchers have concentrated on mothers' mental health and not paid attention to that of the father, and yet fathers play an enormous role in their children's lives. As an example, we know that postnatal depression in fathers is linked to depression suffered by their own teenage daughters. Ensuring the father has both good physical and mental health is vital as the results of not doing this can have profound consequences[227].

Fathers exert influence on their children's development and mental health through both their direct interactions as well as their indirect interactions (e.g. providing instrumental or emotional support to their partners). For instance, a father's function as a source of emotional support tends to enhance the quality of the mother-child relationship and, in turn, facilitates positive adjustment by children[1]. Conversely, when fathers are unsupportive and marital conflict is high, children may suffer.

New parenthood is a time of huge change in both men's and women's lives. It can create several new pressures and stresses associated with lifestyle changes, from changes in the couple's relationship, getting used to a new baby in the family home, and worries about money, to general anxiety around the new feelings of responsibility and now may include the new fears around the Covid-19 pandemic - all exacerbated by sleep deprivation! In addition to this, new fathers may also experience increased pressure to be a 'supportive partner', and struggle with trying to balance the various demands of their family, work, and personal needs.

Poor mental health in fathers can affect their child's behavioral, social, cognitive, and emotional development, and contribute negatively to their health as well as their partners. It is vital that dads are supported, nurtured and listened to on the parenting journey.

Sue Atkins – Expert Parenting Coach

When both parents are depressed, they are least likely to be following good-health guidelines with their babies – e.g. putting them to sleep on their back, breastfeeding, not putting them to bed with a bottle, etc[1]. Furthermore, parental attitudes to mental health and mental illness will very much influence their children's attitude toward seeking help[229]. If a parent experiences a high level of stigma and avoids reaching out for assistance, their children are also more likely to be affected by stigma, and adopt avoidant strategies, preventing essential early help.

This will all, of course, have an impact on the father's ability to bond and be positively involved, with his child. Establishing "a secure attachment with a caregiver is a fundamental building block for good mental health"[230]for a child and that "warm attachment relationships and play between children and their fathers can have a huge impact on self-esteem, social competence and managing adversity".

We know that enduring poor mental health can mean that the relationship between the father and his baby can be deeply affected. A strong bond is needed between an infant and both parents to ensure a healthy development for that child. We need to provide more support for fathers' mental health and to enhance the relationship with their infants. Dr Andrew Mayers

Fatherhood involvement is indeed very important, and it's not accurate to say that parenting children aged 0-5 is just mothering. Both parents play crucial roles in a child's development. Here are some reasons why fatherhood involvement is significant[231,232]:

Child Outcomes:

- Children with involved fathers tend to have a higher IQ, better school readiness, improved social skills, enhanced emotional regulation, and greater empathy.
- They also exhibit increased attachment, emotional security, popularity, and independence.

Paternal Outcomes:

- Fathers who are actively involved in their children's lives experience fewer mental health issues.
- They also report increased confidence, parenting satisfaction, and relationship satisfaction.

Maternal Outcomes:

- Mothers also benefit from the father's involvement, experiencing fewer mental health issues.
- They also show increased responsiveness, confidence, and affection.

Parenting of children 0-5 Child Outcomes:

- Kindlon, 1995)- Higher IQ, school readiness, social skills, emotional regulation, and empathy- Increased attachment, emotional security, popularity, independence
- Paternal Outcomes: (Sethna et al., 2015; Singley et al., 2017)- Fewer mental health issues
- Increased confidence, parenting satisfaction, and relationship satisfaction
- Maternal Outcomes: (Mallette et al., 2019; Maselko et al., 2019)
- Fewer mental health issues
- Increased responsiveness, confidence, and affection

However, 62% of the dads surveyed by Fathers Network Scotland in 2019 felt that their mental health difficulties did get in the way of forging good connections with their children[313] Paulson et al (2006) also found that depressed fathers are less likely to read with, sing songs and tell stories to their babies than other fathers – and then depressed mothers[314].

"I was so not interested in my baby; I was what I do know now depressed. I couldn't even bring myself into the room and decided to hide away in my office at home. It was only after speaking with you that I had to seek help for myself my family and my wonderful baby. It was hard at first, but it was the best thing and the touch tips, feel and just talking to my baby who is now 2 years of age was wonderful. I had to get the help first, to be able to focus, I had lost confidence in myself as a man and a father which were signs of my deep depression I was told".

Support must be given to fathers about mental health, both before and after the birth. Expectant and new fathers whose partners suffer from mental health vulnerabilities need to be helped to understand what she is going through and help support her. The men's mental health also needs to be included in the picture – for two reasons: a vulnerable man will need support from both his partner and professionals if he is to recover; and also, because poor mental health in fathers has huge and often long-lasting impact on both their partner and their children. Adrienne Burgess[215].

Da Costa et al, in 2017, found that paternal postnatal depression can negatively impact infant and child development. Guiterrez-Galve et al's large research study questioned the mechanisms of risk transmission from fathers who were depressed during the postnatal period to their children's depression at the age of 18 years[233]. It found that fathers' depression appeared to affect their child's conduct and, not only was it associated with their child's depression at 18 years of age, but it also appeared to influence emotional problems with their daughters, too, particularly if their mother was also depressed. Shaheen et al's 2019 research also indicated that giving perinatal and postnatal mental health assessments to fathers could help to prevent future childhood behavioral problems[234].

Further, and linked to this, is the point noted by Khan that fathers will often make "compensatory adjustments to mitigate any impact of maternal mental illness on child mental health and development… [and the father's good mental health, therefore, acts as a protective factor for children's mental health."

Paul Ramchandani is the LEGO Professor of Play in Education, Development, and Learning at the University of Cambridge[1]. He is also the Director of the PEDAL Research Centre, where he leads a research team investigating the role of play in children's early development[235].

His research is focused on early child development, with a particular interest in child and parental play and the prevention of emotional and behavioral difficulties. Much of his work has explored the role of fathers, as well as mothers, in children's lives and development.

One of his studies suggests that children whose fathers make time to play with them from a very young age may find it easier to control their behavior and emotions as they grow up. The study found that fathers engage in more physical play even with the youngest children, opting for activities such as tickling, chasing, and piggyback rides. This seems to help children learn to control their feelings and may also make them better at regulating their behavior later on, as they enter settings where those skills are important – especially school[236].

However, Professor Ramchandani emphasizes that it's important not to overstate the impact of father-child play as there are limits to what the research can tell us[235]. But it does seem that children who get a reasonable amount of playtime with their father benefit as a group.

• Early prevention programs that emphasize the importance of looking after parents' mental health and the impact it can have on their child's development are crucial for promoting overall family well-being. These programs aim to provide parents with the knowledge, skills, and support they need to navigate the challenges of parenthood and promote positive parent-child interactions.

Research has shown that core parenting knowledge, attitudes, and practices are strongly associated with healthy child development. By equipping parents with information about child development, effective communication strategies, stress management techniques, and self-care practices, these programs can help parents better understand and meet their child's needs while also taking care of their mental health[236].

Early prevention programs can take various forms, including antenatal classes, parenting workshops, home visiting programs, and online resources. These programs often cover topics such as understanding child development milestones, building secure attachments, managing stress and emotions, fostering positive discipline strategies, and accessing support networks.

Yes, there is a link between postnatal depression and depression in teenagers. Research has found that postnatal depression in fathers is linked to emotional problems for their teenage daughters[237]. Almost one in 20 new fathers suffered depression in the weeks after their child was born[237]. The research, based on a sample of more than 3,000 families in Bristol, UK, also identified a link between post-natal depression in men and depression in their daughters as they reached adulthood[237]. At 18, girls whose fathers had experienced depression after their birth were themselves at greater risk of the condition. The increased risk applied only to daughters; sons were not affected[237].

One reason for this "handing on" effect could be that post-natal depression in fathers is sometimes linked with an increased level of maternal depression. This might mean that family life is more disrupted for everyone with higher levels of stress for all.

It may also be that having one or both parents with depression affects how parents interact with their children.

These findings highlight the importance of recognising and treating depression in fathers during the postnatal period and call on health professionals to consider both parents when one reports depression[275].

ADVERSE CHILDHOOD EXPERIENCES (ACES)

Adverse Childhood Experiences (ACEs) are potentially traumatic events that occur in childhood. ACEs can include violence, abuse, and growing up in a family with mental health or substance use problems. These experiences can have a significant impact on a child's life and development[238,239,240]

ACEs can be a single event, or prolonged threats to, and breaches of, the young person's safety, security, trust, or bodily integrity. Examples of ACEs include physical abuse, sexual abuse, emotional abuse, living with someone who abused drugs or alcohol, exposure to domestic violence, living with someone who has gone to prison, living with someone with serious mental illness, and losing a parent through divorce, death, or abandonment[238].

The effects of ACEs on our physical and mental health are significant. They can increase the risk of certain health problems in adulthood, such as cancer and heart disease, as well as increase the risk of mental health difficulties, violence, and becoming a victim of violence.

In addition to promoting positive parent-child interactions, early prevention programs can also address the impact of adverse childhood experiences (ACEs) on parental mental health. ACEs, such as childhood abuse, neglect, or household dysfunction, can have long-lasting effects on individuals' mental health and well-being. By providing support and resources to parents who have experienced ACEs, these programs can help break the cycle of intergenerational trauma and promote healthier family dynamics.

"I had gone through what I know now as adverse childhood experiences, it all made sense how I was acting out as a new father. I was lucky I had the support and

understanding of what had happened to me and be a better father".

It is important to ensure that these programs are accessible to all parents, regardless of their socioeconomic status or background. This includes providing information and resources in multiple languages, offering culturally sensitive support, and addressing barriers to participation, such as transportation or childcare.

By investing in early prevention programs that prioritize parental mental health and child development, society can reap long-term benefits. These programs have the potential to improve family well-being, enhance parenting skills, reduce the risk of mental health issues in both parents and children and contribute to positive outcomes for individuals and communities.

Research on the extent to which fathers struggle with their mental health during times when Adverse Childhood Experiences (ACEs) have occurred is limited. However, there is growing recognition of the impact of ACEs on parental mental health and the intergenerational transmission of trauma.

Studies have shown that individuals who have experienced ACEs, including childhood abuse, neglect, or household dysfunction, are at an increased risk of mental health issues later in life. This includes both mothers and fathers. The effects of ACEs can manifest in various ways, such as depression, anxiety, substance abuse, and difficulties in forming healthy relationships.

While research specifically focusing on fathers' mental health in the context of ACEs is limited, it is reasonable to assume that fathers can experience significant distress and challenges in coping with the effects of their childhood trauma. The impact of ACEs on fathers' mental health can have implications for their parenting abilities, family dynamics, and the well-being of their children.

It is important to note that the effects of ACEs are not deterministic, and individuals can develop resilience and seek support to overcome the challenges they face. Recognizing the potential impact of ACEs on fathers' mental health is crucial for providing appropriate support and interventions.

Further research is needed to better understand the specific experiences and struggles of fathers in relation to ACEs and their mental health. This research can help inform the development of targeted interventions and support services that address the unique needs of fathers who have experienced ACEs.

- New fathers who have suffered ACEs may struggle with their mental health due to the pressures and changes of fatherhood, such as financial responsibility, relationship issues, lifestyle adjustments, and lack of sleep.
- New fathers who have suffered ACEs may also struggle with their emotional regulation, attachment, and parenting skills, as they may have difficulties in expressing, coping, and bonding with their feelings and their children.
- New fathers who have suffered ACEs may benefit from seeking professional help, such as counselling, therapy, or support groups, to address their trauma and improve their mental health and well-being.

1001 CRITICAL DAYS

The 1001 Critical Days is a unique period for a baby that sets the foundations for lifelong emotional and physical well-being. This term refers to the time from conception to the age of 2. It's a period of rapid development which lays the foundations for lifelong health and wellbeing[241,242]

The development of a baby's brain begins in the womb and continues rapidly for the first two years after birth.

During Pregnancy:

- A baby's brain is one of the first organs to form, and it grows rapidly throughout pregnancy[241].
- Early neural connections develop in the spinal cord that help your baby to make tiny movements in the uterus.
- As your pregnancy progresses through the first trimester, the cerebellum helps your baby suck and swallow, while the brain stem enables them to contract their diaphragm and chest muscles.
- In your second trimester, your baby may hear their first sounds as the temporal lobe continues to develop the connections needed for hearing.

- In the third trimester, your baby’s brain development ramps up, and the whole organ separates into the right hemisphere and the left hemisphere.

From Newborn to 2 Years:

- At birth, your baby’s brain is around a quarter the size of an adult’s brain. By the end of their first year, this will have doubled in size.
- Most of your baby’s behavior at birth is controlled by the brain stem, such as breathing, sleeping, and swallowing.
- Sight is one of your baby's least developed senses at birth. Your newborn can see only about 20cm to 30cm away. However, by the time they are nine months, the visual areas of their cortex have developed enough that they can see almost as well as you.
- During your baby's first year, their hearing also develops, followed by early language and
- The communication skills, such as babbling, facial expressions and gestures, and cognitive skills.

first years of life are critical to your baby's brain development. It's when your baby's brain grows most rapidly and adapts according to the experiences and interactions, they have. Their brain is very flexible, with millions of new connections being formed especially in their first year. That's why positive early life experiences that nurture and respond to your baby's needs are so important[339].

"It was only after finding out on the course, how important this is for our baby I acted. Why is this not mentioned in antenatal classes".

The concept was developed as part of the early year's healthy development review and outlines 6 areas for action to improve the health outcomes of all babies. These areas include seamless support for families, a welcoming hub for families, the information families need when they need it, an empowered Start for Life workforce, continually improving the Start for Life offer, and leadership for change.

"We know that enduring poor mental health can mean that the relationship between the father and his baby can be deeply affected. A strong bond is needed between an infant and both parents to ensure a healthy development for that child. We need to provide more support for fathers' mental health and to enhance the relationship with their infant". Dr Andy Mayers

The 1001 Critical Days Manifesto is a cross-party manifesto setting out a vision for the provision of services in the UK for this early year's period. It was launched in 2013 and again in 2015, and it emphasizes the importance of acting early to enhance the outcomes for children[2]. The manifesto seeks to use best practices to guide suggested interventions and calls for the evaluation of new interventions in a rigorous scientific manner.

The first 1001 days of a baby's life, from conception to age two, is a period of rapid development that lays the foundation for lifelong health and well-being. Here's why it's so important:

- Rapid Brain Development: During this time, a baby's brain doubles in size[228,240]. One million neural connections are formed every second during this time.
- Influence of Environment and Experiences: The way our brains develop is a product of the interplay between our genes and our environment. Our environments play a crucial role in shaping the developing brain in the first 1001 days[2]. Foundation for Future Development: Early development shapes the architecture of the brain, which in turn influences a child's ability to take advantage of other developmental opportunities[2].Impact of Parental Well-being: Foetal brain development can be influenced by maternal well-being, and physical and mental health.
- Importance of Caregiver Relationships: After birth, sensitive, responsive interactions and healthy relationships with caregivers are particularly important for early brain development.

This period is a unique opportunity to build the brains of the children who will build the future. Therefore, there is a clear case for reducing adversity and supporting early caregiving in the earliest years of a child's life.

MENS BRAINS CHANGE DURING FATHERHOOD?

The Brain Gets Ready to Learn from Fatherhood

Researchers believe that leading up to the birth of their children, men's brains become more plastic (Martínez-García et al., 2022). In other words, the structures, networks, and pathways in the brains of expectant fathers become less stable and can change more readily[243].

research has shown that the brains of new fathers change when they become dads. A study published in the journal Cerebral Cortex found that a man's brain undergoes a slight shrinkage when his newborn arrives, complementing similar research showing that women undergo cerebral changes during motherhood. Another study found that changes in gray matter, the amygdala, and the increased production of the hormone oxytocin have a positive effect on the brains of new fathers. These changes help fathers to form attachments and bonds by feeling a sense of love and protection[243].

We used to say that being a mum was instinctive, but dads had to learn how to parent. We now know that experience some of the same sort of biological changes that help prepare them for parenthood. Recent studies have shown that the same is true for dads. We see increases in grey and white matter, that's the neurons and their connections, in certain key areas. Dr Anna Machin explains this more in her books and well-received ted x talk.

"That was one of the best things out of the course, seeing the video about the science behind fatherhood. It was a real eye open that my partner didn't know about either".

Dr. Anna Machin, an evolutionary anthropologist from the Department of Experimental Psychology at the University of Oxford, has conducted extensive research on the neurobiology and psychology of human relationships, particularly romantic and parent-child relationships[244].

Her research has revealed significant changes in men when they become fathers. These changes are emotional, biological, and physiological. Brain scans show changes in a man's brain when he becomes a father. Two key changes occur a dramatic drop in testosterone levels and changes in grey matter[244].

New research is showing that like new mums, new dads' brain and hormonal levels also change significantly during pregnancy and the first few months of a baby's life[245]. The hormone oxytocin, often referred to as the female 'love drug', has long been known to support the bonding process between mother & infant. However, it has been discovered that it is not just mum who benefits from the bonding effect of this hormone. Dads and mums who live together during pregnancy have been shown to have similar levels of oxytocin in their blood.

Studies have also shown that these couple's personalities change during this period. They align, enabling them to better empathize with each other, and extraversion in dads-to-be also decreases helping them become more family focused.

Around the time of the birth, dad's testosterone levels drop, by up to a third, making him more likely to want to parent. It also helps dads show greater empathy and affection towards their children and respond to their cries[1]. Dads' brains also change with increases in grey and white matter in areas linked to affectionate care and threat detection, as well as those responsible for problem-solving and planning.

After the birth, skin-to-skin contact with both parents helps newborns adjust to life outside the womb, it also triggers oxytocin release which promotes the bonding process[1]. The hormonal release during skin-to-skin helps dad continue to get close to their baby in the months after the birth, as well as helps to reduce stress[2].

However, at around 3 months things begin to change. Babies start to recognize dad and react with a smile or a giggle. At this stage another hormone comes into play - beta-endorphin. This naturally addictive hormone produces feelings of warmth, closeness, and happiness and is produced when we laugh, sing, dance and most crucially play together.

Several studies (including this 2001 study by the Department of Biology at Queen’s University in Ontario) have shown that male testosterone (known as the male sex hormone) and cortisol (a stressor hormone) levels dip in the first weeks of fatherhood.

While estrogen has been considered the female sex hormone, estradiol (the predominant form of estrogen) plays a key role in nurturing behaviors and male sexual function. When this form of estrogen is present in the male system, it promotes more nurturing behaviors in the father.

Prolactin (referred to as the "mom hormone", as it is used in the female system to promote lactation) also spikes in new fathers. According to a 2002 study, lowered testosterone levels and heightened prolactin levels in the male brain are associated with emotional responses to infant cries in new fathers.

COST TO THE NATION

Mental health problems cost the UK economy at least £117.9 billion annually, according to a report published by the Mental Health Foundation and the London School of Economics and Political Science. This cost is equivalent to around 5% of the UK's GDP. Almost three-quarters of the cost (72%) is due to the lost productivity of people living with mental health conditions and costs incurred by unpaid informal carers who take on a great deal of responsibility in providing mental health support in our communities. Across the UK, there were 10.3 million recorded instances of mental ill-health over a one-year period[247].

Before moving on, it's important to consider one other huge consideration – the cost which perinatal mental health difficulties have to the nation as a whole. Bauer et al published their "The Cost of Perinatal Mental Health Problems" paper in 2014. This paper highlighted the astonishing numbers of people who are affected by perinatal mental illness or disorders and the financial costs to the nation for their care. Perinatal depression, anxiety, and psychosis carry a total long-term cost to society of about £8.1 billion for each one-year cohort of births in the UK. This is equivalent to a cost of just under £10,000 for every single birth in the country.

- Nearly three-quarters (72%) of this cost relates to adverse impacts on the child rather than the mother.

• Over a fifth of total costs (£1.7 billion) are borne by the public sector, with the bulk of these falling on the NHS and social services (£1.2 billion).

• The average cost to society of one case of perinatal depression is around £74,000, of which £23,000 relates to the mother and £51,000 relates to impacts on the child.

• Perinatal anxiety (when it exists alone and is not co-morbid with depression) costs about £35,000 per case, of which £21,000 relates to the mother and £14,000 to the child.

• Perinatal psychosis costs around £53,000 per case, but this is almost certainly a substantial under-estimate because of a lack of evidence about the impact on the child; costs relating to the mother are about £47,000 per case, roughly double the equivalent costs for depression and anxiety.

Mental health disorders are on the rise in every country in the world and could cost the global economy up to $16 trillion between 2010 and 2030. This cost is due to a combination of health care expenses, lost productivity, and the impact on quality of life[347]. It's important to note that these estimates can vary depending on the methods used in the studies.

THE COVID-19 PANDEMIC

has had a significant impact on new fathers. Here are some key findings from various studies[249,250].

The COVID-19 pandemic has significantly affected the ability of fathers to attend scans. Here are some key points: When the pandemic hit, restrictions were introduced on partners attending pregnancy appointments and births. This led to many fathers missing out on milestone moments.

Expectant fathers were often not allowed to accompany mothers-to-be into antenatal scan appointments due to Covid risks. This was despite people being able to mix at pubs and restaurants.

According to data collected for 144 trusts in England, Scotland, and Wales, half of the trusts and health boards were restricting partners from attending at least two of three key moments: the 12-week scan, the 20-week scan, and the duration of labor. Many new fathers felt isolated due to restrictions on maternity care caused by the pandemic. They were often excluded from aspects of their partner's pregnancy and their baby's birth, leading to feelings of loss and disconnection. Despite these challenges, some fathers reported positive impacts. For example, 40% of respondents in one study felt that COVID-19 had a positive impact on their role as a father. Additionally, 52% became more aware of their importance as a father, and 60% felt closer to their children.

However, the pandemic also led to increases in mental health difficulties, alcohol consumption, and suicidal thoughts among parents. This highlights the need for adequate support and resources for new parents during such challenging times. A report by the House of Commons Petitions Committee highlighted the ongoing impact of COVID-19 on new parents, including disruptions to access to support services and economic challenges.

"It was so hard not having the family support about us when we needed it".

These findings underscore the importance of providing support to new fathers during the pandemic, as their experiences can significantly affect their well-being and their family's health.

Consideration of fathers' mental health across cultures and religions has been given little consideration, especially in terms of their attitudes to screening, interventions and treatment, prevention, and the interplay with maternal mental health and child outcome measures. In these challenging times, the impact of COVID-19 is likely to present additional pressures on the family unit, which need to be explored through high-quality research methods, which fully engage users and other stakeholders. - Paul Sutcliffe, Associate Professor, Warwick Medical School.

The COVID-19 pandemic has had a significant impact on new fathers, and while there have been challenges, there have also been some unexpected benefits:

- Increased Bonding Time: The lockdown conditions of the pandemic have allowed many new fathers to spend more time at home with their newborns[5]. This has led to stronger bonds and a better understanding of their children's day-to-day routines[350].

- Reduced Parental Stress: Some fathers reported less avoidant attachment and parental stress during the lockdown[5].
- Improved Relationship Satisfaction: Both fathers and mothers reported better relationship satisfaction and stronger parental alliance during the lockdown[5].
- Boosted Confidence: Being at home with their children has boosted many fathers' confidence in their parenting abilities[350].
- Better Life Satisfaction: Mothers displayed better life satisfaction during the lockdown[252].

It's important to note that while these are potential benefits, the experiences of new fathers during the pandemic can vary greatly depending on individual circumstances[2]. The pandemic has underscored the importance of providing support to new fathers during this transition, as their experiences can significantly affect their well-being and their family's health.

Darwin et al's 2017 study highlighted the fact that many fathers still feel excluded from the whole birth, delivery, and childcare process by health professionals, and Mayers et al's 2020 research explained that although fathers appear to play an important role in supporting their partners, many feel alienated within maternity services.

The COVID-19 pandemic reporting has had a significant impact on mental health worldwide.

Around a third of adults and young people reported that their mental health has worsened since the start of the pandemic1. In adults, the proportion of individuals showing symptoms of depression has almost doubled. People with depressive symptoms were more likely to feel that their finances were being impacted, as well as access to care and essential goods.

The pandemic has had an impact on the number of people using publicly funded mental health services2. On an average month, the NHS talking therapies service was expecting to receive about 150,000 referrals for treatment of common mental health problems such as depression or anxiety. Increased Rates of

Suicidal Thoughts: Lockdown had a major impact on the UK's mental health, including increased rates of suicidal thoughts which we have to unknowledge many were first-time Dads.

"I AM A PARENT NOT AN INFECTION RISK" (Scott Mair, Mark Williams)

The name of the survey came from a quote from a father who was involved in the survey. The full survey can be seen online and highlighted that so many fathers weren't even asked once at any time during the perinatal period about their mental health. It showed that during COVID-19, how fathers felt treated and that the concern was also shown by their partners.

Our survey focused on fathers and birth partners in the perinatal period. As recent studies and during COVID-19 have highlighted, this period can have a heavy impact on the mental health of the dad or the birth partner. We asked 261 participants 17 questions to try and capture the experience of the father/ birth partner, the supporting parent, who is often unheard of and undervalued.

Our report highlighted the need for improving support for fathers/ birth partners and the critical resources that all parents deserve. We also need to address the shortage of healthcare professionals, and the high pressure that healthcare professionals are under. In our view, from the findings of the report, there needs to be a complete overhaul of services and a cultural change in maternity services to support all new parents.

This comes down to government funding and better changes in policies to include fathers/ partners during the perinatal period. After speaking to many healthcare professionals, we feel extra support and better education around paternal mental health is needed. The report also shows that there is still a lot of non-engagement with fathers/ birth partners which has been highlighted by the voices of the parents' needs. Since Covid, there have been good outcomes when fathers/partners have had that extra time at home, which also shows the need for better parental leave from employment.

“Guaranteed access to the labor ward and natal wards as an integral family member”

It is shocking to think that fathers and partners were not asked about mental health. It's simply not good enough. However, let's look at the fact that 22.2% were asked, which is a sign of good practice and again adds to our recommendation of a joined-up approach. The big worry remains that 77.8% of fathers and birth partners who completed our survey were not asked about their mental health, so with all that we do know and in such a stressful and often traumatic time, we are not even on a human level asking how the parents that didn’t give birth are feeling mentally. With research stating that 45% of new mothers report birth trauma (Journal of Perinatal Education), that means dad and partners are witnessing this, but we do not ask simply if they are ok.

“More support and a knowledge base for dads to go to get support”.

When you have someone being asked if they are ok and saying no, you would expect to be offered advice or signposting. Unfortunately, 71.6 % of fathers and birth partners who completed our survey were not offered signposting. There is an argument that there are little resources to signpost to. We also hear often that dad or partner is not the patient, however, there are places to signpost to and some will be listed at the end of the report. Let’s also look, however, at a positive that almost 30% were given signposting.

“Recognition of PND in dads, by healthcare and employers, with proactive resources to address it.

67% or nearly 7 in 10 fathers/ birth partners surveyed said they struggled with their mental health during pregnancy or the perinatal period. We see the impact on fathers that a lack of engagement and acknowledgement during pregnancy has and that this can lead to anxiety which can and often leads to depression after the birth. In some of the comments not understanding complications, their partner of baby might be experiencing increased anxiety.

Fathers polled and previously supported also discuss drastic changes in mood with up to 80 % of parents feeling their mental is impacted by a neonatal stay (RCM, 2022). However, even with a relatively noncomplicated birth, it can cause an impact on mental health and most fathers and partners felt being included and supported could have reduced how severe this impact was.

With 48.7% of dads and birth partners not feeling involved during appointments we know this can have an impact on the father/ birth partner. We hear from fathers/ birth partners regularly who feel excluded during appointments:

"I'd like acknowledgment from healthcare professionals that dads even exist. So many appointments where I wasn't looked at and was actively ignored even when I asked questions."

This was even more alarming. Over 82% of fathers/ birth partners reported feeling stressed, anxious, or depressed during this period, which shows the need for earlier prevention and support. We know that fathers/partners may only engage with services after this period and at crisis and end up in general mental health services which are often overwhelmed without specialist perinatal support. This has a big strain on the mothers/partners' mental health and relationships which often can be prevented.

"Maybe a dad's group to discuss feelings and issues that people are experiencing".

Daniels et al's 2020 research into fathers' experiences when witnessing their partner's birth trauma noted that fathers did not feel that they were getting the support that they needed from healthcare professionals.66.3 % of fathers/birth partners who completed our survey experienced signs of depression in the perinatal period.

Quite often people will experience the above but not realize it is depression, particularly when it comes to alcohol intake. Anger is also an issue. In many men that we have worked with, there can be a reluctance to discuss feelings of anger for fear of repercussions and judgment but this question must be asked.

"We have 3 children and our youngest was born at 34 weeks and required a stay in the neonatal unit. I have never been so scared or felt such a loss of control, as I had to stand by helplessly and watch my seriously ill daughter fight for her life. My mental health took a massive dive during this period and to be honest I didn't know who to talk to and would have been so grateful for support."

A clear plan to help parents navigate support is needed. with organizations working together with parents for all outcomes including perinatal mental health specialists, third-party organizations and charities. Being a new parent can be a big challenge: near-sleepless nights, increased pressure on your relationship, and having much less free time than you used to, especially for parents who have struggled with their mental health previously before the perinatal period. Family members including fathers and birth partners, need to be educated about postnatal depression so they can recognise the symptoms and seek help. The same applies to fathers' depression: both parents need to be trained to recognize the signs and seek help.

"More information about the reality of having a child. e.g. stories of Dads who struggled to connect with their child, found it hard, etc".

There are organisations out there in certain locations offering some support, however, this highlights the need for it to be standard practice across all trusts and areas. 95.7 % of dads and birth partners say they would like an advocate or more support. Dads said hearing from other Dads gave real comfort, but for those who didn't have that service it can be a very isolating and lonely time as we both can attest to. They say men don't talk, but it's a myth. We just need to give the platform and the permission to be vulnerable to everyone.

"Maybe a dad's group to discuss feelings and issues that people are experiencing". Ads and Partners – Their Voice

New dads put a lot of pressure on themselves "One thing that comes up a lot in my work is this belief that you need a new set of skills to be a successful dad, while mums have this natural maternal instinct." In truth, being a parent doesn't come easily to anyone. I wish new dads knew there's no such thing as a perfect Dad. "One thing I tell dads as part of recovery is to get hands-on and be silly with your baby. Move away from thinking that have to be the logical, hunter-gatherer parent while mum is the nurturing parent. Also, trust your instincts; yes, take on information and other people's advice but above else, have faith in your judgement."

"Follow-up appointment/calls after the baby is born to check up on the father. Support groups! Any support would be good really!"

Why, are services just for mums? I am working from home and my wife is away in the week. I have no family around me apart from my sister who helps me. I don't tell my wife, as I feel that I should be able to do this on my own. It's hard and have just had to google some information as health professionals have not engaged with me. I am a parent as well and something needs to be done.

"Health visitors and midwives should involve the fathers more and listen to our concerns".

I am on my own with the baby, my partner left after our son was born and had done this before in other relationships, I was later to find out. I went to a baby appointment and the lady in the hospital asked me where is mum and had to explain that she was not in our people's lives which was upsetting reporting the situation I was now living in every day. I would have been ok with that, but there was no support given to me after the conversation.

"Professionals to talk to them and help them understand what's going on".

We are talking about mental health now, why was I never asked about my mental health? I had already been in services when I was younger after being involved in a car accident which had a big impact on my life. It all came to head when I was to become a father. I was afraid and thought if I told anyone, that social services may be involved.

"I'm a parent, what about the support I need as a father".

The findings are particularly concerning considering that dads fall into the highest risk of suicide group- men aged 21-48. Previous research studies have shown that fathers in the perinatal period are also 47 times more likely to be at of risk suicide.67% also said they are still struggling with their mental health long after becoming a parent. 'I want recognition that we are not secondary in the parenting process'.

Our survey also highlighted how dads and birthing partners can often feel neglected during the pregnancy, birth, and baby process. A massive 51% felt uninvolved or left out during antenatal appointments. One commented that they wanted 'acknowledgment from healthcare professionals that dads even exist. There were so many appointments where I wasn't looked at and was actively ignored even when I asked questions.'

Another said that they wished for 'respect from the medical community – **I felt like a sperm donor rather than a father.**

Previous research shows that struggling dads are less likely to read, sing songs, or tell stories to their babies. This impacts the bond between father and child. Respondents to the survey also commented that the strain of full-time work and parental responsibility needs more recognition in general.

One suggested that '2 weeks paternity leave is pathetic to bond with a new child'. Another commented that 'a lot of focus is on the birthing partner and rightly so, but it's isolating and lonely.' Many also felt that proper recognition of postnatal depression in dads is needed, along with support from health services and employers.

"I understand that the health of the mother is what matters to the physical health of the baby, but I needed help too".

Again, these findings are reflected in the research. For example, Darwin et al's 2017 study highlighted the fact that many fathers still feel excluded from the whole birth, delivery, and childcare process by health professionals, and Mayers et al's 2020 research explained that, although fathers appear to play an important role in supporting their partners, many feel alienated within maternity services.

This latter study highlighted an overall lack of support for many fathers, despite wanting support on how to help their partner, as well as information on their mental health and the support services available. The fathers specifically wanted healthcare professionals to signpost them to someone they could talk to for emotional support, and to be taught coping strategies which would help them to support both their partner and baby. The research further suggested that health professionals and perinatal mental health services need a better understanding of the resources that fathers need to support both their mental health and that of their partner.

"Not once did any health professionals ask him about his mental health, only me".

Darwin et al's report also noted that the language used by men differed from that used by health professionals; for example, they preferred to use the word 'stress', which they said was greater in the postnatal period.

There is also the fact that, when a health visitor enquires about any incidences of domestic abuse, the emphasis often appears to be on violence toward the mother and not towards the father. I have found that some fathers think this is biased and they feel let down by the services. I have encountered four fathers who wanted support as they were victims of abuse from their partner, and the statistics support this: for example, in 2018/19, 576,00 (2.5%) of men and 1.2 million (4.8%) of women were victims of partner abuse, which equates to roughly one male victim for every two female victims. During the same period, 16 men and 80 women were killed by their current or previous partner (Mankind 2020)

"I was asked if my partner was violent towards me, but he was not. It stopped him from communicating with our health visitor".

Daniels et al's 2020 research into fathers' experiences as witnesses to their partner's birth trauma in particular noted that fathers did not feel that they were getting the support that they needed from health care professionals.

"I should have been more included from the beginning".

A mother and father should both complete questionnaires regarding depression and a father should be asked how he is feeling or if there is anything he wants or doesn't understand. These questions are solely aimed at the expectant mother whilst a father has to butt in and speak during a conversation he is only there to witness.

Interestingly, Higgins et al in 2020 found that fathers admitted to not being prepared for parenthood and would have welcomed more direct contact with health professionals to help them achieve their full potential as parents. There is, though, the fact (or myth?) that health professionals are often unable to gain access to fathers as they are at work at key times. One way to combat this potential issue is to provide greater access to information on perinatal mental health via the workplace (see 'Pressures from wider society', below).

MOTHERS VOICE

Mothers often have a deep understanding of their family's emotional dynamics and may be able to recognize if the father is struggling. However, it's important to remember that mental health is complex and can be difficult to understand from the outside. Open communication between partners is crucial. If a father, or any parent, is struggling, they should feel encouraged to express their feelings and seek professional help if necessary. It's a team effort to support each other's mental health in a family.

The mother's voice can play a crucial role in supporting a father's mental health for several reasons:

- Emotional Support: The mother's voice can provide emotional support and reassurance to the father, helping him navigate the challenges of parenthood.
- Communication: Open and honest communication between parents is key to maintaining mental health. The mother's voice can help express feelings, concerns, and expectations, fostering a supportive environment.
- Shared Parenting Experience: The mother's voice can help the father feel included and valued in the parenting experience. This can boost his confidence and reduce feelings of anxiety or being overwhelmed.
- Mental Health Awareness: The mother's voice can help in recognizing signs of mental health issues in the father and encourage him to seek help early.

This was recognized that we have to support mothers and partners, to give them a voice for their concerns. This was the reason me and Scott Mair, published a survey with over 450 mothers and birthing partners. One of the quotes from the survey explains what one mother shared with us.

"My partner went to his GP after much persuasion and was simply prescribed antidepressants. No therapy is available. He is severely affected, and I worry for our marriage and the long-term impact of all of this on our infant son. My amazing husband is a shell of his former self and as a result, my mental state is suffering too."

Supporting anyone with depression can be challenging. It's important to remember to take care of your mental health as well. When I became depressed and engaged with help afterward, Michelles depression came back after looking after me, and worries set in. This of course affected her mental health. If we can support every parent during the perinatal period, it can stop the roots of the cause from developing into all other areas. As mentioned, early prevention to support all new parents in their mental health is key to the timeline of the relationships and struggles after this period.

Remember, both parents need to support each other's mental health. This not only benefits the individual parents but also contributes to the overall well-being of the family.

PATERNITY LEAVE

Paternity Leave provides fathers with time to be involved with their children[251]. This involvement can encourage higher levels of engagement and responsibility.

In another study, Lloyd Frank Philpott explored the effect of paternal leave on men's mental health. The details of this study are not available in the search results, but it indicates a focus on understanding how societal structures and policies can impact the mental health of fathers[252].

The duration of paternal leave is not a stable predictor for father-infant bonding, suggesting that fathers who do not have the opportunity to take long periods of paternal leave can still form strong bonds with their infants.

Fathers' direct interactions with babies are important in the earliest weeks and months of their lives[2]. The more time they spend together, the more fathers become aware of their baby's preferences, and the better they can read and become attuned to their body language and signals.

Physical contact between newborns and fathers nurtures bonding and healthy development. For example, preterm babies in the Neonatal Intensive Care Unit who have "kangaroo care" (skin-to-skin contact) with their fathers experience the same physiological benefits as they do after contact with their mothers[253].

Paternity leave can help bring about very strong relationships with children over time. In some instances, the time spent at home allowed fathers to develop what they characterized as a "special" bond that would last for years to come. These findings underscore the importance of paternity leave in promoting father-infant bonding.

Here are some of the countries that offer the best paternity leave policies:

Finland: Expecting mothers in Finland can start their maternity leave seven weeks before their estimated due date. After that, the government covers 16 additional weeks of paid leave through a maternity grant. The country also offers eight weeks of paid paternity leave.

Sweden: New parents in Sweden are entitled to 480 days of leave at 80% of their normal pay. That's on top of the 18 weeks reserved just for mothers. Sweden is unique in that dads also get 90 paid paternity days reserved just for them.

Japan: Japan offers 30 weeks of paid leave for fathers, by far the most of all the countries studied[254].

These countries have recognized the importance of paternity leave in promoting father-infant bonding and supporting families. However, the specifics of these policies can vary, and it's always important to check the most current regulations.

Discrimination against fathers taking paternity leave is a significant issue in many workplaces. Even though paternity leave comes with multiple benefits and is more widely offered than ever before, many men are not taking it[254].

The reasons for this are multifaceted. Many men cite fears of being discriminated against professionally, missing out on pay raises and promotions, being marginalised, or even mocked as reasons for not taking time off. These concerns are considered to be the effect of deeply ingrained and highly damaging stereotypes around gender[353].

In one instance, a father won a landmark discrimination case after his employer threatened to cut his wages following his request to take paternity leave 354. After his wife was diagnosed with post-natal depression, Madasar Ali requested to take paternity leave from his employer to care for his newborn daughter[2]. Following this request, it was found that the employer stated that if he was to take such leave, they would reduce his pay to the statutory minimum after two weeks[354]. However, women at the firm were entitled to receive 14 weeks' leave at full pay rates in the same circumstances.

"For many fathers, the experience of becoming a parent is closely followed by a return to the workplace two weeks later. To my knowledge, there are rarely processes in place to take account of a father's experiences during his paternity leave (possible trauma, sleep deprivation, upheaval, worry) and there is an expectation that he will get straight back into work. This sends a message that a father should not be impacted by having a baby, nor should his work. The reality is that many fathers struggle to adjust to working alongside their new role as a father and can feel huge pressure and cognitive dissonance as this struggle is not recognised by society or employers.

Dr Blaithin O'Dea - Child Psychologist, Perinatal Community Team, Southern Health NHS.

Research suggests that there is a widespread workplace culture that is putting men off taking up their entitlement to shared parental leave and paternity leave[3]. One in four say they have faced verbal abuse or mockery from co-workers or their employer for being a more engaged dad.

It's important to note that employees are protected by law from workplace discrimination on the grounds of paternity leave or as a result of exercising or seeking to exercise their paternity rights.

Parental leave for new fathers is indeed very important for several reasons[255].

- Parent-Child Bonding: Paternity leave, especially longer leaves of several weeks or months, can promote parent-child bonding. This is a crucial time for new fathers to bond with their newborns, which can have long-term benefits for the child's development.
- Improved Outcomes for Children: Research suggests that children whose fathers take paternity leave have improved outcomes, including better performance in school·
- Increased Gender Equity: When fathers take parental leave, it can help to break down traditional gender roles, both at home and in the workplace. This can lead to a more equitable distribution of childcare and household responsibilities.

- Reduced Likelihood of Divorce: Fathers taking parental leave can strengthen the father-child bond and reduce the likelihood of divorce.
- Benefits for Businesses: All of the research suggests that providing parental leave for new fathers helps businesses attract and retain productive workers, promotes worker commitment, and facilitates greater gender equality.

"I had to juggle everything all at once, I was not expecting it to hit me like it did depression. I wish I had time to bond with my baby and that was taken away after he was unwell in hospital. I had to go back to work in two weeks. When I asked my manager for time off, he told me he only had one week and why I was so special. I soon left the following year after being so unwell".

However, many men are still reluctant to use the benefit because they fear it will negatively impact their jobs or careers. It's crucial to recognize that paid parental leave is not just a 'women's issue.' It's an issue for all parents and for everyone who understands the importance of including men and fathers in caregiving[2].

Therefore, companies need to promote a culture where taking parental leave is normalized and encouraged for all parents. This can help ensure that new fathers don't miss important appointments or milestones due to work commitments.

COST OF NEW FATHERS' MENTAL HEALTH IN SOCIETY

The mental health of new fathers is an important aspect of overall family well-being and has implications for society as a whole. While specific data on the economic cost of new fathers' mental health is limited, we can draw insights from broader research on perinatal mental health and its societal impact[256].

- Prevalence of Mental Health Issues: Approximately 10% of new fathers worldwide experience postnatal depression, highlighting the significance of mental health challenges in this population. Paternal depression and other mental health issues can have long-term consequences if left untreated, affecting the well-being of both fathers and their families.

- Impact on Parent-Child Interaction: The mental health of fathers and other caregivers is crucial for healthy parent-child interactions. Both paternal and maternal depression have been shown to hurt how parents interact with their children. This can affect the child's emotional well-being, cognitive development, and overall family dynamics.
- Societal and Economic Costs: Untreated perinatal mental health problems, including those experienced by new fathers, carry long-term economic and social costs for society. These costs can manifest in various ways, such as increased healthcare utilization, decreased work productivity, and potential strain on social support systems.
- Importance of Support and Treatment: Recognizing and addressing the mental health needs of new fathers is crucial for mitigating the potential costs to society. Providing accessible and effective support services, such as paternal mental health programs, counseling, and therapy, can help alleviate the burden on individuals, families, and society as a whole.

The mental health of both parents during the perinatal period is crucial, not only for their well-being but also for the child's development. Mental illness in either parent can indeed contribute to couple conflict and poorer child development outcomes. Support from partners can play a significant role in preventing the development of maternal perinatal mental health disorders. In cases where disorders do occur, this support can greatly impact the mother's recovery and overall well-being[2].

Furthermore, when a mother is struggling to meet her baby's needs due to her mental health condition, the baby's psychosocial and emotional development may be protected by relationships with other caregivers, including the co-parent. This highlights the importance of a supportive network for the mother and child during this critical period. It's essential to recognize these factors and ensure that appropriate support systems are in place for families during the perinatal period. This can help to mitigate the potential costs and negative impacts associated with perinatal mental health disorders[2].

Becoming a father means inevitable change. It might not be physically visible to the rest of society, but becoming a father impacts internally, in the father-to-be's mind. Many thoughts and feelings are evoked, and some are not always welcome. As with mothers, this can be a source of real shame. What is stirred up inside, if we can bear to notice, at the thought of bringing new life into this world?

Although there may be thoughts and feelings of joy and excitement at the idea of having a new baby, for most men there will be, ordinarily, as there is for women, real fears about this change, and the capacity to be a parent. Why wouldn't there be? It is a developmental change of great significance.

For men, like women, sometimes these thoughts and feelings can be disturbing and may impact not only the relationship with their partner but the relationship with their baby and their mental health. If a man doesn't have a space to be able to share his internal experience this can lead to a real sense of isolation and his mental health can deteriorate seriously or he can start to behave differently.

Without vital support and help, there might be a deterioration in the father's mental health, difficulties within his intimate relationships, an impact on his work, an increase in reliance on addictive substances, risk-taking… and so the list goes on.

No man and no father is the same, and the relationship with their baby, and each baby will be unique and different. That relationship will be informed by so many factors: his relationship with his partner, whether the pregnancy was planned/wanted; his own early life experience of being fathered; his previous traumatic experiences and mental health, and so on. It is complex and thoughts and feelings often are difficult to make sense of on one's own. In parent-infant psychotherapy we recognize that a mother and baby do not exist without a father, and vice versa. They are all interconnected relationally. Inside we have all experienced being an infant, and having parents, whether they have been physically present or not, we will have ideas in our mind about what it means to be good enough parents.

A baby needs a 'good enough' couple; mother and father; who can help him to make sense of the world including his early thoughts and feelings, to help him grow up and become his person not coupled with mummy and not coupled with daddy but tolerating not being part of a couple. This supports his capacity to be alone, to grow independently, and to observe and be observed by others.

"A father is not ancillary to a baby's development and life but is vital. There is always a father in mind, as part of a couple who created the baby in mind, and whether physically present or psychologically available, this will continue to be a factor of curiosity for the child, acknowledged or not, and impact on their mental health. The father's legacy, like the mother's is everlasting". Jane Turner

When it comes to rage and new dads, it's important to recognize that some fathers may experience anger or irritability during the postpartum period. Here are a few key points to consider:

POSTPARTUM RAGE IN FATHERS

Just like new mothers, some new fathers may experience postpartum anger or irritability. This can be attributed to various factors, including hormonal changes, lack of sleep, increased stress, and adjusting to the demands of parenthood[257].

Postpartum depression and anger:

Postpartum depression can also manifest as anger or irritability in new dads. It's estimated that around 1 in 10 fathers experience postpartum depression or anxiety. Symptoms may include sudden outbursts, increased impulsivity, and even violent behavior.

"I have never felt so angry in the first year of fatherhood. I was so angry that I punched the sofa and broke my hand, four months after my son was born" – Mark Williams

Postpartum rage is a mood disruption that causes intense anger, aggression, and agitation in the weeks and months after giving birth. It's sometimes called postpartum anger[2]. This condition can affect anyone who recently gave birth, and it's most common within the first six weeks to one year after childbirth[2].

The symptoms of postpartum rage can vary from person to person, but they often include[258]:

- Difficulty controlling anger and temper.
- Feeling uncontrollably irritable.
- Increased yelling or swearing.
- Hitting or throwing objects.
- Violent urges or thoughts, often directed at a spouse, your baby, or a family member.
- Difficulty switching thoughts from anger to something more positive.
- Anger about things that formerly would not have been bothersome.

Postpartum rage can coincide with other postpartum conditions like postpartum depression and postpartum anxiety. However, it's important to note that you can experience rage without feeling depressed, and having postpartum depression doesn't mean you'll also develop feelings of rage.

If you or someone you know is experiencing these symptoms, it's important to seek help from a healthcare provider. They can provide support and discuss treatment options, which may include support groups, therapy, and medication. If you have thoughts of harming yourself, your baby, or others, it's crucial to seek immediate help.

"I remember feeling this urge of anger that I had never experienced before. My partner was saying things to me and where I could cope before just didn't handle the situation very well. I am still regretting my actions even today after getting help".

Dr Jane Hanely, my mentor since 2012 who has been involved with perinatal mental health (PMH) for over 40 years explains.

I believe that parents deserve the best possible care during the perinatal period, to ensure they enjoy parenthood. It is the way my work emphasizes the importance of recognizing and addressing mental health issues in fathers. We have come a long way in the past ten years to include fathers, but still so much we can do that services can provide that support for fathers in their own right as well.

COPING STRATEGIES

There are various strategies that new dads can employ to manage anger and irritability. These may include practicing self-care, seeking social support, engaging in stress-reducing activities, and learning anger management techniques[259].

It's crucial to remember that anger and irritability in new dads are not uncommon, and seeking help and support is essential for their well-being and the well-being of their family. If you or someone you know is experiencing difficulties, it's recommended to reach out to a healthcare professional for assistance.

Substance abuse can have a significant impact on new fathers and their ability to provide support for their partners' mental health, as well as on the overall well-being of the child. Research suggests that substance abuse among fathers can contribute to various negative outcomes and risks for both the father and the child[259].

One study highlights the importance of recognizing the impact of substance abuse and mental health issues on fathers and the need for effective support systems. It emphasizes that fathers with complex histories, including substance abuse and mental health issues, should not be overlooked in safeguarding efforts for children. Insufficient attention to fathers in the postnatal period can hinder their ability to actively engage and provide support to their partners and children.

It is worth noting that fathers, like mothers, can experience postnatal depression. Hormonal changes, as well as the stressors associated with the transition to fatherhood, can contribute to the development of postnatal depression in fathers. Substance abuse can further exacerbate mental health challenges and increase the risk of depression and other negative outcomes for fathers.

Moreover, substance abuse among fathers can have a direct impact on their parenting abilities and the well-being of their children. Studies have shown that fathers with substance abuse issues may struggle to meet their children's needs and provide a stable and nurturing environment Substance misuse can impair judgment, affect emotional regulation, and lead to inconsistent parenting practices, which can negatively impact child development and well-being.

Recognizing the importance of addressing substance abuse among fathers, there are resources available to support fathers struggling with substance abuse. Organizations such as Fatherhood.gov provide tips and promising practices for fathers dealing with substance abuse and offer guidance on how to have conversations about substance abuse with their children. Programs like "Fathers for Chang3[369] focus on addressing substance abuse, domestic violence, and poor parenting among fathers of young children.

In conclusion, substance abuse among new fathers can have significant implications for their mental health, their ability to support their partners and the well-being of their children. It is crucial to recognize the unique challenges faced by fathers and provide appropriate support and resources to address substance abuse and promote positive mental health outcomes.

UNEXPECTED PREGNANCY

Unexpected pregnancies can indeed lead to depression. This is often referred to as antenatal depression. Symptoms can include feeling sad, a low mood, or tearful a lot of the time, feeling irritable, or getting angry easily, losing interest in other people and the world around you, not wanting to eat or eating more than usual, negative thoughts, such as worrying you will not be able to look after your baby, feeling guilty, hopeless or blaming yourself for your problems, and having problems concentrating or making decisions.

An unintended pregnancy is a risk factor for poor maternal mental health including perinatal depression, stress, and lower levels of psychological well-being and life satisfaction[3]. It may increase the risk of paternal depression and parenting stress.

Unexpected fatherhood can indeed lead to depression. This is often referred to as paternal depression[1]. Symptoms can include feelings of depression and anxiety[260].

"I was ready to go to university, it was my purpose throughout school. I was 19 years of age, and my girlfriend became pregnant and just didn't know what to do. I was scared that I was unable to cope, and this baby was going to ruin my life. Everyone including my family told me that it was my fault and that I had to live up to my responsibility. It was only after I didn't go to university that my girlfriend told me that she stopped taking the pill and she did it not for me to go to university. It was a shock and we split up. Now I can't even see my baby as she has a new boyfriend, and I am in a mountain of debt with a job I hate".

Unintended fatherhood is linked to an increased risk of a man having postnatal depression[4]. Paternal depression is, in turn, linked to a higher risk of depression in their partners and more behavioral problems in their children.

There are many reasons that you might experience mental health problems while your partner is pregnant or after they give birth. But these problems are more likely if you:

- Don't have good support networks in place.
- Are struggling with other stressful life events like moving house, losing your job, or a bereavement?
- Have poor living conditions or are living in poverty.
- Experienced abuse in your childhood.

You might also be coping with:

- extra responsibilities around the house
- financial pressures
- a changing relationship with your partner
- lack of sleep
- looking after several children.

WORK-RELATED STRESS IN FATHERS

Workplace anxiety and depression can indeed have significant effects on families.

Work-related stressors and work-family conflict are important social determinants of mental health[1]. While the impact of these stressors on parents' mental health is well documented, we know comparatively less about their impact on children's mental health[1]. The stressors of work-to-family conflict, increased difficulties in work-family balance since the COVID-19 pandemic, irregular schedules, low esteem derived from work, and job insecurity were all indirectly associated with an increase in parental concern for their children's mental health through increased parents' depressive symptoms[261].

Workplace anxiety can translate into problems at work such as failure to meet deadlines, forgetfulness, inability to concentrate or focus, sick days or lost productivity, and a spillover effect on family life[262]

One study on family members of people with depression found that many felt that their insights and knowledge were ignored by health professionals. They were also more likely to become ill themselves, facing an increased risk of burnout, exhaustion, depression, and psychological distress[376].

It's important to note that help and support are available. If you or someone you know is experiencing these symptoms, it's crucial to seek help from a healthcare professional. With appropriate treatment and support, most people can manage their symptoms.

Work-related stressors and work-family conflict are indeed important social determinants of mental health[1]. While the impact of these stressors on parents' mental health is well documented, we know comparatively less about their impact on children's mental health.

The stressors of work-to-family conflict, increased difficulties in work-family balance since the COVID-19 pandemic, irregular schedules, low esteem derived from work, and job insecurity were all indirectly associated with an increase in parental concern for their children's mental health through increased parents' depressive symptoms.

"My manager didn't have a clue about mental health, we could clearly see that my work was affected due to situations on the shop floor. Of course, when I got home, just felt useless and didn't want to do anything with the family".

Parenting and relationship resources deteriorate when fathers' work–family conflict increases or is sustained; this, in turn, affects children's socio-emotional development and wellbeing[262].

While there is a relative abundance of research focusing on maternal mental health, data on fathers is still limited by comparison[3]. A systematic review of 18 studies confirmed increased paternal stress in the perinatal period, especially around the time of birth[263].

Work-related stress and depression can be caused by a variety of factors, including:

- Long hours and heavy workload: Working for extended periods without adequate rest can lead to burnout, which is a state of chronic physical and mental exhaustion.
- Job insecurity: Uncertainty about the future of one's job can cause significant stress.
- Conflicts with co-workers or bosses: Interpersonal issues in the workplace can create a hostile work environment, leading to stress.
- Lack of control or insecurity: Feeling that you have little control over your work or job security can lead to stress.
- Lack of job satisfaction, boredom, or isolation: Not finding fulfilment in your work, feeling bored, or feeling isolated can contribute to stress.
- Fear of violence, bullying, or harassment: Working in an environment where there is a fear of violence, or where bullying or harassment is prevalent, can lead to significant stress[5].
- Bad relations with other work colleagues: Poor relationships with colleagues can create a negative work environment and contribute to stress.
- Problems with the working environment: Issues such as noise, temperature, overcrowding, and poor facilities can cause stress.

"I was already struggling in my job. I hated every day getting up in the morning. The manager was a bully and I just felt trapped. When my wife was expecting another baby, which was not planned that upped the pressures in my mind. The thought of having to do overtime to provide for the things that

we needed just scared me. After the baby was born and my wife had postnatal depression, this just came too much, and became so unwell. I had everything a great family and friends but feel that the workplace for me was a big factor".

These factors can directly affect mood, leading to symptoms such as irritability, sleep disruption, and cognitive changes like impaired concentration[1]. Over time, these can lead to depression[1]. It's important to address these issues and seek help if you're feeling overwhelmed. Many workplaces have resources available to help manage stress, and professional help is also available.

ALCOHOL

It is the most common for new fathers I have supported over the years to drink more after the baby is born. This may be due to various factors, such as stress, fatigue, social pressure, or coping with the changes in their relationship and lifestyle. Many fathers have drunk more when finding out they are going to be fathers again[2].

The transition to fatherhood is a significant event in a man's life, and it can motivate some parents to change health-related behaviors. However, the health behaviors of fathers, including drinking alcohol, can have a significant impact on families[263,264].

It is a common theme for some fathers to use alcohol as a form of self-medication when dealing with depression. Alcohol can temporarily suppress feelings of isolation, anxiety, or sadness, which may provide temporary relief for some individuals. However, this relief is short-lived and can often lead to a worsening of depressive symptoms over time.

While women are twice as likely to be diagnosed with depression, men are four times more likely to commit suicide. This suggests that men are less likely to seek help and support when feeling anxious, stressed, and depressed. A tendency to use alcohol to cope can make these symptoms worse over time.

It's important to note that while alcohol might seem to provide temporary relief from symptoms of depression, it ultimately contributes to the condition and makes it worse. Therefore, seeking professional help for depression is crucial, and there are many effective treatments available that don't involve alcohol. If you or someone you know is struggling with depression and alcohol use, it's important to reach out to a healthcare provider for help.

"I've always drunk when I'm stressed, even more during that time".

Men who drink during pregnancy may increase the chance of their partner drinking and negatively affect relationship quality. Exposure to intoxicated adults can lead to increased alcohol use in children under 13 years old. Moreover, new evidence has found a link between paternal alcohol consumption before conception and the chances of fetal birth defects[265].

Fathers who drink alcohol regularly before conception are associated with greater chances of birth defects like congenital heart disease, limb anomalies, clefts, and digestive tract anomalies[3]. Paternal alcohol use can lead to decreased newborn birth weight, marked reduction in overall brain size, and impaired cognitive function.

Fatherhood can be an opportunity to change drinking habits, but support for new fathers in this regard is often lacking[1]. It's important to better support fathers during this transition, as it can benefit the whole family and improve health outcomes.

Substance abuse can have a significant impact on new fathers and their ability to parent effectively. Research shows that fathers battling substance use want to reconnect with their children and parents effectively, leading to a sense of pride and a powerful reason to remain sober[266]. Some surveys of men in treatment reveal that a very high percentage – between 80% – 96% – believe that they require support in their role as fathers.

Substance abuse can limit a parent's ability to be positively involved in their children's lives. It can also lead to negative outcomes for parents and their children. Substance abuse can impact a person's ability to make sound decisions; fulfil responsibilities in the home, workplace, and school; and maintain relationships.

"I was drinking more and more since my daughter was born. I had gone through so much before becoming a father and always had used drink to cope with life pressures and the things that had happened to me in my childhood. I was to learn positive coping skills and that was the turning point in my life. I had to learn the coping skills first, to replace the drink that keeping me sane in my mind and give me brain a break".

While drug addiction in pregnant women can affect fetal development, drug addiction in fathers doesn't normally affect the baby at the time of birth. Addiction can affect sperm quality and development, but these defects usually cause early miscarriage rather than birth defects.

SUBSTANCE ABUSE

In the book "Fathers and Perinatal Mental Health which Dr Jane Hanley and I wrote together highlighted substance abuse. book explores the way in which fathers' mental health has presented in the past and how it presents now. It looks at the father's attitudes towards his mental well-being and how he may self-manage and self-medicate.

This is an important issue that affects many families and children. Substance abuse is the long-term misuse of drugs and/or alcohol by a parent or carer. It can cause social, mental, physical, and legal problems for the parent and their children. Most parents and carers who drink alcohol or use drugs do so in moderation, which doesn't present an increased risk of harm to their children. However, parents and carers who misuse substances can have chaotic, unpredictable lifestyles and may struggle to recognise and meet their children's needs[268].

Substance abuse can cause social, mental, physical, and legal problems for the person and their family. Some of the most common types of substance abuse are:

- Alcohol abuse: This is when a person drinks more than the recommended daily limit of alcohol, which can affect their health, behavior, and relationships. Alcohol abuse can result in an increased risk of several serious health issues, such as brain damage, liver damage, heart disease, and hypertension.

- Tobacco abuse: This is when a person smokes or chews tobacco, which contains nicotine, a highly addictive substance. Tobacco abuse can cause many diseases and cancers, such as lung cancer, mouth cancer, and stroke. Tobacco abuse can also affect the health of others through second-hand smoke.
- Opioid abuse: This is when a person uses opioids, which are a class of painkillers and depressants, either in illegal forms like heroin or in legal forms like prescription medicines. Opioid abuse can cause physical dependence, withdrawal symptoms, respiratory depression, and overdose.
- Stimulant abuse: This is when a person uses stimulants, which are drugs that increase energy, alertness, or productivity, such as cocaine, methamphetamine, or amphetamines. Stimulant abuse can cause hyperthermia, hostility, mood swings, seizures, psychosis, and heart failure.
- Hallucinogen abuse: This is when a person uses hallucinogens, which are drugs that alter the perception of reality and distort the senses, such as LSD, PCP, DMT, or mushrooms. Hallucinogen abuse can cause hallucinations, paranoia, anxiety, panic, and flashbacks.
- Inhalant abuse: This is when a person inhales solvents, aerosols, gases, or nitrites, which are substances that can be found in household or industrial products. Inhalant abuse can cause brain damage, nerve damage, organ damage, and sudden death.
- Novel psychoactive substance abuse: This is when a person uses novel psychoactive substances, which are synthetic or natural substances that mimic the effects of other drugs, such as cannabis, ecstasy, or ketamine. These substances are also known as "legal highs" or "designer drugs". Novel psychoactive substance abuse can cause unpredictable and harmful effects, such as agitation, psychosis, seizures, and coma.

"I never used drugs ever before becoming a father, I needed something to give me a lift and I was working in mental health services as well. It was brought up with the manager, after they found out and that changed everything as

I had to admit I had a problem which was better for me in the long term. I am so happy now; I was in a tunnel and didn't see any way to get help".

EATING DISORDERS

Eating Disorders can indeed occur in new fathers, although they are not as commonly discussed or studied as they are in new mothers[2]. The stress and changes that come with parenthood can trigger disordered eating behaviors[269,270].

These disorders can manifest in various ways, such as excessive concern about body image, extreme dieting, binge eating, or compulsive exercise[2]. It's important to note that men often don't disclose their disordered-eating behaviours, and health-care providers don't always think to screen men for symptoms.

The role of fathers in their children's eating disorders is also significant. Fathers can play a profound role in their child's recovery from an eating disorder[2]. Research has shown that when fathers are more involved in treatment sessions, it predicts better outcomes for their kids.

If you or someone you know is struggling with an eating disorder, it's important to seek help from a healthcare professional. Early intervention can lead to more successful treatment outcomes.

Body image issues are a common concern for many men. Almost half of UK men say poor body image has affected their mental health[1]. This can be due to a variety of factors, including media portrayals of the "ideal man", societal expectations, and personal experiences.

Here are some key points about body image in men[2,269,270]:

- Media Influence: Men may have body image concerns because of media portrayals of the "ideal man" or because of the pressure put on men to meet societal expectations.
- Societal Expectations: There is peer pressure among teenage boys and men to be physically 'tough' and 'strong'.

- Personal Experiences: Body image issues can be a result of trauma connected with bullying, sexual trauma, or other childhood trauma.
- Muscle Dysmorphia: In particular, the condition muscle dysmorphia, or "bigorexia," disproportionately affects men.
- Pandemic Impact: During the pandemic, isolation and lack of social and physical activity has led to a spike in disordered eating and negative body image issues in men.

It's a myth that it's only women and girls who suffer with 'eating disorders. The National Association for Males with Eating Disorders estimates that 25% to 40% of people with eating disorders are men and boys. The issue for boys, men and fathers to getting help is stigma, together with a lack of understanding about the size and presentation of eating disorders in the male population can mean that eating disorders are not identified or treated early enough.

"I was always the "The fat kid" growing up, being the biggest one among my friends. It got even worse when I became a father, not sure why but I know I didn't want my child to see me as this horrible looking person".

It's important to note that everyone's body is unique and it's okay to not fit into societal standards of beauty. If you or someone you know is struggling with body image issues, it's important to seek help from a healthcare professional.

GAMBLING

When it comes to the topic of gambling and new dads, there are a few different aspects to consider. Let's explore them further:

Some possible reasons for new dads to gamble could be to alleviate the stress and pressure associated with the new responsibilities of parenthood, as a way to socialize with other dads who also gamble, as a means of entertainment or excitement, or to try and supplement their income. However, it's important to remember that gambling can become addictive and cause financial, emotional, and interpersonal problems. Seeking professional help or support can be beneficial if gambling has become a problem[271,272].

Gambling can indeed have a significant impact on families. Here are some of the potential effects:

- Material Deprivation: Gambling can lead to financial difficulties, which can result in material deprivation for the family.
- Domestic Violence: There can be an increase in domestic violence in families where a member has a gambling problem.
- Divorce and Separation: Gambling problems can strain relationships to the point of causing separations or divorce.
- Child Abuse and Neglect: In some cases, children in the family may experience neglect or abuse as a result of the gambling problem.
- Emotional Problems: Family members, including children, parents, siblings, and grandparents, can experience emotional problems due to the stress and instability caused by gambling.
- Reduced Household Budgets: The partners of people who gamble harmfully, their children, their wider family and friends, and other social contacts, can also be harmed. There can be multiple knock-on effects, including reduced household budgets.

I have always had a problem with gambling, but it gets even worse after my daughter was born, I had. I was losing so much money and even took out a loan without my wife knowing to try to win my money back. I felt that it was a distraction as my wife was struggling with her mental health after a traumatic birth, which I felt panic and seeing the baby heart beat lower in the hospital.

Video games can be addictive for several reasons[273]:

Psychological Tricks: Video games use psychological tricks to be habit-forming. They often replicate strategies from the gambling and retail industries to ensure that players keep coming back[389].

- Neurochemistry & Behaviour Reward System: There are direct video game effects on the brain such as neurochemistry and behavior reward system[391].
- High Degree of Immersion: The high degree of immersion in video games can make them addictive[391].
- Thrill-Seeking Nature: The thrill-seeking nature of the games can also contribute to their addictiveness391.
- Sense of Freedom, Purpose/Progress, and Social Connection: Video games can meet our basic psychological need for a sense of freedom, purpose/progress, and social connection[390].

However, it's important to note that while playing video games can be a fun pastime, and there are some potential benefits, there are health risks associated with too much gaming. They include repetitive stress injuries, vision problems, sleep deprivation, depression, and possibly addiction to playing[1].

These effects can indeed lead to the breakdown of family relationships. It's important to seek help if gambling is causing issues within a family. There are many resources and support groups available for individuals and families affected by gambling.

"I remember ending up in a casino in Swansea and I didn't even gamble. It was just a distraction" – Mark Williams

GAMING

Many fathers enjoy gaming as a hobby, and it can provide a form of entertainment and relaxation. Gaming allows them to unwind and have some personal time. It can also be a way for new dads to connect with friends and maintain social connections, especially if they have limited time for in-person interactions[274].

Balancing gaming and fatherhood:

While gaming can be a source of enjoyment, it's important for new dads to find a balance between gaming and their responsibilities as fathers. Prioritizing family time, taking care of their child's needs, and being present in their child's life are crucial aspects of fatherhood. It's essential to ensure that gaming does not interfere with these responsibilities.

Gaming solutions for sleep-deprived new dads:

Becoming a new father often means experiencing sleep deprivation due to the demands of caring for a newborn. However, there are gaming solutions available for sleep-deprived dads. For example, portable gaming devices or mobile gaming apps can allow dads to enjoy gaming during their downtime or while taking care of their child. These options provide flexibility and convenience for gaming sessions.

As a new father I was gaming even more than ever. I was losing control and had to stay awake to check the baby. I would have my game console right by the left-hand side of the cot. My girlfriend would be fast asleep and would not know. It was affecting my working life and of course our relationship was starting to fail. I felt like a failure myself as a new father.

MENTAL HEALTH AND HUMAN RIGHTS

The Universal Declaration of Human Rights (UDHR), proclaimed by the United Nations General Assembly in 1948, sets out fundamental human rights to be universally protected. It's against the law to discriminate against anyone because of their sex, religion, disability or certain other personal characteristics ('protected characteristics.

As of 2023, Clinical guideline [CG192] Published This guideline covers recognising, assessing and treating mental health problems in women who are planning to have a baby, are pregnant, or have had a baby or been pregnant in the past year[275]. It covers depression, anxiety disorders, eating disorders, drug- and alcohol-use disorders and severe mental illness (such as psychosis, bipolar disorder and schizophrenia). It promotes early detection and good management of mental health problems to improve women's quality of life during pregnancy and in the year after giving birth.

This is concerning, as the mental health and well-being of fathers/partners are just as important as that of mothers in the postnatal period. It is crucial that fathers/partners are included in the conversation and have access to support and resources to ensure the best outcomes for both the baby and the family as a whole....

To find out more about mental health, human rights, and how to support your mental health, as well as the mental health of others in the UK, there are several resources available:

• Mental Health Foundation (MHF) - The MHF is a UK charity that provides information, resources, and support on various aspects of mental health. They have a dedicated section on their website that covers mental health and human rights, including articles, guides, and campaigns.

• Equality and Human Rights Commission (EHRC) - The EHRC is an independent body in the UK that promotes and enforces equality and human rights laws. They provide guidance, resources, and publications on various topics, including discrimination and human rights about mental health.

• Mind - Mind is a leading mental health charity in the UK. They offer a wide range of resources, information, and support for individuals experiencing mental health problems, as well as their families and friends. Their website has specific sections on legal rights, discrimination, and advocating for better mental health services.

• Rethink Mental Illness - Rethink Mental Illness is another UK-based charity that focuses on improving the lives of people affected by mental illness. They provide information, advice, and support through their helpline, online resources, and local services. They also have resources specifically addressing legal rights and discrimination.

• NHS Choices - The National Health Service (NHS) website provides information and resources on mental health conditions, treatments, and support services available in the UK. You can find information about your rights as a patient, access to mental health services, and guidance on how to navigate the healthcare system.

• Local Support Services - Depending on your location, there may be local support services, advocacy groups, or community organizations that focus on mental health and human rights. These can include local mental health charities, community centres, or social service agencies. Conducting a search online or reaching out to your local authority can help you discover relevant resources in your area.

It's important to remember that laws and resources may vary depending on your specific circumstances and country of residence. Therefore, it's recommended to consult with local organizations and authorities for more tailored information and support.

World Health Organization (WHO) and Office of the High Commissioner for Human Rights (OHCHR) Publication: "Mental health, human rights, and legislation: guidance and practice" - This publication provides guidance and practical information on how to ensure that laws, policies, and services related to mental health are in line with human rights conventions. You can access this publication to gain a comprehensive understanding of mental health and human rights.

• WHO Mental Health website - The WHO website offers a wealth of information on mental health, including resources, guidelines, and reports. You can explore their mental health section to find specific topics related to mental health and human rights.

• National and International Mental Health Organizations - There are various mental health organizations that focus on promoting mental health and advocating for human rights in mental health. Examples include Mental Health America, National Alliance on Mental Illness (NAMI), and Human Rights Watch. Visiting their websites or reaching out to them can provide you with valuable information and resources.

• Educational Institutions - Many universities and academic institutions offer courses or programs related to mental health and human rights. You can explore online courses, workshops, or certificate programs that cover these topics.

• Local Community Resources - Community centres, counselling centres, and mental health clinics often provide educational materials, workshops, and support groups related to mental health and human rights. Contacting these resources in your local area can help you access the information and support you need.

• Books and Publications - There are numerous books and publications available that cover the intersection of mental health and human rights. These can range from academic texts to personal narratives and self-help guides. Visiting bookstores, libraries, or online platforms can help you find relevant reading materials.

The Quality Rights initiative aims to support countries to assess and improve the quality of care in mental health and related services and to promote the rights of people with psychosocial, intellectual and cognitive disabilities.

CONCLUSION[275]

Supporting new fathers is crucial for several reasons:

- Child Development: Fathers can have deep and lasting effects on their child's brain, emotions, and body development[1]. An engaged and supportive dad can help children develop in a more positive way, such as being more confident with exploring the world, finding it easier to regulate their own feelings, and being able to build better social relationships with their peers in childhood.
- Father's Mental Health: New fathers can experience challenges throughout their partner's pregnancy, and during the first few years of their child's life. They might suffer from high levels of anxiety about their newfound roles and responsibilities, their relationship with their partner, or their relationships with the new baby. Supporting new fathers can help them cope with these challenges and contribute to their mental health.
- Lower suicide rates in Men/Fathers. Here are some strategies: Raise Awareness: Many people are unaware that new fathers can experience postnatal depression and other mental health issues. Raising awareness about these issues can help new fathers feel less alone and more understood.
- Gender Equality: Despite the evidence that shows that dads are important to child development and can be at risk of experiencing mental health difficulties, there is very little support for new fathers out there[1]. Gender inequality still exists in early parenthood, and services can often still reflect more traditional

family structures[1]. Supporting new fathers can help address this inequality.

- Family Dynamics: The role of fathers has increased over the years, with dads now being more present in their children's lives than ever before[1]. This is due to a range of reasons, such as more women going to work and providing for their family economically, evolving attitudes to fatherhood, and the increase in same-sex parenting[1]. Supporting new fathers can help them navigate these changing family dynamics.

In conclusion, supporting new fathers is not only beneficial for the fathers themselves but also for their children, partners, and society as a whole. It contributes to healthier family dynamics, better child development, and a more equitable society. Therefore, it's vitally important for dads to receive the support they need.

I had been fighting to get fathers and perinatal mental health on the agenda for thirteen years and was close many times, even at Westminster when we sat in the room and the very same day, they called a snap election. It was our luck at the time that the member of parliament didn't get in again.

It was Chris and Owen from Future men that changed that for me. They wanted to add to the agenda of fatherhood and include perinatal mental health. The charity had been pushing agendas on fathers for fourteen years at Westminster and they even did a survey.

The survey reveals that over half (52%) of men in the UK feel pressured by society's expectations of them, and that 40% suffer from anxiety as a result.

Future Men's YouGov poll reveals a crisis of masculinity as more than a third of young men feel unfairly treated and forgotten by society, with social media identified as a key source of negative behavioural role models.

- 37% of young men feels society still expects them to "be the breadwinner".
- 49% of UK adults believe that 'not being able to provide financially' would cause a man to feel emasculated.
- 51% of young men believe that society expects them to "man up" when faced with challenges.

• A third (34%) of men under 35 feel that struggling with mental health makes them less masculine.

• Over half (51%) felt that "crying in front of others" would make them feel 'less masculine'.

• 29% of UK men feel forgotten/left behind due to society's expectations of them.

High percentage of young boys and men – will become fathers in the future. Mark Williams

Becoming a dad can be a challenging and rewarding experience, but it can also affect your emotional wellbeing in various ways. These issues are normal and understandable, but they can also have a negative impact on your health, your relationship with your partner, and your ability to bond with your baby. That's why it's important that early prevention support needs addressing.

It is indeed discrimination that fathers are not getting the support they need to be involved and equal parents. There are many ways that fathers are discriminated against in the family courts, in the workplace, and in the society. Some of the examples are:

- Fathers are less likely to get custody of their children in divorce cases, even if they are fit and willing parents. According to a study, 83% of mothers receive custody of their children in divorces.
- Fathers are often expected to pay child support and alimony, but they may not have enough access or contact with their children. According to a report, only 22% of fathers who live apart from their children see them more than once a week.
- Fathers are not given enough parental leave or flexible work arrangements to care for their children, especially in the early years. According to a survey, only 14% of fathers take more than two weeks of paternity leave, and 44% of fathers say they experience work-family conflict.

Fathers are stereotyped as incompetent, absent, or abusive parents, and they face social stigma and prejudice if they choose to be stay-at-home dads or primary caregivers. According to a study, 69% of people agree that a father who stays home to care for children is less of a man.

These forms of discrimination are not only unfair and harmful to fathers, but also to their children, their partners, and society. Children benefit from having a close and positive relationship with both parents, regardless of their marital status or gender. Partners benefit from having a supportive and equal partner who shares the responsibilities and joys of parenting. Society benefits from having a diverse and inclusive culture that values and respects all forms of families and parenting.

Therefore, it is important to challenge and change the discrimination that fathers face and to promote and support the rights and roles of fathers in their families and communities. Some of the ways to do this are:

- Advocating for legal and policy reforms that ensure equal rights and opportunities for fathers in the family courts, such as shared parenting, joint custody, and fair child support.
- Campaigning for better and more flexible parental leave and work arrangements for fathers, such as paid paternity leave, parental leave for fathers, and telecommuting options.
- Educating and raising awareness about the benefits and challenges of fatherhood, and the diversity and complexity of fatherhood experiences, such as through books, documentaries, websites, and support groups.
- Celebrating and honoring the contributions and achievements of fathers, and the positive impact they have on their children, their partners, and society, such as through events, awards, and media.

Could physics one day contribute to the understanding and treatment of mental health issues? Just a theory I have had over recent years.

- Quantitative Analysis: Physics-based techniques such as functional magnetic resonance imaging can be used for quantitative studies of mental health. This could potentially lead to a better understanding of mental illnesses.

- Addressing Systemic Issues: Physicists are also addressing systemic issues within academia that contribute to mental health problems, such as the pressure to publish, the precarity of contracts, and systemic sexism and racism.

However, it's important to note that while physics can provide tools and foster supportive communities, the treatment of mental health issues often requires a multidisciplinary approach, including medical intervention and psychological therapy1. Physics is just one piece of the puzzle in addressing mental health issues. What I do know, is that we have to start looking at different ways in the world of mental health to prevent illnesses from developing in later life, that of course starts during pregnancy.

New dads need to be asked how they are feeling, and they need to be supported and encouraged to share their emotions and concerns. So next time you see a new father, ask him "How Are You Dad".

KEY RECOMMENDATIONS FOR CHANGE: Fathers Reaching Out - Why dads Matter[1,275].

More support for paternal mental health during the perinatal period, in order to assist the father in becoming the best version of himself, ensuring that he is able to provide support for the mother's mental health, as well as protecting against any negative impact that this could have on the child, overall giving rise to better outcomes for the child in the longer term*.

Enquiries into paternal deaths are an important aspect of understanding and addressing the health and well-being of fathers. While maternal mortality has traditionally received more attention, recognizing and addressing paternal deaths can provide valuable insights to improve overall family health outcomes. Just as with MBRRACE-UK's efforts to reduce maternal and infant deaths, it would be beneficial to have similar initiatives focusing on paternal mortality.

Conducting investigations and audits into paternal deaths can help identify the causes and contributing factors, leading to a better understanding of the unique challenges faced by fathers and the potential gaps in current healthcare systems and policies. This information can then be used to develop targeted interventions and strategies to prevent future deaths and improve overall paternal health and well-being.

By highlighting the causes and outcomes of paternal deaths, policymakers and healthcare providers can be encouraged to consider specific measures to address the needs of fathers, including mental health support, access to quality healthcare, education on fatherhood, and involvement in prenatal and postnatal care. This can lead to improved services and policies that better support fathers' health and overall family outcomes.

In summary, conducting inquiries into paternal deaths, similar to the approach taken for maternal deaths, can provide valuable data and insights to inform policies, interventions, and healthcare practices aimed at reducing mortality rates among fathers and improving the overall well-being of families.

The introduction and use of appropriate methods of mental health screening for fathers-to-be/partners during the perinatal period are a significant step towards supporting their emotional well-being. Mental health screening can help identify and address any potential mental health concerns, ensuring that fathers receive the necessary support and treatment they may require.

Integrating mental health screening into routine perinatal care for fathers can have several benefits. Firstly, it increases awareness about the importance of mental health in fathers and encourages open conversations about their emotional well-being. Screening can also help healthcare providers identify symptoms of mood disorders, anxiety, or other mental health conditions early on, enabling timely interventions and support.

Implementing appropriate methods of mental health screening for fathers-to-be/partners should involve validated tools and questionnaires designed specifically for this population. These screening tools should be sensitive to a range of mental health conditions, including depression, anxiety, stress, and adjustment disorders. Additionally, it is crucial to consider cultural and contextual factors that may influence fathers' mental health experiences.

Once screening is conducted, it is essential to ensure there are appropriate resources and referral pathways in place to provide further assessment, support, and treatment if needed. This may include access to mental health professionals, counseling services, support groups, or educational programs tailored to fathers' needs.

By integrating mental health screening into perinatal care for fathers, we can promote early detection and intervention, ultimately improving their well-being and fostering healthier family dynamics. It also helps reduce stigma surrounding men's mental health and encourages a more inclusive approach to perinatal care that acknowledges the significance of paternal mental health.

Specialist mental health services for new fathers are available in all areas of the UK to address the specific mental health needs and challenges they may face during the perinatal period. There are several reasons why these services have been developed and made accessible across the country:

Recognition of the importance of paternal mental health: Research has shown that fathers can also experience mental health difficulties during the perinatal period. It is now widely acknowledged that the well-being of both parents significantly impacts the overall family dynamics and the development of the child. Therefore, there is a growing understanding of the need to provide specialized support for new fathers.

Increasing awareness of men's mental health: Over the years, there has been increasing recognition of men's mental health issues and the importance of addressing them. This awareness has led to a greater focus on providing specialized services and resources specifically tailored to support fathers' mental health needs.

Evolving understanding of gender roles and parenting: Society's understanding of gender roles and parenting has evolved, emphasizing the importance of involving fathers more actively in the perinatal journey. This shift has resulted in a greater recognition of the unique challenges and emotional experiences faced by new fathers, leading to the development of specialized services to support them.

Drive towards holistic and inclusive perinatal care: The field of perinatal mental health has been moving towards a more holistic and inclusive approach that considers the mental health needs of both parents. By ensuring that specialist mental health services for new fathers are available in all areas of the UK, healthcare providers are prioritizing the well-being of fathers and working towards creating more inclusive perinatal care pathways.

Commitment to improving overall family well-being: Providing specialized mental health services for new fathers aligns with the broader goal of improving overall family well-being. By offering comprehensive support to fathers, it contributes to healthier family dynamics, stronger relationships, and better outcomes for both parents and children.

A map of paternal mental health services for new fathers, covering dad-focused antenatal programs, apps, online communities where safeguarding would be assured, and/or sources of information.

The provision of services that concentrate on fathers' emotional needs and ways of managing anger and distress, to help fathers understand and express what they are feeling and to promote other, more positive, ways of coping.

To help address some of these issues, I would like to see[2]:

- Dads-to-be and new dads often seek support networks to share their worries and concerns. While there may not be an extensive list of dads-only support groups across the UK, there are initiatives and organizations that provide support specifically for fathers.
- Specialist mental health services for new fathers are available in all areas of the UK.
- A map of paternal mental health services for new fathers, covering dad-focused antenatal programs, apps, online communities where safeguarding would be assured, and/or sources of information.
- Advocacy services in hospitals which make links with new parents, giving them information on resources and support that are available, but which can be hard to find.

- The provision of services which concentrate on fathers' emotional needs and ways of managing anger and distress to help fathers understand and express what they are feeling and to promote other, more positive, ways of coping.
- Enquiries into paternal deaths, in the same way as MBRRACE-UK68 (Mothers and Babies: Reducing Risk through Audits and Confidential Enquiries across the UK) is reporting on maternal deaths, highlighting causes and outcomes to make policy users consider ways in which they can reduce the deaths of mothers and infants in the future.
- Dads-to-be and new dads often seek support networks to share their worries and concerns. While there may not be an extensive list of dads-only support groups across the UK, there are initiatives and organizations that provide support specifically for fathers.
- Specialist mental health services for new fathers are available in all areas of the UK.
- A map of paternal mental health services for new fathers, covering dad-focused antenatal programs, apps, online communities where safeguarding would be assured, and/or sources of information.
- Advocacy services in hospitals that make links with new parents, giving them information on resources and support that are available, but which can be hard to find.
- The provision of services that concentrate on fathers' emotional needs and ways of managing anger and distress to help fathers understand and express what they are feeling and to promote other, more positive, ways of coping.
- Enquiries into paternal deaths, in the same way as MBRRACE-UK68 (Mothers and Babies: Reducing Risk through Audits and Confidential Enquiries across the UK) is reporting on maternal deaths, highlighting causes and outcomes in order to make policy users consider ways in which they can reduce the deaths of mothers and infants in the future.
- More research and data into the extent to which fathers were struggling with their own mental health during times when Adverse Childhood Experiences (ACEs) have occurred.

- Social media can indeed have a significant impact on parental mental health, especially when parents perceive others' lives as perfect or compare themselves negatively. While further research is needed to fully understand this issue and develop effective strategies, here are some potential ways to tackle the mental health impact of social media:
- Raise awareness: Education and awareness campaigns can be implemented to help parents understand the potential negative impacts of comparing themselves to others on social media. By recognizing that what is portrayed online may not reflect reality, parents may be less likely to feel inadequate or overwhelmed.
- Encourage digital well-being: Promote healthy digital habits by encouraging parents to limit their time spent on social media and engage in activities that promote well-being. This may involve setting boundaries, establishing tech-free times or areas in the home, and finding alternative ways to relax and connect with loved ones.
- Foster supportive online communities: Encouraging the creation of safe and supportive online communities for parents can be beneficial. These communities should focus on sharing authentic experiences, providing emotional support, and offering practical advice. Moderation should be in place to ensure the community remains positive, respectful, and free from harmful comparisons.
- Promote self-compassion: Help parents develop self-compassion by emphasizing that perfection doesn't exist and that it's okay to have struggles. Encourage them to practice self-care, prioritize their well-being, and seek support when needed. This can help reduce the negative impact of social media comparisons and promote a more positive self-image.
- Advocate for responsible social media use: Engage with social media platforms to encourage the development of features that promote well-being, such as easy access to mental health resources or tools for managing screen time. Collaboration between mental health organizations, parenting groups, and social media platforms can contribute to creating healthier online environments.

- Support offline connections: Encourage parents to focus on building and nurturing meaningful relationships in their offline lives. Strengthening connections with family, friends, and local parenting communities can provide additional support, reduce feelings of isolation, and foster a sense of belonging.
- It is important to recognize that tackling the mental health impact of social media requires a multi-faceted approach involving individuals, communities, and society as a whole. Supportive and understanding environments, along with self-care practices, can help parents build resilience and maintain their mental well-being in the face of unrealistic portrayals on social med.
- Raising awareness of perinatal mental health issues in relation to fatherhood is crucial. Here are some information and resources that can be made available in the workplace:
- Educational Materials: Provide pamphlets, brochures, or posters that explain perinatal mental health issues that fathers may face. These materials can include signs and symptoms of mental health problems, risk factors, and ways to seek support.
- Workshops and Training: Organize workshops or training sessions for employees to learn about perinatal mental health issues. Invite mental health professionals or experts to provide insights on how to recognize and address these issues effectively.
- Employee Assistance Programs (EAP): Ensure that EAPs include information, resources, and support for perinatal mental health. EAPs can provide confidential counselling services, access to mental health professionals, and resources for both fathers and their partners.
- Online Resources: Curate a list of reliable online resources specifically tailored to perinatal mental health for fathers. This could include websites, articles, podcasts, or videos that offer guidance, coping strategies, and stories of other fathers' experiences.
- Peer Support Networks: Encourage the formation of peer support networks within the workplace. These networks can provide a safe space for fathers to share their experiences,

exchange advice, and connect with others who may be going through similar challenges.

- Flexible Work Policies: Consider implementing flexible work policies that support fathers during the perinatal period. This can include options for paternity leave, reduced working hours, or remote working arrangements to accommodate their responsibilities and provide necessary support.
- Mental Health Champions: Appoint individuals within the workplace as mental health champions, who can serve as points of contact for employees seeking guidance or support related to perinatal mental health. These champions can undergo training to better understand the unique challenges faced by fathers during this time.
- Collaboration with Community Organizations: Establish partnerships with local organizations focused on perinatal mental health to expand available resources and support for fathers. Collaborate on events, share information, and refer employees to these organizations for additional help if needed.
- Communication Channels: Utilize internal communication channels such as newsletters, intranet portals, or webinars to regularly share information, resources, and success stories related to perinatal mental health. This can help create a culture of openness and support within the workplace.

Remember that creating a supportive workplace environment involves an ongoing effort. By providing information, resources, and support, employers can play a vital role in promoting perinatal mental health awareness among fathers and fostering a more compassionate and understanding workplace culture. (especially considering that, for many men, unaccustomed to or uncomfortable with sharing their feelings/asking for help, this might be the only way for them to do this).

PREPARING FOR AND EDJUSTING TO FATHERHOOD[275]:

- Increased availability of dad-specific/dad-focused resources which enable dads to gain the information that they need in order to be properly prepared for parenthood.

- Greater access to support for both dads (and/or dads-to-be) individually and parents (and/or parents-to-be) as a couple in developing communication skills and other relevant tools which will help them throughout the challenges of the perinatal period.
- Early prevention programmes, covering both the importance of looking after our own mental health and the impact that this can have on our child's development, made available to all parents.
- Advocacy services in hospitals which make links with new parents, giving them information on resources and support that are available, but which can be hard to find.
- An emphasis on educating children on parenthood, perhaps during their final year at school, to help prepare them for their future roles. The provision of better support for new parents/new fathers on how to educate and raise their children with the necessary skills, principles and values to enable them to be the role models for the next generation. Improved engagement and involvement of dads and partners by healthcare professionals throughout the perinatal period with reference to all elements of the antenatal, birth and postnatal experiences.

One reason is the lifestyle changes that often occur after becoming a parent. The demands of caring for a newborn, sleep deprivation, and increased stress levels can disrupt established routines and make it more challenging for fathers to engage in healthy behaviours. This may lead to less physical activity, poor dietary choices, and weight gain over time.

Additionally, the presence of a new baby can impact a father's social life and leisure activities. Fathers may spend less time engaging in activities that promote physical fitness, such as sports or exercise, as they prioritize caregiving responsibilities. This change in routine and reduced opportunities for physical activity can further contribute to an increase in BMI.

It is essential to note that individual experiences may vary, and not all fathers will experience a significant increase in BMI after becoming parents. However, these trends highlight the importance of prioritizing self-care, maintaining a healthy lifestyle, and seeking support when needed.

The provision of information to men about the changes that may occur in their body during the perinatal period. The provision of services which concentrate on fathers' emotional needs and ways of managing anger and distress. This would greatly help fathers to understand and express what they are feeling and to promote other, more positive, ways of coping.

Accessing support:

• More innovative ways of sharing information on the online support groups and sources of information available, so that men who are struggling are more easily able to find and access these.

• More dads-only support groups across the UK, enabling dads-to-be and new dads to seek out and find the support networks that they need in order to share their worries and concerns.

• The development of more online support groups for dads-to-be and new dads.

• Consideration of whether and how organisations and employers can introduce 'back to work' plans for new dads, to ensure that they were able to cope with their workload alongside the pressures and challenges of new fatherhood, specifically during the first year of their baby's life.

• Every parent being asked whether they have been the victim of domestic abuse, with information on support and opportunities for further conversations available for both partners.

To help address some of these issues, I would like to see:

More support for paternal mental health during the perinatal period, in order to assist the father in becoming the best version of himself, ensuring that he is able to provide support for the mother's mental health, as well as protecting against any negative impact that this could have on the child, overall giving rise to better outcomes for the child in the longer term.

Providing more support for paternal mental health during the perinatal period is crucial for ensuring that fathers can become the best versions of themselves, support the mother's mental health, and protect against any negative impact on the child. By prioritizing paternal mental health, we can contribute to better outcomes for the child in the long term.

Research has shown that fathers can experience mental health challenges during the perinatal period, which includes the time before and after the birth of a child. These challenges can range from stress and anxiety to depression and postpartum disorders. It is important to recognize that fathers' mental health is interconnected with the well-being of the entire family, including the mother and child.

By providing support for paternal mental health, we can create an environment where fathers feel empowered, informed, and equipped to navigate the challenges of parenthood. This support can take various forms, including:

• Access to information and resources: Providing fathers with information about perinatal mental health, common challenges, and coping strategies can help them better understand their own experiences and seek appropriate support when needed. Online resources, educational materials, and workshops can be valuable sources of information.

• Mental health screening and assessment: Incorporating mental health screening and assessment for fathers during the perinatal period can help identify those who may be at risk or experiencing mental health difficulties. This can facilitate early intervention and appropriate support.

• Peer support and counselling: Creating spaces for fathers to connect with other fathers who may be going through similar experiences can be beneficial. Peer support groups, counselling services, and helplines specifically tailored for fathers can provide a safe and non-judgmental space for sharing concerns, seeking advice, and receiving emotional support.

• Involvement in antenatal and postnatal care: Encouraging fathers' active involvement in antenatal and postnatal care can foster their sense of connection and responsibility. This can include attending prenatal appointments, participating in parenting classes, and engaging in caregiving activities.

• Workplace support: Recognizing the importance of work-life balance and providing workplace policies that support fathers' involvement in family life can contribute to their overall well-being. Flexible working arrangements, parental leave policies, and employee assistance programs can help fathers manage their responsibilities and prioritize their mental health.

By implementing these measures, we can create a supportive environment that acknowledges the importance of paternal mental health and its impact on the well-being of the entire family. This approach can lead to better outcomes for fathers, mothers, and children in the longer term.

FATHERHOOD AND MENTAL HEALTH[275]

The role of a father continues to be crucial after the postnatal period. Fatherhood can have a significant impact on a man's mental health. The transition to fatherhood can be a joyous time, but it can also bring about stress, anxiety, and changes in mood after the postnatal period. Fatherhood can have a significant impact on a man's mental health. The transition to fatherhood at each stage of the child's life can be a joyous time, but it can also bring about stress, anxiety, and changes in mood.

Mental Health History: If you have a history of mental health issues, fatherhood can potentially exacerbate these challenges and impact your overall well-being. Mental health problems can indeed make daily tasks more challenging.

Parenting is a unique journey for each individual, and there's no one-size-fits-all manual. Each child is different, and what works for one might not work for another. Showing your child love and affection helps them feel secure and valued but may feel different if the father is struggling with his mental health and wants to isolate himself.

Again, the impact on children we have to take into account that father's mental health plays a crucial role in the well-being of his children. When a father is mentally healthy, he is better able to provide emotional support and create a stable environment for his children. Fathers can face significant struggles when their child is unwell throughout their journey and issues that may come up throughout school. Fathers' wellbeing should be looked upon not just in the postnatal period but beyond his journey and that many factors may come into account.

The journey of fatherhood to teenagers is a unique and transformative experience. This is a period of significant growth and change, both physically and emotionally. Fathers need to be prepared to guide their teenagers through these changes, providing support and understanding.

Open and honest communication is crucial during this time. Teenagers are forming their own identities and may have questions or concerns that they need to discuss. That communication may be a breakdown and more feeling of anger and frustration if the father has issues with his mental health.

Teenagers are striving for independence, so it's important for fathers to set clear and consistent boundaries. This helps teenagers understand what is expected of them. When someone is depressed, this may be overwhelming and harder to set these grounds in the first place,

Role Model: Fathers serve as role models for their teenagers. They can influence their teenager's behaviour, attitudes, and beliefs through their own actions. It is clear again; this may affect his role and be aware that many parents are depressed and still can be great role models. Many children have gone into working in these sectors after seeing their parents' struggle.

Emotional Support: Teenagers may experience a range of emotions during this time. Fathers need to provide emotional support and help their teenagers navigate these feelings. Education and Career Guidance: As teenagers start to think about their future, fathers can play a key role in providing advice and guidance about education and career options.

Child Poverty Action Group's annual cost of a child report cost of raising a child to the age of 18 can vary greatly depending on various factors such as location, income, and lifestyle. However, here are some estimates:

In the UK, the average cost of raising a child to 18 was estimated to be £157,562 for a couple and £208,735 for a single parent, including housing and childcare. This equates to

£11,596 a year or £966 a month for a single parent and £8,753 a year or £729 a month for a couple1.

Please note that these are average costs, and the actual cost can vary greatly depending on various factors such as location, lifestyle, and individual circumstances.

It's crucial to pay attention to a father's mental health at all times. Mental health is just as important as physical health children often model their parents' behaviours. This is a well-known concept in psychology known as "social learning theory" which suggests that people, especially children, learn by observing others.

Behavioural Imitation: Children tend to imitate the behaviours they observe in their parents. This can include everything from mannerisms and speech patterns to attitudes and responses to situations. children often model their parents' behaviours, attitudes, and values, and this continues into adulthood and can significantly influence how they behave when they become parents themselves.

Emotional Responses: Children often learn how to express and manage their emotions by watching their parents. For example, if parents handle stress in healthy ways, children are likely to develop similar coping mechanisms. This phenomenon is part of the social learning theory, which suggests that people learn by observing others and how they may parent themselves.

Social Interactions: Parents' interactions with others serve as a model for children's social behaviour. This includes how parents treat family members, friends, and strangers. If the father has become depressed, this may affect how he his seeing the world and that may be taken forward when their children became parents.

Values and Beliefs: Parents' values and beliefs are often passed down to their children through modelling. This includes views on topics like honesty, hard work, and kindness. The way parents were raised often influences their own parenting styles. If their parents were authoritative, they might adopt the same approach. If their parents were permissive or neglectful, they might choose to raise their children differently. Fathers' behaviours again may affect this when feeling depressed.

Health and Lifestyle Habits: Children often adopt health and lifestyle habits from their parents. This includes dietary habits, physical activity levels, and attitudes towards health and wellness. Depression can significantly impact a person's ability to maintain good health habits. Depression often causes fatigue and a lack of energy, which can make it difficult to find the motivation to exercise, prepare healthy meals, or maintain other good health habits.

Remember, while children are heavily influenced by their parents, they are also influenced by other factors such as their peers, teachers, and their own individual experiences. They should be treated with the same level of care and attention. Children tend to imitate the behaviours they observe in their parents, which can include everything from mannerisms and speech.

FATHERS SUPPORT[275]

Errol Murray's experience highlights the challenges many new fathers face. Balancing work and family life can be difficult, especially when there's a long commute involved. The exhaustion from work and travel can limit the quality time spent with the child and affect communication with the partner. This situation is even more challenging when there's a lack of a local support network.

It's important for new parents, like Errol, to seek support when needed. This could be in the form of parenting groups, counseling, or simply reaching out to friends and family. Employers can also play a role by providing flexible working arrangements or parental leave policies that support a better work-life balance. Remember, it's okay to ask for help and take care of your own well-being too. After all, a happy parent makes for a happy child.

Errol set up Leeds Dads is a voluntary organisation based in Leeds, UK, that brings together a diverse community of fathers for social interaction and support[1]. They host various events such as dad walks, meetups, forest school sessions, soft play, and more[1]. Their mission is to inspire dads to take an active parenting role so that they can have a positive impact in strengthening their family unit[2].

Leeds Dads provides a thriving community for dads in Leeds, offering parenting advice, friendship, and wellbeing support. They ensure that dads-to-be and new dads are provided with knowledge and encouragement to have the greatest impact in their children's early years[2]. They also promote positive physical and mental health for dads across the city, through engaging activities for them and their children[275].

In general, fathers may be less likely to talk about their mental health compared to mothers. This is likely due to a variety of societal and cultural factors that can influence how men are socialized to express their emotions. In many cultures, men are expected to embody traditional qualities such as stoicism, emotional neutrality, and self-reliance, and may hesitate to discuss their feelings or ask for help.

However, it's important to note that this is not universal, and many fathers do talk about their mental health and seek support when they need it. There is also a growing awareness and recognition of the importance of mental health among fathers, and more resources and support services are becoming available to help men cope with mental health challenges.

It's important to encourage open and honest conversations about mental health and to normalize seeking help when needed. fathers' mental health is just as important as mothers and seeking help is a sign of strength, not weakness.

In my experience of running hundreds of sessions for fathers, that once one father tends to open up, another one will follow. This opens the groups up to conversations, where they feel safe to do so and tell everyone about their experiences. When I share my experiences at the opening of the group, this tends to help fathers feel that they are not the only ones, and they can be honest and feel less judged.

Bonding and attachment with your baby as a father are crucial for their emotional and cognitive development. Here are some suggestions to help foster bonding and attachment:

- Spend quality time together: Make it a priority to spend one-on-one time with your baby every day. Engage in activities like cuddling, talking, singing, reading, or simply being present and attentive to their needs.
- Participate in caregiving tasks: Take an active role in caring for your baby's basic needs, such as feeding, bathing, and changing diapers. This allows you to establish a routine and create a bond through nurturing.
- Skin-to-skin contact: Practice skin-to-skin contact with your baby. Holding your baby against your bare chest has been shown to promote bonding, regulate their body temperature, and reduce stress for both of you.
- Engage in playtime: Play is a vital part of bonding. Get down on the floor and play with your baby using toys, games, or even just making funny faces. Follow their cues, respond to their gestures and sounds, and create positive interactions.
- Be responsive and attuned: Respond promptly to your baby's needs and cues. By being consistently responsive, you build trust and help them feel secure in your presence. This lays the foundation for a strong attachment.
- Communicate and interact: Talk, sing, and make eye contact with your baby. Your voice, touch, and facial expressions are powerful ways to communicate love and connection. Engaging in positive interactions stimulates brain development and strengthens your bond.
- Take care of yourself: Prioritize self-care to ensure you are emotionally available and present for your baby. Get enough rest, eat well, exercise, and seek support when needed. Taking

care of your own well-being contributes to your ability to form a healthy attachment.

Remember, bonding and attachment take time and may not happen overnight. Be patient, consistent, and flexible as you navigate your unique relationship with your baby. Every interaction counts, no matter how small, and your love and dedication will contribute to building a strong and loving bond over time.

When it comes to paternal mental health services for new fathers in the UK, there are various resources available, including dad-focused antenatal programs, apps, online communities, and sources of information. While a comprehensive map of all these services may not exist, here are some options to consider.

It's important to note that while online communities can provide valuable support, ensuring safeguarding is essential. When seeking online communities or forums, look for platforms that prioritize safety, moderation, and have clear guidelines in place.

Additionally, the NHS and local authorities in the UK are increasingly recognizing the importance of paternal mental health. They are working towards improving services and support for fathers during the perinatal period.

Remember, the availability of specific services may vary depending on your location. It's recommended to explore local resources, speak with healthcare professionals, and reach out to organizations mentioned above for further information and support.

These groups can be found for a range of issues, including mental health, addiction, chronic illness, grief, and many more. Support groups can be facilitated by professionals or led by peers who have experienced similar challenges. Some support groups meet in person, while others may be held virtually or via phone. The purpose of a support group is to provide emotional and social support to its members and empower them to take steps towards overcoming their challenges[275].

- Improved mental health and well-being.
- Reduced feelings of isolation and loneliness.
- Increased self-esteem and self-confidence.

- Learning from others who have similar experiences.
- Gaining new perspectives and insights.
- Access to resources and information.
- Opportunities for personal growth and development.
- Feeling supported and understood.
- Increased sense of belonging and community.
- Ability to cope with difficult situations more effectively.

Overall, support groups provide a safe and supportive environment for individuals to share their thoughts, feelings, and experiences while receiving support, guidance, and encouragement from others who understand.

The frequency of the meetings and the duration of each meeting will depend on the purpose of the discussion group, the availability of the participants, and the resources of the group. Some groups may meet weekly, biweekly, or monthly, and each meeting may last between 30 minutes to several hours.

The meeting place could be a community centre, a coffee shop, a library, or online, depending on the preference and availability of the participants. Virtual meetings can offer the convenience of connecting with people from different locations, but in-person meetings can provide social interaction and a sense of community.

If the meetings are going to be virtual, the best way to communicate will depend on the technology and platform preferred by the participants. Zoom, Facetime, Skype, Google Meet, or other similar tools can be used. The age group and who is welcome to join will depend on the focus and purpose of the discussion group. Some groups may be open to all adults, while others may focus on specific topics or interests[275].

The support group leader can be anyone who has the skills and experience to facilitate the group and encourage participation. Alternatively, a moderator or facilitator can be hired or appointed to lead the group. The meeting can be open or closed, depending on the privacy and comfort level of the participants. Open meetings allow anyone to join at any time, while closed meetings require participants to register and commit to attend regularly.

The group rules and guidelines will depend on the topic and focus of the discussion group. Rules for confidentiality, respect, and active listening are common in most support groups. The number of participants will depend on the purpose and resources of the group. Some groups may benefit from having a small, intimate setting, while others may thrive in larger, diverse groups. Encourage participation.

During the support group meeting, try to encourage participation from all members. Some members may be more vocal than others, so it's important to give everyone a chance to share their thoughts and feelings.

Try to create a safe and non-judgmental environment where members feel comfortable sharing their experiences. Prompt them with open-ended questions and validate their feelings by acknowledging their perspective.

It's important to remember that everyone is on their own journey and may not be at the same place in their healing process. Encourage members to listen to each other and respect differing opinions without judgment. End the meeting with gratitude.

After the meeting, take a moment to appreciate and thank the group members for attending and sharing their time and experiences. It's important to remind them that they're not alone in their struggles and that the support group is a valuable resource for them.

Encourage them to continue attending and participating in future meetings. And don't forget to express your own gratitude for the opportunity to facilitate the support group and be a part of their journey towards healing.

Here are a few more to keep your support group going successfully:

- Foster a safe and inclusive environment: Ensure that everyone feels welcomed and respected in the group. Encourage open communication and establish ground rules to maintain a safe space for sharing.
- Maintain regular meeting schedules: Consistency is key in keeping a support group running. Set a regular meeting schedule and stick to it, allowing members to plan their attendance accordingly.

- Rotate leadership roles: Share the responsibility of facilitating meetings among group members. This not only lightens your load but also encourages active participation and ownership within the group.
- Provide resources and information: Stay informed about relevant resources, articles, books, or workshops related to the topics discussed in your support group. Share these resources with members to enhance their understanding and encourage personal growth.
- Encourage member engagement: Actively involve members in the support group by assigning tasks or roles, such as note-taking or leading discussions on specific topics. This promotes a sense of belonging and increases member investment in the group.
- Offer additional activities or events: Organize occasional social activities or guest speakers to help members connect outside of regular meetings. This can strengthen the sense of community within the group and provide opportunities for further support and learning.
- Adapt to changing needs: Evaluate the needs of your support group regularly and be willing to adapt your approach based on feedback and evolving circumstances. This flexibility ensures that the group remains relevant and beneficial to its members.
- Remember, the success of a support group relies on the collective effort of its members and facilitators. By creating a nurturing environment, encouraging engagement, and adapting as needed, you can help your support group thrive.

Starting and running a support group can be challenging and requires a significant amount of effort and organization. It's important to recognize the administrative work involved, such as scheduling meetings, maintaining communication with group members, and ensuring a positive and inclusive atmosphere. Giving up after a few meetings is common for many who attempt to start their own support groups without fully understanding the commitment involved.

Joining an established support group, whether in-person or online, can be a great alternative. It allows you to benefit from the expertise and experience of others while focusing on your own personal growth. Exploring existing support groups, like the free support groups offered by Men's Group, can provide you with a supportive community and the opportunity to connect with others who share similar experiences and challenges.

Ultimately, whether you choose to start your own support group or join an existing one, it's crucial to consider the effort and commitment required to ensure its success.

Dialectical behaviour therapy[2]

(DBT) is a type of talking therapy that helps people who feel emotions very intensely. It is based on cognitive behavioural therapy (CBT), but it also focuses on accepting who you are at the same time. DBT teaches you skills to manage your emotions, cope with stress, and improve your relationships. DBT can help with problems like self-harm, suicide attempts, depression, and borderline personality disorder (BPD

DBT usually involves both individual and group sessions. In individual sessions, you work with a therapist to identify and change unhelpful thoughts and behaviours. In group sessions, you learn and practice skills such as mindfulness, distress tolerance, emotion regulation, and interpersonal effectiveness. You may also have phone coaching from your therapist between sessions to help you apply the skills in your daily life.

Cognitive behavioural therapy[2]

(CBT) is a type of talking therapy that aims to help you manage problems by changing how you think and act. Trauma-focused CBT uses a range of psychological techniques to help you come to terms with the traumatic event.

For example, your therapist may ask you to face your traumatic memories by describing aspects of your experience in detail. During this process, your therapist helps you cope with any distress you feel while identifying any beliefs you have about the experience that may be unhelpful.

Your therapist can help you gain control of your fear and distress by reviewing with you any conclusions you have drawn about your experience (for example, feeling you're to blame for what happened, or fear that it may happen again).

You may also be encouraged to gradually restart any activities you have avoided since your experience, such as driving a car if you had an accident.

You'll usually have eight to twelve weekly sessions of trauma-focused CBT, although fewer may be needed. Sessions usually last for around sixty to ninety minutes.

Eye movement desensitisation and reprocessing[2]

(EMDR) is a psychological treatment that's been found to reduce the symptoms of PTSD. It involves recalling the traumatic incident in detail while making eye movements, usually by following the movement of your therapist's finger.

Other methods may include the therapist tapping their finger or playing sounds. It's not clear exactly how EMDR works, but it may help you change the negative way you think about a traumatic experience.

Psychodynamic psychotherapy involves talking more about how your past influences what happens in the present and the choices you make. It tends to last longer than CBT and counselling. Sessions are an hour long and can continue for a year or more.

There are different types of psychodynamic psychotherapy, but they all aim to help you understand more about yourself, improve your relationships, and get more out of life. Psychodynamic psychotherapy can be especially useful for people with long-term or recurring problems to find the cause of their difficulties.

There's some evidence that psychodynamic psychotherapy can help depression and some eating disorders. NHS psychodynamic psychotherapists normally work in a hospital or clinic, where you'll see them as an outpatient. Private psychodynamic psychotherapists often work from home.

Family therapy, a therapist (or pair of therapists) works with the whole family. The therapist explores their views and relationships to understand the problems the family is having. It helps family members communicate better with each other.

Sessions can last from forty-five minutes to an hour and a half, and usually take place several weeks apart. You may be offered family therapy if the whole family is in difficulty. This may be because one member of the family has a serious problem that's affecting the rest of the family. Family therapists deal with lots of different issues, including:

- Child and adolescent behavioural problems
- Mental health conditions, illness, and disability in the family
- Separation, divorce, and stepfamily life
- Domestic violence
- Drug addiction or alcohol addiction

Relationship counselling[2]

Relationship counselling, or couples therapy, can help when a relationship is in crisis (after an affair, for example). Both partners talk in confidence to a counsellor or therapist to explore what has gone wrong in the relationship and how to change things for the better. It can help couples learn more about each other's needs and communicate better.

Ideally, both partners should attend the weekly hour-long sessions, but they can still help if just one person attends. Yes, relationship counselling can help couples communicate better and resolve their conflicts. According to the British Association for Counselling and Psychotherapy (BACP), relationship counselling can help improve the way you relate to those around you and allow you to break free from old patterns of behaviour[3]. Counsellors can provide a supportive and non-judgmental environment to help you identify issues or problems in a relationship and find a way through those difficulties[3].

Relationship counselling can also help you understand your own and your partner's feelings and needs, and how they affect your relationship. You can learn to express your emotions and thoughts more clearly and constructively, and to listen to your partner more attentively and empathically[1]. Relationship counselling can also help you cope with difficult life events, such as bereavement, illness, or separation, that can put a strain on your relationship.

If you are interested in relationship counselling, you can find a qualified and experienced counsellor who can help you with your specific situation on the BACP website[3]. You can also talk to your GP or a local NHS talking therapies service[2] to find out more about the options and benefits of relationship counselling.

Group therapy[2]

In group therapy, up to around twelve people meet, together with a therapist. It's a useful way for people who share a common problem to get support and advice from each other. It can help

you realize you're not alone in your experiences, which is itself beneficial.
Dads Group therapy is a form of psychotherapy that involves one or more therapists working with a small group of people who share similar issues or goals. Group therapy can help dads to learn from each other, support each other, and improve their mental health and well-being.
Some people prefer to be part of a group or find that it suits them better than individual therapy.

Interpersonal therapy[2]

This is a talking treatment that helps people with depression to identify and address problems in their relationships with family, partners, and friends.
Behavioural activation is a talking therapy that encourages people to develop more positive behaviours, such as planning activities and doing constructive things that they would usually avoid doing.
Interpersonal therapy is a type of psychotherapy that focuses on improving your relationships and social interactions. It can help you cope with mental health conditions such as depression, anxiety, and post-traumatic stress disorder (PTSD) by helping you understand and change how you think and feel about yourself and others. Interpersonal therapy usually lasts for 12 to 16 sessions, and each session is about an hour long.
Identifying the main interpersonal problems that are affecting your mental health, such as grief, role transitions, interpersonal disputes, or social isolation. Exploring how your emotions, thoughts, and behaviours are influenced by your interpersonal problems, and how they affect your relationships in return. Setting goals and strategies to improve your interpersonal skills and resolve your interpersonal problems. Practicing new ways of communicating and relating to others and getting feedback from your therapist. Reviewing your progress and achievements and planning for the future[13].
Interpersonal therapy can help you develop a better sense of yourself and your needs and enhance your ability to connect and

communicate with others. It can also help you cope with stress, improve your mood, and increase your self-esteem.

Mindfulness-based therapies[2]

Mindfulness-based therapies help you focus on your thoughts and feelings without becoming overwhelmed by them. They can be used to help treat depression, stress, anxiety, and addiction.
Mindfulness-based stress reduction (MBSR) incorporates techniques such as meditation, gentle yoga, and mind-body exercises to help people learn how to cope with stress.
Mindfulness-based cognitive therapy (MBCT) combines mindfulness techniques like meditation and breathing exercises with cognitive therapy. The National Institute for Health and Care Excellence (NICE) recommends MBCT to help people avoid repeated bouts of depression.

Art therapy

What is Art Therapy?: Art therapy is a technique rooted in the idea that creative expression can foster healing and mental well-being1. It is a tool therapists use to help patients interpret, express, and resolve their emotions and thoughts.

How Does it Work?: Patients work with an art therapist to explore their emotions, understand conflicts or feelings that are causing them distress, and use art to help them find resolutions to those issues. The creation or appreciation of art is used to help people explore emotions, develop self-awareness, cope with stress, boost self-esteem, and work on social skills.

Gayle Berry Book "Fathers Light" explains that Fatherhood is an emotional transition for men and yet it often is not treated in this way. Feelings around fatherhood are not shared in the same way as feelings around motherhood. Many men enter into the unknown without a guide, feeling lost and alone. When a father shares his experience, it enables vulnerability, honesty, growth and reflection. This collection of poems has been written by fathers from all over the world. They have opened their hearts to share their experiences of journeying with their children and navigating the joys and challenges of fatherhood.

USEFUL ORGANISATIONS IN THE UK[275]

There are many organisations that support fathers, very few when it comes to their mental health. There are some areas that can provide extra support thought the groups such as Leeds Dads and Dads in Mind part of bluebells in Bristol.

Listed below are some organisations that I have found to offer good help and support to dads and men across the UK. Please note, though, that this is not an exhaustive list:

Birth Trauma Association: Provides support for anyone affected by birth trauma, including partners.

The Hub of Hope is a mental health support database that brings together local, national, peer, community, charity, private and NHS mental health support and services in one place for the first time.

Dads House: This organization supports single fathers and their children. They offer a range of services including a community food bank, drug and alcohol testing, and a cost-of-living crisis support.

Families Need Fathers (FNF): FNF is a leading UK charity that has been supporting dads, mums, and grandparents to have personal contact and meaningful relationships with their children following parental separation since 1974.

Fathers Institute – The Fatherhood Institute is a UK charity working to build a society that values, prepares, and supports men as involved fathers and caregivers. Our work focuses on research, policy and other areas of fatherhood.

Fathers Network Scotland - Fathers Network Scotland is a charity that aims to improve children's lives through the positive involvement of dads, father-figures and whole families.

The DadPad is for all fathers who want to give their child the very best start in life. Whether he is about to become a first-time dad or wants to ensure that he can still cover all the bases with a new addition to the family, the DadPad is the low-cost, high-value resource that dad will want to always have within arm's reach.

Dad Matters: This organization provides support for dads, including resources for improving access to services and help with job search, training, and employment.

NAPAC: The National Association for People Abused in Childhood (NAPAC) offers support to adult survivors of all forms of child abuse. They provide a free, confidential support line.

Supporting Male Victims: The UK government has a policy paper on supporting male victims of crimes that fall within the violence against women and girl's space.

Men's Advice Line: This is a confidential helpline for male victims of domestic abuse. They offer non-judgmental information and support.

Mankind: Another resource for male victims of domestic abuse.

Rape Crisis England and Wales: They run a rape and sexual abuse support line.

Autistic Parents UK: This is an Autistic-led Charity (CIO) committed to supporting Autistic parents in a number of ways. They offer online peer support groups (larger and smaller groups), monthly webinars and live Q&A sessions, monthly book giveaways, local peer support groups, volunteer-led one to one peer support sessions, and professional training.

National Autistic Society: They provide guides for navigating family relationships, and advice for parents, siblings, and children on how to support their autistic family member[2]. They also have a collection of useful resources to download, including cards to let people know that you, your child or somebody you are with is autistic, and that some extra time in certain situations might be helpful.

Teenage mothers and young fathers: support framework: This framework helps local healthcare commissioners and service providers review support arrangements for young parents in their area.

Young Fathers - Young Parents Advice: This page covers five key things that young fathers may need to understand and think about when children's services become involved with their child.

Young Dads Collective: The Young Dads Collective (YDC) works to improve the lives of young dads and their children by tackling the social exclusion that locks out young dads' potential.

Men's Mental Health Groups in UK

Andy's Man Club is a UK charitable organisation that provides a safe environment for men to come together and talk about issues and problems they have faced or are currently. There's no referral, no registration, and no charge. Even the brew and biscuits are free.! They have over 100 free support groups nationwide. regardless of age, circumstances, or experiences.

Talk Club: Talk Club is a UK male mental health charity that helps men improve their mental health. They offer peer-to-peer talking groups, talking therapies, and business support.

Mental Health Foundation: The Mental Health Foundation provides information and resources on men's mental health.

Men's Group UK: Men's Group UK offers various sub-groups that address specific needs such as depression, addiction, chronic pain, social anxiety, and more.
Remember, it's okay to seek help and connect with others who are in the same situation. These groups can provide valuable

advice, support, and a sense of community. Don't hesitate to reach out to them.

Perinatal Mental Health Support

Perinatal mental health services are crucial in supporting pregnant women and new mothers. In the UK, the NHS provides a range of services to support perinatal mental health.

Specialist Perinatal Mental Health (PMH) Services: These services provide care and treatment for women with complex mental health needs during the perinatal period. They also support the developing relationship between parent and baby and offer advice for planning a pregnancy.

Maternal Mental Health Services: The NHS has set up these services, which combine maternity, reproductive health, and psychological therapy for women. They provide critical care for women whose mental health suffers after experiencing birth trauma or baby loss.

Community Care: The NHS aims to ensure that by 2023/24, at least 66,000 women with moderate/complex to severe PMH difficulties can access care and support in the community.

The Breastfeeding Network: Offers nationwide support about breastfeeding and perinatal mental health.

The Maternal Mental Health Alliance UK is a charity and network of over 100 organisations that aims to improve the mental health and wellbeing of women and their families during pregnancy and the first postnatal year. It works through awareness, education and action, and campaigns for equitable access to high quality services for women with, or at high risk of, perinatal mental health problems.

Action on Postpartum Psychosis (APP) is a national charity that supports and advocates for mums and families affected by postpartum psychosis (PP), a severe but treatable mental illness that begins in the days and weeks after giving birth.

Acknowledgements

First, I want to say thank you to all the parents I have spoken with over the years, we put their trust in me and wanted me to be a voice for their concerns. It has been an honour to speak up on their behalf while gaining the education to write this book. There are so many people to thank when it comes to supporting me on the journey and without missing anyone out, I would like to say thanks for everything, and you know who you are. Last my wife, Michelle who has supported me when there were times, I just wanted to give up mostly in the early years and turned down paid roles to earn far less money to continue the fight for parents. My friends and Family who are always there for us, I'm blessed to have so many closes friends that are always there for me. Last my son Ethan, who without you coming into this world, we wouldn't have helped so many families. I brought purpose into my life, being a father and loved every minute so far.

Selected Bibliography for Mark Williams (275)

Publications

• Daddy Blues– Trigger Publishing

• Fathers and Perinatal Mental Health: A Guide for Recognition, Treatment and Management– Routledge (co-authored with Dr Jane Hanley)

Supporting Parents and Families with Perinatal Mental Health: A Guide for Professionals - Jessica Kingsley Publishers (co-authored with Dr Jane Hanley)

Unconventional – Publish Nation

Journals

• Father's Reaching Out: Postnatal depression support for partners – Journal of Health

Visiting (2013)

• Fathers Reaching Out – Midwives (2013)

• Meeting the mental health needs of new fathers – Nursing Times (2016) Hanley, J and Williams, M (2020).

• Assessing and managing paternal mental health issues – Nursing Times (2017) Hanley, J and Williams, M (2020).

• An insider perspective on the NHS England decision to screen fathers for depression – Williams, M

Australian Fatherhood Research Bulletin (2019) Williams, M

• The Importance of Fathers Mental Health – EC Psychology and Psychiatry (2019)

• Fathers' perinatal mental health – British Journal of Midwifery (2020) Hanley, J and Williams, M (2020).

• What is the risk of perinatal anxiety and depression if you have ADHD Midwifery Forum 203(12), 2023

A Father and Partner's Guide to Support Through Pregnancy and Beyond – All4Birth M Williams

M Williams All4Birth, 2 2022 How Are You Dad - In the labor ward

International Education of Parents Journal. Postnatal Depression and Father's. Postnatal Depression and Father's M Williams 2019

Fathers and Listening Visits. M Williams Listening Visits in Perinatal Mental Health -Chapter 5, 69-76

National Press

The Guardian, The Telegraph, Metro, The Mirror, The Irish Times, The Express, The Daily, Metro,
Mail, The Independent and overseas publications

Television Appearances
BBC Breakfast, ITV Good Morning Britain, BBC 2 Victoria Derbyshire,
Sky News, Channel 5, Today (US) BBC/ITV Wales News, GB News, Channel 4 and The Mental Health show.

Radio Appearances
BBC Radio 4: Woman's Hour, World Service BBC Radio 5, BBC Radio 2: Jeremy Vine Show
BBC local radio: Wales; Scotland; Berkshire; Bristol; Humberside; Lincolnshire; London. Manchester,
Manchester; Norfolk; Nottingham; Three Counties; Shropshire; Solent; Stoke; Surrey; Tees.
Wiltshire, Independent radio: Heart; LBC; Talk Sport
Non-UK radio stations in: Australia; Brazil; Canada; Columbia, USA; Germany; Finland, Ireland; New
Zealand; and Zimbabwe

Appearances in Television and Radio Documentaries
• 2014: "Our Stories", with Denise Welch
• 2014: "My secret past: My post-baby breakdown", Channel 5 with Jennifer Ellison
• 2016: "My Parental Pain", by Alexandra Gatenby [shortlisted in the Mind Media Awards
Student Journalist category 2016120]
• 2019: "Fathers on the edge", by Rosie Dowsing [awarded the Mind Media Awards
Student Journalist 2019122]
• 2019: BBC Radio 4's "Dads and the Delivery Room"
2021: Daddy Blues Film by Parvinder Shergill. Amazon Prime

Magazine and Online Features

• I'm a Dad Who Suffered Postnatal Depression – happiful (2017)
• One Man's Story Of Suffering From Male Postnatal Depression – ELLE (2017)
• Conference one-to-one: how are you, dad? – Community Practitioner (2018)
• Mental health doesn't have a gender – Motherdom (2019)
Suffering in Silence: The Dads Dealing with Birth Trauma – Men's Health
Male postnatal depression: Why men struggle in silence BBC.
Postnatal depression in dads: 'I didn't know men could struggle too – BBC.
'It's OK not to be OK': Fathers reveal their experience of postnatal depression- ITV.
Huffington Post – PTSD is common in Fathers.

Book Contributions
DAD: Untold stories of Fatherhood, Love, Mental Health and Masculinity
Let's talk about the first year of parenting (New Parents)
The New Dad's Survival Guide: What to Expect in the First Year and Beyond
Mark has contributed to over twenty books at time of writing this book.

TEDx Talk
The Importance of father's mental health.

References

(1) Fathers Reaching Out – Why Dads Matter
(2) Fathers and Perinatal Mental Health Book (Routledge, J Hanley, M Williams)
(3)Nhs.uk/mental-health/conditions/post-natal-depression/overview.
(4) Sad dads: paternal postpartum depression
(5) When Fathers Begin to Falter: A Comprehensive Review on Paternal Perinatal Depression

(6) Healthyplace.com/other-info/mental-illness-overview/the-history-of-mental-illness
(7) Sciencemuseum.org.uk/objects-and-stories/mental-health.
(8)gingerbread.org.uk/find-information/parenting-perspectives/single-dads/
(9) whatadad.org-/2023/06/how-stay-at-home-dads-cope/
(10)psychologytoday.com/intl/blog/the-baby-scientist/202306/why-so-many-lgbtq-families-are-thriving
(11) sdlgbtn.com/children-of-gay-couples-how-to-choose-what-to-call-your-parents/
(12) The changing role of the modern-day father. https://www.apa.org/pi/families/resources/changing-father.
(13) Fatherhood In the Past And Fatherhood Today; What Changed?
(14) The Changing Role of Fathers In The Last Thirty Years.
(15) History of Fatherhood during the Nineteenth and Twentieth ... - EHNE. ehne.fr/en/encyclopedia/themes/gender-and-europe/demographic-transition-sexual-revolutions/history-fatherhood-during-nineteenth-and-twentieth centuries.
(16) britannica.com/event/womens-movement
(17) BBC News - Should dads be in the delivery room? http://news.bbc.co.uk/2/hi/8377099.stm.
(18) Midwifery Today Michel Odent the heart and science of birth. https://www.midwiferytoday.com/speakers/michel-odent/.
(19) The first male nurses | Nursing History Now - Royal College of Nursing. rcn.org.uk/magazines/History/2020/Nursing-History-Now-first-men-nurses-on-register.
(20) ihv.org.uk/about-us/history-of-health-visiting
(21) Fathers across cultures: The importance, roles, and diverse practices .... https://psycnet.apa.org/record/2015-46469-000.
(22) An Anthropology of Dads: Exploring fatherhood in eHRAF. hraf.yale.edu/an-anthropology-of-dads-exploring-fatherhood-in-ehraf/
(23)rf.org.uk/report/understanding-fathering-masculinity-diversity-and-change
(24)childpsychotherapy.org.uk/resources-families/understanding-childhood/fathers-understanding-vital-role-fathers-father-figures

(25) bps.org.uk/psychologist/focus-fathers-child-mental-health-interventions
(26) Mental Health Stigma | Psychology Today. https://www.psychologytoday.com/us/basics/mental-health-stigma.
(27) Stigma around mental health - Mind. https://www.mind.org.uk/information-support/types-of-mental-health-problems/mental-health-problems-introduction/stigma-misconceptions/.
(28) Stigma and discrimination | Mental Health Foundation. mentalhealth.org.uk/explore-mental-health/a-z-topics/stigma-and-discrimination.
(29) ACP - Fathers - Understanding the Vital Role That Fathers, & Father Figures, Play in Children's Emotional Development
(30) "What Can I Do to Not Have This Life"? A Qualitative Study of Paternal Postnatal Depression Experiences among Fathers in the United Kingdom.
(31)Mentalhealth-uk.org/help-and-information/conditions/anxiety-disorders/types.
(32)NHS.uk/mental-health/conditions/generalised-anxiety-disorder/overview.
(33) WHO.int/newsroom/factsheets/detail/anxiety-disorders.
(34) Prevalence and course of anxiety disorders (and symptom levels) in men across the perinatal period: A systematic review.
(35) Bps.org.uk/psychologist/psychological-plan-perinatal-care
(36) raisingchildren.net.au/pregnancy/health-wellbeing/mental-health/antenatal-postnatal-anxiety
(37)bmcpregnancychildbirth.biomedcentral.com/articles/10.1186/s12884-021-04188-4
(38) Introduction to the Analytical Methodologies for the Analysis of Microplastics.
(39)Nichd.nih.gov/health/topics/preconceptioncare/conditioninfo/stress.
(40) Medicalnewstoday.com/articles/how-much-stress-is-too-much-when-pregnant.
(41) Ohsu.edu/school-of-medicine/moore-institute/stress-and-placenta

(42)Britishjournalofmidwifery.com/content/research/subsequent-childbirth-after-previous-traumatic-birth-experience-womens-choices-and-evaluatios.
(43)Mentalhealth.org.uk/explore-mental-health/publications/becoming-dad.
(44) nationalelfservice.net/populations-and-settings/perinatal-mental-health/perinatal-mental-health-problems-in-fathers-are-common-and-legitimate-but-we-need-better-ways-to-reach-and-help-them/
(45)bmcpregnancychildbirth.biomedcentral.com/counter/pdf/10.1186/s12884-017-1229-4.pdf
(46) who.int/newsroom/fact-sheets/detail/mental-disorders
(47)cambridge.org/core/journals/the-british-journal-of-psychiatry/article/prevalence-of-antenatal-and-postnatal-anxiety-systematic-review-and-metaanalysis
(48) Anxiety among fathers is higher than recently reported, new study suggests. https://medicalxpress.com/news/2021-04-anxiety-fathers-higher.html.
(49) Anxiety among fathers is higher than recently reported, new study suggests. https://medicalxpress.com/news/2021-04-anxiety-fathers-higher.pdf.
(50) A narrative review of the relationship between parenting and anxiety .... .tandfonline.com/doi/pdf/10.1080/02673843.2021.1980067.
(51) lordslibrary.parliament.uk/coroners-determination-of-suicide-bill
(52) bps.org.uk/psychologist/dads-get-sad-too
(53) Mentalhealth.bmj.com/content/25/4/148
(54) who.int/data/gho/data/themes/mental-health/suicide-rates
(55) Why Do Some Dads Faint During a Delivery? [HELPFUL TIPS]. https://fatherresource.org/dad-faints-during-a-delivery/.
(56) Are dads a help or a hindrance in the labour ward - Irish Examiner. https://www.irishexaminer.com/lifestyle/arid-20249485.html.
(57) Maternity ward dads: Kick them out or welcome them in? https://www.bbc.co.uk/news/uk-scotland-51234420.
(58) Tips for Dads in the Delivery Room (Like How to Not Pass Out). https://www.motherrisingbirth.com/2019/04/tips-for-dads-in-the-delivery-room.html.

(59) Identifying individuals with undiagnosed post-traumatic stressdisorder.bmcpsychiatry.biomedcentral.com/articles/10.1186/s12888-022-04267-6.
(60) PTSD Differential Diagnosis: Is It PSTD or Something Else? - Psych Central. https://psychcentral.com/ptsd/differential-diagnosis-of-ptsd-symptoms.
(61) fatherhoodinstitute.org/
(62) bmjopen.bmj.com/content/9/9/e030792
(63)myscience.ca/en/news/wire/high_rates_of_postpartum_depression_and_anxiety_in_canadian_fathers-2022-utoronto
(64) neurosciencenews.com/paternal-child-depression-20975/
(65) frontiersin.org/articles/10.3389/fpsyg.2022.1044664/full
(66)prism.ucalgary.ca/server/api/core/bitstreams/3c0b6850-44be-4588-bf7e-ee0dee39249c/content
(67)bmcpregnancychildbirth.biomedcentral.com/articles/10.1186/s12884-021-03657-0
(68)bmcpregnancychildbirth.biomedcentral.com/articles/10.1186/s12884-020-03228-9
(69) jomh.org/articles/10.31083/jomh.v17i1.324
(70)familyincluded.com/postnatal-depression-fathers-relationship-families-china/
(71)academic.oup.com/bmb/article/101/1/57/26216e
(72) Father involvement, maternal depression and child nutritional outcomes in Soweto, South Africa
(73) Postnatal depression and its effects on child development: a review of evidence from low- and middle-income countries
(74) Screening fathers for postpartum depression in a maternal-child health clinic: a program evaluation in a midwest urban academic medical center.
(75) African Journal of Primary Health Care & Family Medicine
(76)bmcpregnancychildbirth.biomedcentral.com/articles/10.1186/s12884-023-05966-y
(77) Epidemiology of postnatal depression and its associated factors in Africa: A systematic review and meta-analysis
(78) onlinelibrary.wiley.com/doi/pdf/10.1111/mcn.13177
(79) Postpartum depression in mothers and fathers: a structural equation model
(80) Paternal Postnatal Depression Among Fathers of Newborn in Saudi Arabia

(81) link.springer.com/chapter/10.1007/978-3-030-56499-5_9
(82)sciencenorway.no/depression-mental-health-pregnancy/a-mothers-postnatal-depression-can-be-passed-on-to-the-father/1777874
(83)link.springer.com/chapter/10.1007/978-3-030-56499-5_9
(84) bmjopen.bmj.com/content/13/1/e063391
(85)bmcpregnancychildbirth.biomedcentral.com/articles/10.1186/s12884-023-05966-y
(86)publications.aap.org/pediatrics/article/145/1/e20191193/36978/A-Call-to-Action-Screening-Fathers-for-Perinatal?autologincheck=redirected
(87)bmcpregnancychildbirth.biomedcentral.com/articles/10.1186/1471-2393-12-75
(88) Supporting women who develop poor postnatal mental health: what support do fathers receive to support their partner and their own mental health?
(89) sciencedaily.com/releases/2017/09/170905145535.htm
(90) bmjopen.bmj.com/content/9/1/e024803
(91) article, fathering factors – 12/2018
(92) Parents' mental health affected by neonatal care
By Julie Griffiths on 20 July 2018
(93) Neonatal care: parents may need long-term psychological support evidence.nihr.ac.uk
(94) link.springer.com/article/10.1007/s10880-022-09902-8
(95) link.springer.com/article/10.1007/s11089-023-01098-4
(96).rcm.org.uk/news-views/news/parents-mental-health-affected-by-neonatal-care/
(97)evidence.nihr.ac.uk/alert/neonatal-care-parents-may-need-long-term-psychological-support/
(98) Miscarriage information and support - for dads and partners - Tommy's. https://www.tommys.org/baby-loss-support/dads-and-partners/miscarriage-support.
(99) Baby Loss and Mental Health: for Dads and Partners | Tommy's. https://www.tommys.org/baby-loss-support/dads-and-partners/your-mental-health-and-wellbeing-after-loss.
(100) Miscarriage and Perinatal Loss – Dad Matters. https://dadmatters.org.uk/loss/.
(101) Miscarriage - Afterwards - NHS. /conditions/miscarriage/afterwards/

(102)/Sad-Dad-Exploration-Postnatal-Depression/dp/185343230X
(103) .goodreads.com/book/show/21892329-
(104)england.nhs.uk/wp-content/uploads/2021/03/Good-practice-guide-March-2021.pdf
(105) /path-perinatal.eu/uk/professionals-page/
(106)hee.nhs.uk/sites/default/files/documents0Perinatal.pdf
(107)pmhn.scot.nhs.uk/wp-content/uploads/2020/08/Role-definitions-Part-1.pdf
(108)oxfordhealthbrc.nihr.ac.uk/our-work/oxppl/pregnancy-and-the-perinatal-period/
(109)Wellbeing article 1-1225,2021
(110)nhs.uk/mental-health/self-help/tips-and-support/mindfulness
(111) Parents' mental health affected by neonatal care - RCM. https://www.rcm.org.uk/news-views/news/parents-mental-health-affected-by-neonatal-care/.
(112) Neonatal care: parents may need long-term support - NIHR Evidence. https://evidence.nihr.ac.uk/alert/neonatal-care-parents-may-need-long-term-psychological-support/.
(113) Mental wellbeing support on the neonatal intensive care unit (NICU). https://www.uhs.nhs.uk/Media/UHS-website-2019/Patientinformation/Neonatal/Mental-wellbeing-support-on-the-neonatal-intensive-care-unit-NICU-2291-PIL.pdf.
(114) 45 percent of parents experience depression, anxiety and ... - ScienceDaily. sciencedaily.com/releases/2017/09/170915095203.htm.
(115) bmjopen.bmj.com/content/9/1/e02487-8
(116) Social services and your family | Family Lives. familylives.org.uk/advice/your-family/social-services-and-your-family/social-services-and-your-family.
(117)tommys.org/pregnancy-information/im-pregnant/mental-wellbeing/tokophobia-fear-giving-birth
(118) verywellmind.com/tokophobia-overview-4684507
(119)nct.org.uk/pregnancy/how-you-might-be-feeling/fear-childbirth-and-tokophobia
(120) The Paternal Experience of Fear of Childbirth: An Integrative Review - MDPI. https://www.mdpi.com/1660-4601/18/3/1231.

(121) The effect of midwifery-led counseling on expectant fathers' fear of .... bmcpregnancychildbirth.biomedcentral.com/articles/10.1186/s12884-022-04638-7.
(122)healthline.com/health/mental-health/time-anxiety
(123)my.clevelandclinic.org/health/diseases/22579-chronophobia-fear-of-time
(124) choosingtherapy.com/time-anxiety/
(125) Can Lack of Sleep Cause Symptoms of Psychosis? - Psych Central. https://psychcentral.com/health/sleep-deprivation-psychosis.
(126) Sleep Deprivation & Psychosis: What's The Connection? - Mind Diagnostics. https://www.mind-diagnostics.org/blog/psychosis/sleep-deprivation-psychosis-whats-the-connection.
(127) bmjopen.bmj.com/content/bmjopen/9/9/e030792.full.pdf
(128) https://bmjopen.bmj.com/content/9/1/e024803
(129) Fatherhood Institute Research Summary: FATHERS AND POSTNATAL DEPRESSION.fatherhoodinstitute.org/2018/fatherhood-institute-research-summary-fathers-and-postnatal-depression/.
(130) Supporting women who develop poor postnatal mental health: what support ...
(131) Paternal Post-Natal Depression - IT Medical Team. itmedicalteam.pl/articles/paternal-postnatal-depression.pdf.
(132) Postnatal depression and fatherhood – what is the fathers' role? bristol.ac.uk/blackwell/funding/case-studies/2018/postnatal-depression-and-fatherhood.html.
(133)bmcpregnancychildbirth.biomedcentral.com/articles/10.1186/s12884-022-04392-w
(134) gh.bmj.com/content/8/Suppl_2/e011086
(135)nct.org.uk/life-parent/your-relationship-couple/relationship-changes/changes-your-relationships-after-having-baby
(136) orcid.org/0000-0003-0743-7208
(137)rcm.org.uk/media/2358/pressure-points-postnatal-care-planning.pdf
(138) creativecommons.org/licenses/by/3.0/igo/

(139)familylaw.co.uk/news_and_comment/should-children-spend-equal-time-with-each-parent-as-the-starting-point
(140fnf.org.uk/news-events-2/press-releases/167-press-releases
(141) htheconversation.com/the-myth-of-the-fatherless-society-73166
(142)www.shoutoutuk.org/2020/06/25/the-famine-of-fatherlessness/
(143)spectator.co.uk/article/rod-liddle-is-right-about-black-boys-and-absent-dads/
(144) New parents face up to six years of sleep deprivation, study says.
https://www.theguardian.com/lifeandstyle/2019/feb/26/parenthood-sleep-deprivation-after-birth-mothers-hit-hardest-research.
(145) Exactly how bad is long-term sleep deprivation for the health of new .... https://www.independent.co.uk/life-style/health-and-families/sleep-one-rem-b1941646.html.
(146) How to cope with sleep deprivation when you have a newborn. https://www.babycenter.com/baby/newborn-baby/sleep-deprivation_7750.
(147) Effective Strategies for Managing Lack of Sleep Postpartum | Sleep.com. sleep.com/sleep-health/postpartum-depression-and-sleep.
(148)fqmagazine.co.uk/being-dad/item/105-biggest-myths-fatherhood-busted
(149) babycentre.co.uk/a539837/five-myths-of-fatherhood
(150) opus.lib.uts.edu.au/handle/10453/133110
(151) europepmc.org/article/MED/30289768
(152) /creativecommons.org/licenses/by/4.0/
(153)kclpure.kcl.ac.uk/portal/en/publications/mental-health-and-wellbeing-during-the-transition-to-fatherhood-a
(154) Supporting women who develop poor postnatal mental health: what support do fathers receive to support their partner and their own mental health?
(155)bmcpregnancychildbirth.biomedcentral.com/counter/pdf/10.1186/s12884-017-1229-4.pdf
(156)mentalhealth.org.uk/explore-mental-health/blogs/fathers-day-focus-young-fathers-and-mental-health
(157) nct.org.uk/about-us/media/news/dads-distress-many-new-fathers-are-worried-about-their-mental-health

(158) Statistics on Male Victims of Domestic Abuse - Mankind. https://mankind.org.uk/statistics/statistics-on-male-victims-of-domestic-abuse/.
(159) Domestic abuse victim characteristics, England and Wales –
(160) Involving and supporting partners and other family members in - NHS England. https://www.england.nhs.uk/wp-content/uploads/2021/03/Good-practice-guide-March-2021.pdf.
(161) Mother and baby units (MBUs) | Royal College of Psychiatrists. https://www.rcpsych.ac.uk/mental-health/treatments-and-wellbeing/mother-and-baby-units-%28mbus%29.
(162) West of Scotland Mother and Baby Unit - NHSGGC. https://www.nhsggc.scot/hospitals-services/services-a-to-z/perinatal-mental-health-service/west-of-scotland-mother-and-baby-unit/.
(163) Parent and Child Fostering - Foster Care Associates - the FCA./www.thefca.co.uk/about-fostering/types-of-fostering/parent-and-child-fostering/.
(164) Postpartum Psychosis for Carers - Royal College of Psychiatrists.www.rcpsych.ac.uk/mental-health/mental-illnesses-and-mental-health-problems/postpartum-psychosis-in-carers?psychologis.
(165) Postpartum psychosis - NHS. https://www.nhs.uk/mental-health/conditions/post-partum-psychosis/.
(166) Postpartum psychosis | Royal College of Psychiatrists. /www.rcpsych.ac.uk/mental-health/mental-illnesses-and-mental-health-problems/postpartum-psychosis.
(167) Postpartum depression - Symptoms, diagnosis and treatment | BMJ Best .... https://bestpractice.bmj.com/topics/en-gb/512.
(168) Postpartum Depression | CAMH - The Centre for Addiction and Mental Health. camh.ca/en/health-info/mental-illness-and-addiction-index/postpartum-depression
(169) Dads with ADHD: Learning to Parent with ADHD - ADDitude.
(170) The Relationship Between Dopamine and ADHD - Very well Mind.
(171) The Link Between Dopamine and ADHD | Better Help.

(172) Autistic Parents: Challenges, Strengths, and Finding Support.
(173) Support and Tips for Autistic Adults - Very well Health.
(174) The Joys and Challenges of Being a Father with Autism. https://inclusive-solutions.com/blog/the-joys-and-challenges-of-being-a-father-with-autism/.
(175) undefined. https://www.researchgate.net/profile/Lloyd-
(176) Challenges That Still Exist for the Deaf Community - verywellhealth.com/what-challenges-still-exist-for-the-deaf-community-4153447.
(177) Parenting While Legally Blind: Secrets of a Visually Impaired New Dad. fatherly.com/love-money/legally-blind-parenting-secrets-of-a-visually-impaired-new-dad.
(178) Deaf blindness - Sense.org.uk/information-and-advice/conditions/deaf blindness/.
(179) Deaf blindness Overview | National Centre on Deaf blindness. Nationaldb.org/info-center/deaf-blindness-overview.
(180) icphs2019.org/the-struggles-and-successes-of-deaf-people
(181) A qualitative exploratory study of UK first-time fathers' experiences, mental health and wellbeing needs during their transition to fatherhood
(182) fatherandchild.org.nz/magazine/issue-19/the-role-model-crisis/
(183) bps.org.uk/psychologist/fathers-behaviours-and-childrens-problems
(184).thejournalthattalksback.com/am-i-the-bleep/how-to-deal-with-feeling-excluded-by-family-and-friends
(185) psychcentral.com/blog/childhood-neglect/2020/01
(186) irr.org.uk/research/statistics/health/
(187 Black, Asian and minority ethnic (BAME) communities. mentalhealth.org.uk/explore-mental-health/a-z-topics/black-asian-and-minority-ethnic-bame-communities.
(188) Existing inequalities have made mental health of BAME groupsmind.org.uk/news-campaigns/news/existing-inequalities-have-made-mental-health-of-bame-groups-worse-during-pandemic-says-mind/.
(189) Health and mental health statistics - Institute of Race Relations. https://irr.org.uk/research/statistics/health/.
(190) .fflag.org.uk/

(191) LGBTIQ+ people: statistics | Mental Health Foundation. https://www.mentalhealth.org.uk/explore-mental-health/statistics/lgbtiq-people-statistics.
(192) LGB people 'more likely to have mental health issues' - BBC. https://www.bbc.co.uk/news/health-57739132.
(193) LGBTQ Mental Health Issues - familydoctor.org. https://familydoctor.org/lgbtq-mental-health-issues/.
(194) Mental health and illness statistics among LGBTQ+: The prevalence of .... https://thriveworks.com/blog/mental-health-and-illness-statistics-lgbtq/.
(195) The 5 Biggest Issues Facing LGBTQ Families Today - Fatherly. https://www.fatherly.com/love-money/big-issues-facing-lgbtq-families-today.
(196) Lesbian and Gay Parenting - American Psychological Association (APA). https://www.apa.org/pi/lgbt/resources/parenting.
(197) Understanding resilience in same sex parented families: the work, love .... https://bmcpublichealth.biomedcentral.com/articles/10.1186/1471-2458-10-115.
(198) Becoming the legal parents of your child | HFEA.
(199) Rhod Gilbert: Stand Up to Infertility review – a very male taboo. https://www.theguardian.com/tv-and-radio/2021/jan/31/rhod-gilbert-stand-up-to-infertility-review-a-very-male-taboo.
(200) Rhod Gilbert's fatherhood hopes after cancer treatment - BBC. https://www.bbc.com/news/uk-wales-67260176.
(201)bmjopen.bmj.com/content/bmjopen/9/9/e030792.full.pdf
(202) https://opus.lib.uts.edu.au/handle/10453/133110
(203) Young people's mental and emotional health: Trajectories and drivers in .... https://epi.org.uk/publications-and-research/young-peoples-mental-and-emotional-health/.
(204) Engaging teenage boys in mental health support. https://www.kcl.ac.uk/engaging-teenage-boys-in-mental-health-support.
(205) Boys experience depression differently than girls. Here's why that matters. https://www.sciencenews.org/article/boys-experience-depression-differently-girls.
(206) https://creativecommons.org/licenses/by/2.0/igo/

(207) https://creativecommons.org/licenses/by/3.0/igo/
(208) Mental healthcare for asylum-seekers and refugees residing in the .... https://ijmhs.biomedcentral.com/articles/10.1186/s13033-021-00473-z.
(209) Asylum seeker and refugee mental health - Royal College of Psychiatrists. https://www.rcpsych.ac.uk/international/humanitarian-resources/asylum-seeker-and-refugee-mental-health.
(210) Unique health challenges for refugees and asylum seekers. https://www.bma.org.uk/advice-and-support/ethics/refugees-overseas-visitors-and-vulnerable-migrants/refugee-and-asylum-seeker-patient-health-toolkit/unique-health-challenges-for-refugees-and-asylum-seekers.
(211)Article- 215,243 prison fr.
(212) petertatchellfoundation.org/prisoners-advice/
(213) prisonersadvice.org.uk/
(214) Fathers Behind Bars: The Problem & Solution for ... - Prison Fellowship. https://www.prisonfellowship.org/2014/10/fathers-behind-bars-the-problem-solution-for-americas-children/.
(215) Children with a parent or relative in prison | Barnardo's. https://www.barnardos.org.uk/get-support/support-for-parents-and-carers/children-with-a-parent-in-prison.
(216)ons.gov.uk/peoplepopulationandcommunity/crimeandjustice/bulletins/childabuseinenglandandwales/march2020
(217)gov.uk/government/publications/supporting-male-victims/supporting-male-victims-accessible
(218)ons.gov.uk/aboutus/transparencyandgovernance/freedomofinformationfoi/childsexualabusestatistics
(219)ons.gov.uk/peoplepopulationandcommunity/crimeandjustice/datasets/childsexualabuseappendixtables
(220)ons.gov.uk/peoplepopulationandcommunity/crimeandjustice/articles/childabuseextentandnatureenglandandwales/yearendingmarch2019
(221)statista.com/statistics/303514/child-cruelty-abuse-in-england-and-wales-uk-y-on-y/
(222) nhs.uk/live-well/addiction-support/addiction-what-is-it/

(223)romper.com/life/baby-massage-lower-postnatal-depression-symptoms-mothers-study-2023
(224)lancastergeneralhealth.org/health-hub-home/2021/september/the-effects-of-social-media-on-mental-health
(225) New Fathers, Mental Health and Digital Communication. Authors: Paul Hodkinson , Ranjana Das
(226)
(241).gov.uk/government/publications/the-best-start-for-life-a-vision-for-the-1001-critical-days
(242)nspcc.org.uk/globalassets/documents/news/critical-days-manifesto.pdf
(243) neurosciencenews.com/fatherhood-men-brain-21997/
(244) annamachin.com/science-behind-human-behaviour/
(245) fathersnetwork.org.uk/dads_change_during_pregnancy
(246) sciencedaily.com/releases/2010/08/100820101207.htm
(247) bigthink.com/neuropsych/neuroscience-of-fatherhood/
(248) maternalmentalhealthalliance.org/about-maternal-mental-health/counting-costs/
(249) New fathers felt isolated by maternity restrictions but bonded better ....
(250) New fatherhood in a pandemic: Challenges and resources for new fathers ....
(251) Association of Paternity Leave with Impaired Father–Infant Bonding
(252) Frontiers | Paternal Leave and Father-Infant Bonding: Findings From the ....
(253) How Paternity Leave Helps Dads and Babies Bond - Greater Good.
(254) Paternity leave benefits extend beyond personal | McKinsey.
(255)dad.info/article/family/relationships/having-kids/why-is-paternity-leave-important-a-dad-s-perspective/
(256)dol.gov/sites/dolgov/files/OASP/legacy/files/PaternityBrief.pdf
(257) Postpartum Rage: Uncontrollable Anger After Birth — Talkspace.talkspace.com/mental-health/conditions/articles/postpartum-rage/.

(258) Postpartum Rage: Causes, Symptoms, and Treatment - Healthline. healthline.com/health/postpartum rage.
(259) parentingforbrain.com/angry-parents/
(260) https://psychcentral.com/health/what-is-mom-rage-and-when-is-it-a-sign-of-bigger-mental-health-issue
(261)managers.org.uk/knowledge-and-insights/article/new-study-reveals-stress-facing-working-fathers/
(262)hbr.org/2017/03/balancing-parenting-and-work-stress-a-guide
(263) .nhs.uk/every-mind-matters/lifes-challenges/work-related-stress/
(264) nhs.uk/conditions/alcohol-misuse/
(265) health.harvard.edu/addiction/alcohol-abuse
(266)mayoclinic.org/diseases-conditions/alcohol-use-disorder/symptoms-causes/syc-20369243
(267) afro.who.int/health-topics/substance-abuse
(268) nhs.uk/live-well/addiction-support/addiction-what-is-it/
(269) Father–daughter relationship and the severity of eating disorders. https://www.cambridge.org/core/journals/european-psychiatry/article/abs/fatherdaughter-relationship-and-the-severity-of-eating-disorders/ADE127A68ECDF8B525A5F799E27D708B.
(270) Body image affects half of men's mental health, new study shows. https://www.bbc.co.uk/news/newsbeat-56904488.
(271)citizensadvice.org.uk/debt-and-money/gambling-problems/if-youre-worried-about-someones-gambling/
(272)patientslounge.com/mental-health/If-You-Love-a-Compulsive-Gambler-Some-Tips-to-Protect-Yourself
(273) bbc.co.uk/news/education-50056136
(274) The health effects of too much gaming - Harvard Health. https://www.health.harvard.edu/blog/the-health-effects-of-too-much-gaming-2020122221645
(275) Publications by Mark Williams

Milton Keynes UK
Ingram Content Group UK Ltd.
UKHW020657290124
436892UK00018B/652

9 781916 981669